# Android Programming In Kotlin: Starting with an App

### Using Android Studio 3

### First Edition

## Mike James

## I/O Press
## I Programmer Library

Mike James Android Programming In Kotlin: Starting with an App

1st Edition

ISBN Paperback: 978-1871962543

First Printing, 2017
Revision 0


Published by IO Press         www.iopress.info

In association with I Programmer     www.i-programmer.info

# Preface

Android programming is an attractive proposition. There are more Android users than any other smartphone or tablet and this makes it a potentially huge market. Android devices are relatively cheap and this makes it suitable for implementing smaller scale projects. Finally the tools that you need are free to download and use and you don't need anyone's permission to get started.

The only difficulty is that the Android is a tough system to master. It is easy enough to get started as Android Studio will build you a Hello World app in a few minutes, but what you do next is more difficult. The good news is that Kotlin is a language that makes working with Java and Android much easier. You cannot get away from Java in Android as it is the language used for the libraries that your apps are built on, but Kotlin makes writing code so much easier and it works with Java code perfectly. As a programmer who has worked in both Java and Kotlin, I can vouch for the fact that Kotlin is a pleasure to work with and an excellent choice.

You can get a surprisingly long way in Android programming by simply copying and pasting code from other programs that roughly do what you want, but the results are usually unreliable and disappointing. To create a good app there is no substitute for understanding how the system works and appreciating its strong points and its limitations.

This book aims not only to show you how common tasks are done in Android, but to make sure that you understand the reasons they are done in a particular way. This means covering not just the what but also the why. The good news is that this isn't as difficult as you might expect because Android does have repeating patterns and ways of doing things and once you have seen something in action you find it generalizes to components you haven't encountered.

This isn't a book full of complete examples and case studies. In fact the examples are stripped down to their bare minimum to avoid having to present lines of irrelevant and repetitious code and to let you see what is essential. It also isn't a complete treatment of everything Android. A single book that covered every aspect of the Android system would be too large to pick up and carry. Instead it focuses on the things you need to know to write a simple app. It focuses on creating the user interface (UI) because this is what you spend most of your time working on even if the app in question is sophisticated. At least 90% of the effort in creating any app goes into building and perfecting the UI and this makes it the key place to start. In this book you will find out how to build an app with a single Activity and a UI. If you master this level of the art then you will find it much easier to push on into unknown territory.

3

It is assumed that you can program, but not necessarily in Kotlin or Java – any general object-oriented language will do as a starting point. As long as you are happy with the idea of a loop, conditional, function and what objects are, then you should have no problem working with Kotlin and Android.

Finally the development tool used is the latest version of Android Studio because it doesn't make sense not to use it or to use anything else.

This is the place to start.

Mike James
December 2017

This book is a revised and updated version of the series of *Android Adventures With Android Studio* on the I Programmer website:

**www.i-programmer.info**

There are additional articles on I Programmer that form the basis of the more advanced books that are still in preparation. After updating and revision, *Android Adventures – Mastering Fragments* will be published in print as **Android Programming: Mastering Fragments & Dialogs**. The first draft of **Android Programming: Structuring a Complex App**, which goes further into threading, concurrency, life cycle and other topics crucial to a real world app, is currently work in progress on the website.

To keep informed about forthcoming titles in the **Android Programming** series visit the publisher's website:

**www.iopress.info**

This is also where you will also find errata, update information to keep up with changes in Android Studio and Android itself and, most importantly, the code from the books. You can also provide feedback to help improve future editions of **Android Programming**.

# Table of Contents

**Chapter 7**
**The ConstraintLayout**                                                  **135**

**Chapter 8**
**Programming The UI**                                                      **165**

**Chapter 9**
**Menus – Toolbar**                                                         **177**

## Chapter 17
## Android The Kotlin Way     301

# Chapter 1

# Getting Started With Android Studio

Android represents a big potential market. It is also the most open of the "big" phone and tablet platforms. You can write a program for an Android and let your friends have a copy, keep it to yourself or put it on sale in an app store.

Android phones and tablets are comparatively cheap and this makes it easier to get started. What is even better, all the tools you need to create an Android app are free. You don't need to pay anything to create, or distribute, your Android apps. If you want to sell them using a well known marketplace there may something to pay – there is a one-time fee of $25 to register for Google Play, but you don't have to use any particular distribution method.

All that stands between you and your Android app is your imagination and programming ability. I can't do much to improve your imagination, but I can help with the programming side of things. If you are new to Android programming this is the place to start.

In this book I will show you the fundamentals of Android programming. Not the tips and tricks, but how to think about what is going on. You'll be introduced to the general principles that will make it possible for you to master anything that you encounter that is new in the future. It isn't possible to cover all of Android in one book as the subject is very large. Instead we focus on the basics of creating a User Interface (UI) as all apps have to have some way of interacting with a user.

There are many ways to create an Android app but Google's Android Studio is an easy to use Android IDE – Integrated Development Environment – and it is now the recommended way of doing the job.

Before Android Studio you had to use the Eclipse IDE and set up the SDK and other pieces of software needed. This wasn't difficult, but Android Studio eliminates extra steps and it makes programming Android easy. Put simply, it is the way of the future and so worth your investment in learning it.

With the release of Android Studio Google stopped work on the Eclipse plugin and this means that Android Studio really is the only way to develop apps from now on.

## The Language Choice

With the release of Android Studio 3 you now have a choice of programming in Java or Kotlin. The advantage of Java is that it is a well known and well supported language. If you already program in Java or want to acquire the skill then you might well be better off starting with ***Android Programming In Java: Starting with an App ISBN: 978-1871962550***

Kotlin may be a be a new language but it is already well supported for the simple reason that it is 100% compatible with Java. The Android libraries are all written in Java, but Kotlin can make use of them with no problems. It is this that makes Kotlin Android development possible. What is more, you aren't restricted to Kotlin in a project. You can add Java code to your new Kotlin project and you can add Kotlin code to an existing Java project.

Put simply, there is very little risk involved in moving to Kotlin and there is a lot to be gained. Kotlin is a much simpler and cleaner language than Java. It has had the benefit of seeing how Java evolved and avoiding those mistakes. Kotlin attempts to get straight to the point. In Java you tend to write some code over and over and it can be time consuming and hides the simplicity of what you are trying to do. Whenever this happens Kotlin modifies the language so that you can express what you are doing succinctly. Programmers moving from Java to Kotlin generally find that they like it because they get more done with less typing. Programmers who only know Kotlin don't know how lucky they are!

Kotlin does things differently from Java and while you can pick up the language as you go you might like to read ***Programmer's Guide To Kotlin ISBN:978-1871962536***. It isn't necessary, as long as you know Java or another object-oriented language, you can pick up Kotlin as you develop your Android apps but I recommend learning the finer points of the language sooner or later. It pays off to know your language.

The way Kotlin is used and the ways it changes Android programming in particular are introduced as we go along. However, the final chapter is a brief look at the major influences of Kotlin on Android programming. If you want a quick overview before you start then read the final chapter, but in many ways it makes more sense to read it as a summary after you have encountered the ideas in context.

The bottom line is that, unless you have a commitment to Java, you probably should start new projects in Kotlin and convert existing projects to Kotlin a bit at a time.

## What You Need to Know

You need to be able to program in a modern object-oriented language. Java would be best as it is closest to Kotlin, but C++, C#, Visual Basic or anything similar are close enough in spirit to Java for you to be able to cope. You might well need to look things up about the specifics of particular features of Kotlin, but most of the time it should be obvious, or obvious with the help of a few comments.

It isn't necessary to be an expert programmer because for a lot of Android programming you are simply using the features and facilities provided. That is, a lot of Android programming is just a matter of following the rules.

However, if you hope to produce something unique and useful you will at some point have to add something of your own – and here creativity and skill are required. So you might not need to be an expert programmer to get started, but you need to become one by the time you create your amazing app.

Fortunately practice is a good teacher and so learning to make the most of Android Studio will actually help you learn to code.

## Making a Start

I'm not going to spend a lot of time explaining how to install Android Studio in a step-by-step way as the Android website does a good job and it is more likely to be up-to-date. It is worth, however, going over the basic principles.

https://developer.android.com/studio/

The installer will download everything you need including the JDK.

**Windows:**

1. Launch the downloaded EXE file,

   `android-studio-bundle-<version>.exe`.

2. Follow the setup wizard to install Android Studio.

**Mac OS X:**

1. Open the downloaded DMG file,

   `android-studio-bundle-<version>.dmg`

2. Drag and drop Android Studio into the Applications folder.

**Linux:**

1. Unpack the downloaded ZIP file,

   `android-studio-bundle-<version>.tgz,`

   into an appropriate location for your applications.

2. To launch Android Studio, navigate to the

   `android-studio/bin/`

   directory in a terminal and execute studio.sh. You may want to add

   `android-studio/bin/`

   to your PATH environmental variable so that you can start Android Studio from any directory.

Accept any defaults that the setup program offers you – unless you have a good reason not to. It installs not only Android Studio, but the SDK and the virtual device system that lets you test your application.

*Software Development Kit*

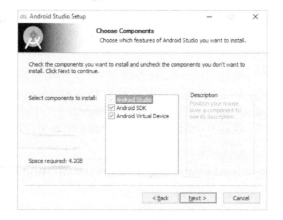

In most cases Android Studio just installs with no problem.

Now you should be able to run Android Studio. If not the most likely cause of the problem is the JDK and so re-installation is a best first option.

*Java Development Kit*

## Your First Program

You can opt to start Android Studio after the installation. You will probably not get straight to Android Studio the first time it starts as it downloads updates to itself and to the Android SDK. You just have to be patient.

When it finally gets going you will see the Android Studio welcome screen:

Android Studio
Version 3.0

✴ Start a new Android Studio project
▷ Open an existing Android Studio project
⬇ Check out project from Version Control ▾
⊡ Profile or debug APK
▨ Import project (Gradle, Eclipse ADT, etc.)
▨ Import an Android code sample

⚙ Configure ▾   Get Help ▾

If you have already created some programs you might well see them listed in Recent projects.

Assuming this is your first project select the option:

Start a new Android Studio project

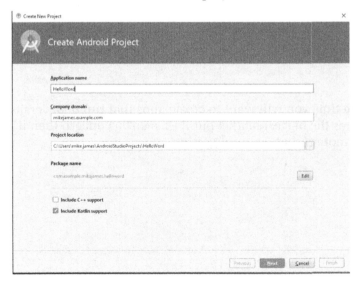

You can ignore the details of the new project for the moment. All you have to do is supply a name for your application – HelloWorld in this case. Also make sure you have Include Kotlin support ticked – this is what makes the project use Kotlin rather than Java. Accept the other defaults that Android Studio has filled in for you.

When you click Next you are given the chance to pick what devices you are targeting. Again simply accept the defaults:

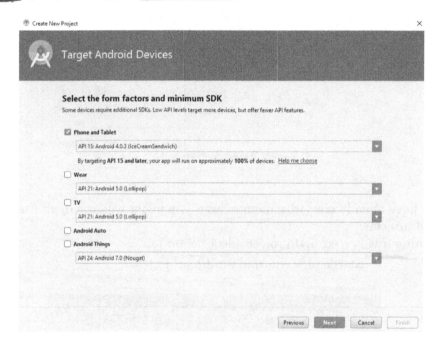

Most of the time you will want to create apps that run on a version of Android that captures the biggest market but if this isn't a concern then it can be better to select a more recent Android version.

Phone I am Using has Android "Pie" OS!!!

The next page lets you select a template for your project. In this case change the selection to Basic Activity. This gives you some additional generated code which makes the app easier to create an app that looks right. Every Android application consists of at least one Activity and this template generates a project with a single Activity ready for you to customize:

On the next page you can assign custom names for the various components of your project that the template generates. For a real project you would assign names that were meaningful but in this case you can accept the defaults:

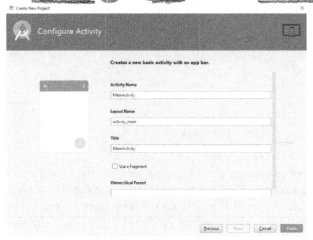

Finally you can click the Finish button and wait as Android Studio creates all the files you need. Even a simple Android project has lots of files so again it all takes time.

# First Look

When everything is ready you will see Android Studio for the first time. As long as everything has worked you should eventually, it takes about three minutes or more, be presented with a view of your new project starting off in the Layout Editor:

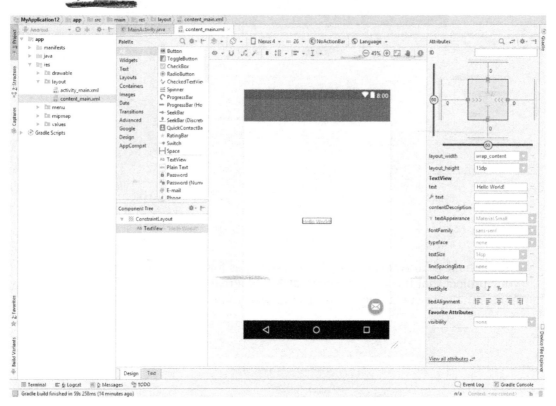

## Problems?

If you get any error messages then the chances are that your project hasn't finished being processed. Wait a little while longer for the activity to stop. If you look at the status line at the bottom of the window you will see a message saying "Gradle Build Finished" when Android Studio has finished with your new project.

If you still have problems it is worth trying the **File,Invalidate Caches/Restart** command. This usually works for "Missing styles" and similar errors.

# The IDE

Although there looks like a lot to master in Android Studio's user interface, most of it you will only visit occasionally. The key things to notice are that moving from left to right you have:

- The Project window
- The tool Palette and the Component Tree window
- The Layout Editor
- The Attributes window

Most of the time you will be using the Project window and the Attributes window. You will also see different editors depending on what sort of file you have selected. In this case you have by default a layout file, **content_main.xml**, selected and hence you have a layout editor in the middle of the screen.

Before we go into layout, which is one of the main topics of this book, it is important that you know a little about the file structure of a project so that you can navigate to its different parts.

## Basic Project Structure

When the project has finished building all of the files created can be viewed by opening the Projects tab. The main thing to notice is that there are a great many folders and files:

It seems almost unbelievable that the simplest Android app you can create involves so many files.

Don't panic. Most of the files that have been created are auto-generated and most of the time you don't need to know anything about them, let alone open or edit them. In fact opening and editing auto-generated files really isn't a good idea.

So let's focus on the files that matter to us.

For our simple program there are only two important files. One of them determines the behavior of the Activity:

MainActivity.kt

The other determines the visual appearance, or View, of the app:

content_main.xml

You can set which Activity is the one that the system starts, but by default it is the single activity that you created and named when you set up the project. You can change the default names but for the moment leave them as they are.

Despite this being a Kotlin project, the java directory, from your point of view, is where most of the construction of your app occurs, so make sure you know where it is. The res directory is where you store all of the resources, layouts, bitmaps, etc, that your app needs.

So while things look complicated at the moment the only two project files that matter to you, and your project, are MainActivity.kt in the java folder and content_main.xml in the res folder.

The two other folders in the java folder are concerned with creating tests for your program. This is not something that we need to worry about when first starting to write Android apps.

## Anatomy of an Activity

An Android app is made up of one or more Activity classes.

You can think of an Activity as being something like a web page complete with HTML to determine what displays and JavaScript to determine what it does.

In the case of an Activity the layout is determined by the XML file in resource (res) folder, this is often called the View and the behavior is determined by the Kotlin or Java code in the java folder.

The XML can be thought of as a markup language much like HTML or XAML. It defines an initial layout for the screen when the app first runs. It is possible to generate new layout components at runtime from the Java file. In fact, if you really want to, you can dispense with the XML file and generate everything from code, but as you will discover the XML markup approach is much the best way to do the job because of the availability of the Layout Editor.

So to be 100% clear in a Kotlin project:

- The kt file contains the code that makes your app behave in particular ways.
- The .xml layout file contains a definition of the initial UI, the View, of your app.

## Hello Layout Editor

Let's take a look at the two files that have been generated for our initial Hello World application beginning with the XML layout. Double click on content_main.xml file in the Project tab and the file will open (if it isn't already open). If it is already open you can also select its tab displayed just above the editor area. You can select any file that is open for editing by selecting its tab.

You can work with the XML directly to define where all the buttons and text go, and later you will learn how to edit it when things go wrong or to fine tune it. However, Android Studio provides you with a very nice interactive editor – the Layout Editor and this is worth using.

As you become more experienced the idea of switching between a design view and an XML view will become second nature. Think of the interactive editor as a very easy way of generating the XML that otherwise would take you ages to get right. If you look at the bottom left you will see two tabs – Design and Text:

only see 1
in upper right,
"Design"

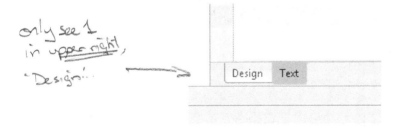

You can switch between editing the XML as text, and editing it in the drag-and-drop Layout Editor simply by clicking on the tab. If you now click on the tab the window will display the Layout Editor but be patient the first time you do this it might take a few moments.

The Layout Editor looks a little too much to take in when you first see it but you will quickly get used to it. On the left is a Palette of all of the components or controls - buttons, text, checkboxes and so on - that you can place on the design surface:

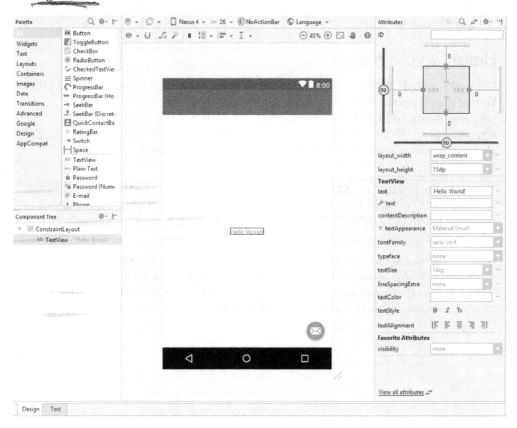

In the middle is the design surface and this defaults to the screen size and appearance of the Nexus 5. You can select other devices to work with.

default device
is " 5.0, 1080×1920, 420dpi (Pixel)"

22

There are, in fact, two views of the layout that you can use, the design and the blueprint. By default you are shown the design view but you can display either view using the menu at the top left of the design area.

*default is "design + blueprint"*

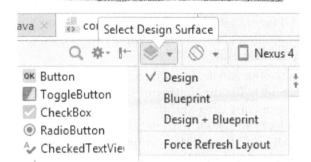

You can display both views together but in most cases available screen area is the main issue and showing just one is the best option. The design view shows you the layout as a close approximation to how it will appear on a real device. The blueprint view doesn't try to render the UI realistically but it does provide you will more layout information to help you position and size elements. Use whichever you are most happy with.

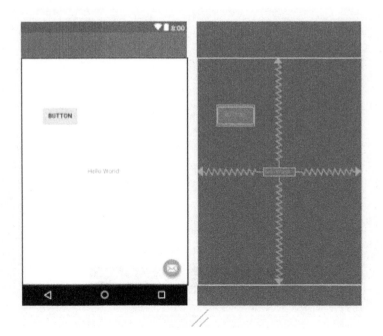

23

On the left, below the Palette, you have the Component Tree which shows you the structure of your layout, that is how different UI components are contained inside others. It shows you the structure of the XML file in an easier to use form. You can use the Component Tree as an easy way of to select individual UI components by clicking on their names. You can also drag-and-drop UI components onto the Component Tree to position them accurately within the hierarchy.

*Know this!!* (handwritten margin note)

On the right you have the Attributes window that can be used to set the attributes, such as width, height, color and so on of any component in the layout. If you have used any drag-and-drop Layout Editor then this will seem familiar and if you have struggled with detailed layout using a markup language, be it HTML, XAML or XML, you will appreciate how easy the Layout Editor makes building and testing a UI.

In the case of our sample program the only component is a single TextView already containing the text "Hello World". A TextView is the standard component to use when all we want to do is to display some static text.

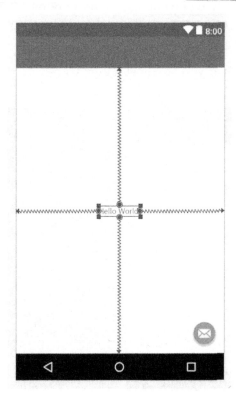

You can modify the greeting text if you want to. Select the TextView component either on the design or in the Component Tree and use the Attributes window to find its Text attribute. Change this to read "Hello Android World":

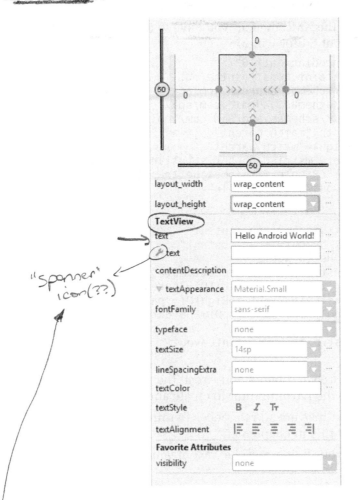

"spanner" icon(??)

Use the text field without the spanner icon. The properties with the spanner icon next to them are used to set values that only show in the Layout Editor. In this case the text field without the spanner icon is the one that controls what appears in your app at runtime.

You can use the Layout Editor to create any UI you care to and you really don't have to get involved in the XML that corresponds to the layout – unless things go wrong or you need to do something so sophisticated that the Layout Editor doesn't support it.

## Inspecting the XML

The Layout Editor will automatically generate the XML needed to create the layout for you and modify it as you change the layout.

If you really want to see the XML then all you have to do is select the Text tab at the bottom of the Layout Editor window:

```xml
<?xml version="1.0" encoding="utf-8"?>
<android.support.constraint.ConstraintLayout
xmlns:android="http://schemas.android.com/apk/res/android"
    xmlns:app="http://schemas.android.com/apk/res-auto"
    xmlns:tools="http://schemas.android.com/tools"
    android:layout_width="match_parent"
    android:layout_height="match_parent"
    app:layout_behavior="@string/appbar_scrolling_view_behavior"
    tools:context="com.example.mikejames.helloworld1.MainActivity"
    tools:showIn="@layout/activity_main">

    <TextView
        android:layout_width="wrap_content"
        android:layout_height="wrap_content"
        android:text="Hello World!"
        app:layout_constraintBottom_toBottomOf="parent"
        app:layout_constraintLeft_toLeftOf="parent"
        app:layout_constraintRight_toRightOf="parent"
        app:layout_constraintTop_toTopOf="parent" />

</android.support.constraint.ConstraintLayout>
```

You should find it fairly easy to understand – read the <TextView> tag for example – but leave it to the Layout Editor to create and modify it.

The quantities starting with @ are all references to things defined elsewhere in resource files, more of this in chapter 11.

We will return to the Layout Editor and the XML it generates in many later chapters.

## The Kotlin

If you double click on the MainActivity.kt file, or just select the
MainActivity.kt tab, you will see the code it contains. Some of the code might
be hidden but you can inspect it if you want to by clicking the + button to
expand it.

The important part of the code is:

```
class MainActivity : AppCompatActivity() {

    override fun onCreate(savedInstanceState: Bundle?) {
        super.onCreate(savedInstanceState)
        setContentView(R.layout.activity_main)
```

You can ignore the instructions that follow the setContentView function
because these set up the standard "extras" that every Android application now
supports – a floating ActionBar.

There are two other functions below the onCreate function but ignore these
for the moment. They implement features you didn't really ask for which can
be useful, but not when you are just getting started.

The onCreate function is the only thing that matters at the moment. This
function is called when your app is run and it is expected to create the view
and do the actions the Activity is concerned with.

As our Activity doesn't really do anything much the only thing onCreate has
to do is first call the inherited OnCreate method, super.onCreate, to do all the
standard things and then use the setContentView function to select the XML
file that determines the layout of the Activities screen.

The line:

```
setContentView(R.layout.activity_main)
```

is the most important of all and really the only one that actually does
anything. It gets the resource object R that represents the layout as defined by
the XML file created by the Layout Editor and makes it the current
ContentView, i.e. it is what is displayed on the screen. In other words, it
makes the connection between the layout you have defined using the Layout
Editor and stored in the XML file, and the user interface that appears on the
device's screen.

You may be puzzled as to why you edited a resource file called
content_main.xml and yet the Kotlin is loading a resource file called
activity_main.xml

The answer is that to make extending your app easier Android Studio creates
two layout files, activity_main.xml that creates the "standard" controls that

are displayed and content_main.xml that you use to design your custom UI. Of course, activity_main.xml contains a reference to content_main.xml. This makes things more complicated for the beginner but it is a simplification later.

We have more to learn about the resource object R but you can see that its main role is to form a link between your Java code and the resources that have been created as XML files by the Layout Editor.

As this is all our Activity does this is all the code we need. While I agree it is hardly an "activity" it is enough to see the basic outline of an Android app and to see how to get it running – which is our next job.

## Getting Started with the Emulator

There are two distinct ways of running an Android app using Android Studio. You can use the emulator or a real Android device. Eventually you will have to discover how to run an app on a real connected Android device because the emulator only allows you to test a subset of things and it is slow. However, for the moment running your first app on an emulator is quite enough to get started.

All you have to do is click the green run icon in the top toolbar – or use the Run,Run "app" menu item. When you do this for the first time it will take a while for the app to be compiled. Subsequent runs are much faster due to optimizations introduced in Android Studio 3.

When your app is ready to be compiled you will see a dialog box appear which allows you to either select a running emulator or start one going:

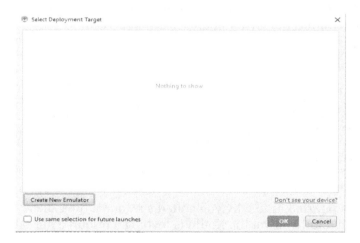

If no emulators are listed then you will have to create one. Select the Create New Emulator button. This will present a dialog box where you can select the device you want to test on.

The default is the Nexus 5 running Nougat API 25 and for a first test you might as well use this. If you need other devices you can use the AVD (Android Virtual Device) Manager to define them.

If you see a message on the right of the screen "HAXM is not installed" then it is a good idea to click the Install Haxm link just below. HAXM is an accelerator that is used on Intel machines to make the Android Emulator run faster. You don't need it but it does speed things up:

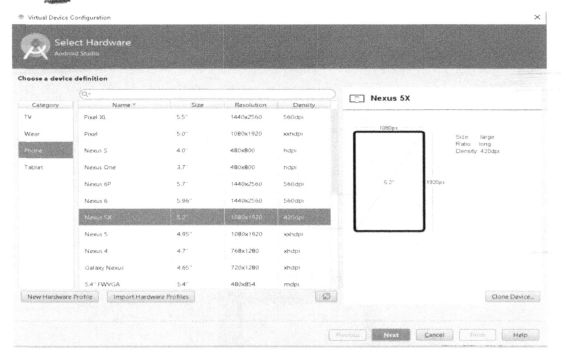

You can accept all of the defaults in this first run. You can monitor the loading of the emulation in the Run window which appears automatically at the bottom of Android Studio. You may see some warnings appear – these can mostly be ignored.

The whole process takes some time the first time you do it. After the first time the emulator is already running and the instant run feature tries to re-run your app with the minimum changes:

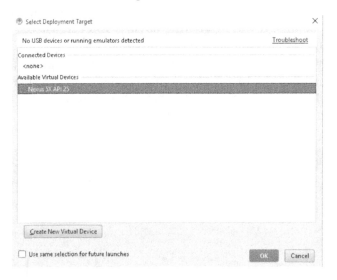

Finally, remember to wait until the Android operating system is loaded and you see the familiar home screen before you start to wonder where your app is. Even when it is loaded it is a good idea to give it a few seconds for Android Studio to notice it and to upload your app:

In our case this isn't particularly impressive – just the words "Hello Android World!", but when you think of the journey traveled it really should impress.

From this point you can now modify the code or the layout and run the app again to see the effects of the changes. If anything goes wrong and you get in a mess then simply delete the project and create it again from scratch.

You still have a lot to discover about how to extend the app and make it useful, but the adventure has begun.

phone: "Build #"
PKQ1.190414.001

# Summary

- Android Studio makes creating Android apps a lot easier than other approaches and it is currently the only official way to do the job.

- An app has at least one Activity and this defines a screen layout, the View, and a behavior. An Activity doesn't have to have a UI, but in most cases it does have one.

- To create a simple application use the Basic Activity template with no extras selected.

- The screen layout is controlled by an XML markup file, Main_Activity.xml, stored in the res directory. There is also content_main.xml, which is where we place our custom UI controls.

- Android Studio provides a drag-and-drop Layout Editor that allows you to create a UI without having to work directly with the XML.

- The behavior of the app is controlled by a Kotlin file, MainActivity.kt in our case, stored in the java folder. You can edit the code in the Kotlin file directly in Android Studio. The code has to load and display the layout defined in the XML file.

- To run an app you need either an emulator based AVD or a real Android device connected to the machine.

- When you run the app you can select which AVD or which hardware device is used to test it. When you first start simply use the default AVD, a Nexus 5.

- You can modify and re-run your app without having to restart the AVD or any real hardware connected to the machine.

# Chapter 2

# Activity and User Interface

So you know how to create an Android app, but do you really know how it works? In this chapter we look at how to create a user interface (UI) and how to hook it up to the code in the Activity.

We discovered in Chapter 1 how to use Android Studio to build the simplest possible app. On the way we discovered that an Android app consists of two parts – an Activity and a View. The Activity is the code that does something and the View provides the user interface (UI). You can think of this duality as being similar to the HTML page and the JavaScript that runs to make it do something, or as a XAML form and the code behind.

The key idea is that an Activity is the code that works with a UI screen defined by the View. This isn't quite accurate in that an Activity can change its view so that one chunk of code can support a number of different views. However, there are advantages to using one Activity per view because, for example, this how the Android back button navigates your app – from Activity to Activity.

A complex app nearly always consists of multiple Activities that the user can move between like web pages but a simple app can manage quite well with just one Activity. There is no hard and fast rule as to how many Activities your app has to have, but it has to have least one.

If you are wondering if an Activity can exist without a View the answer is that it can but it doesn't make much sense as this would leave the user with no way to interact with your app. Activities are active when their View is presented to the user.

It really is a great simplification to think in terms of an Activity as a single screen with a user interface.

If you want something to run without a UI then what you want is a service or a content provider which is beyond the scope of this book.

It is also worth making clear at this early stage that an Activity has only one thread of execution – the UI thread – and you need to be careful not to perform any long running task because this would block the UI and make your app seem to freeze. That is, an Activity can only do one thing at a time and this includes interacting with the user. If you write a program using a single activity and it does a complicated calculation when the user clicks a button then the activity will not be able to respond to any additional clicks or anything that happens in the UI until it finishes the calculation.

In most cases the whole purpose of the Activity that is associated with the UI is to look after the UI and this is what this book is mostly about.

Also notice that creating additional Activities doesn't create new threads. Only one Activity is active at any given time, more of this later when we consider the Activity lifecycle in detail.

In this book we are going to concentrate on the single screen UI Activity because it is the most common app building block you will encounter, and it is even where most complex apps start from.

## The MainActivity

Start-up Activity (by default)

There is one activity in every project that is nominated as the one to be launched when your app starts. If you use Android Studio to create a new Basic Activity app called **SimpleButton** and accept all the defaults, the startup Activity is called MainActivity by default. You can change which Activity starts the app by changing a line in the app's manifest.

The Manifest is a project file we haven't discussed before because if you are using Android Studio you can mostly ignore it and allow Android Studio to construct and maintain it for you, but it is better if you know it exists and what it does.

The Manifest is stored in the app/manifests directory and is called AndroidManifest.xml.

It is an XML file that tells the Android system everything it needs to know about your app, including what permission it requires to run on a device.

In particular it lists all of the activities and which one is the one to use to start the app.

If you open the generated Manifest, by double-clicking on it, you will see a little way down the file:

```
<activity
 android:name=".MainActivity"
 android:label="SimpleButton" >
```

This defines the Activity the system has created for you and the lines just below this define it as the startup Activity:

```
 <intent-filter>
  <action android:name="android.intent.action.MAIN" />
  <category android:name="android.intent.category.LAUNCHER" />
  </intent-filter>
</activity>
```

34

Notice that the choice of which Activity starts the app has nothing to do with what you call it, i.e. calling it MainActivity isn't enough.

For the moment you can rely on Android Studio to look after the Manifest for you. In most cases you will only need to edit it directly when you need to correct an error or add something advanced.

## Inside the Activity

The generated Activity has one class, **MainActivity**, which holds all of the methods and properties of your activity.

It also has three generated methods:

- onCreate
- onCreateOptionsMenu
- onOptionsItemSelected

The last two are obviously connected to the working of the **OptionsMenu**, which is an important topic but one that can be ignored for the moment. Not all Activities need to have an OptionsMenu and you could even delete these methods if you don't want to support an options menu.

All three of these methods are event handlers. That is they are called when the event that they are named after occurs. The whole of an Android app is a collection of nothing but event handlers and their helper functions.

The most important method generated by Android Studio is onCreate. This is an event handler and it is called when your app is created and is where we do all the initialization and setting up for the entire app. It is also generally the place we show the app's main UI screen.

Let's take another look at the first two lines of generated code for onCreate, which are the most important:

```
override fun onCreate(savedInstanceState: Bundle?) {
    super.onCreate(savedInstanceState)
    setContentView(R.layout.activity_main)
```

The onCreate event handler is passed a Bundle object called savedInstanceState. This is intended to preserve state information between invocations of your app and we will see how this is used later. In this case no data has been saved and so savedInstanceState is null – but you still have to pass it on to the inherited onCreate method. You will learn a lot more about Bundle in Chapter 12.

The final instruction calls setContentView, which is a method that has a number of different overloaded forms. In this case we pass an integer that indicates which XML file describes the layout to be used for the view. The setContentView method uses this to create all of the components of your UI as defined in the XML file. That is, this is the connection between the layout you created using the Layout Editor and the layout that appears on the device's screen.

It is worth looking a little closer at the way that the layout file is specified because this is a general way that Android lets you access resources. There is a whole chapter about resources later but it is still worth an introduction now.

The R object is constructed by the system to allow you to access the resources you have placed in the resource directories. For example, in onCreate the use of R.layout.activity_main returns an integer value, its id, that allows the setContentView method to find the activity_main XML layout file. In general all resources are found via the R object, think of it as an index of resources.

## View and ViewGroup

So far so good, but it is important to realize that what happens next is that the XML file is rendered as a set of View objects. That is, Java objects that are all sub-classes of the View object. The entire UI and graphics system is implemented as a hierarchy of components derived from the View class.

If you have used almost any GUI framework, AWT, Swing, XAML, etc, this idea will not be new to you. For example, a button is a class derived from View and to create a button all you have to do is create an instance of the Button class. You can of course create as many buttons as you like simply by creating more instances.

This leaves open the question of where the button appears in the layout?

The answer to this is that there are ViewGroup objects which act as containers for other View objects. You can set the position of the child View objects or just allow them to be controlled by various layout rules, more of which later. You can opt to create the entire UI in code by creating and working with instances of View objects and this is something demonstrated in Chapter 7.

So to be 100% clear all of the UI objects are defined in code and every UI object, such as a button, has a class with a similar name that lets you create the UI in code. In fact this is the only way to create the UI but there are other ways of specifying it. Instead of writing code to create the UI you can specify what you want in an XML file and then use supplied code to display it. This is what setContentView does – it reads the XML file you specify and creates objects that implement the UI.

This means you could create the UI by manually writing an XML file that defines view objects and how they nest one within another and rely on the system to create the view object hierarchy for you. Although this is possible, it is much easier to use the Layout Editor to create the XML file and then allow the system to create the objects for you from the generated XML file. That is, you can drag-and-drop a button onto the Layout Editor and it will automatically generate the XML needed to create it and specify where it is and all of the other details you set.

That is, at the surface level there are three ways to create the UI:

1.  You can write code to generate the necessary objects.

2.  You can write XML tags and use the system to convert the XML to the same objects.

3.  You can use the Layout Editor to interactively create the UI and generate the XML file which is then converted into the Java objects needed. You can think of this as:

    ```
    drag-and-drop layout -> XML -> View objects
    ```

Being able to work with the UI in an interactive editor is one of the great advantages of using Android Studio and, even if you know how to edit the XML layout file directly, it isn't a feature you should ignore. It is nearly always a good idea to use the layout editor as the first step and apply any tweaks, if necessary, to the XML file later.

## Creating Our First UI

To see how all of this fits together let's add a button and a textView object. You probably already know that a button is for pressing and you can guess that a textView is used to show the user some text.

First remove the Hello World text that is generated automatically when you create a new blank Activity. Load the content_main.xml file by opening it from the project view.

The content_main.xml is where you create all of your UI. There is another layout file, but as explained in Chapter 1 this simply provides the standard elements in a UI like the AppBar. Notice that because of this you can see UI components in the Layout Editor that you cannot edit - they belong to the other layout file. To remove "Hello World" all you have to do is select it and press the delete key:

Notice that there is an undo command, Ctrl-Z, if you delete something by mistake.

Next select the button in the Widgets section of the Palette by clicking on it:

If you now place the cursor over the design area you will discover that as you move it various alignments are indicated by lines:

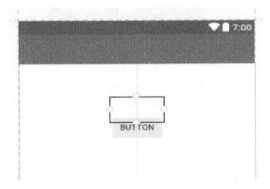

To position the button simply click and a full button, complete with the default caption Button, will appear.

However, simply dropping the button on the design surface isn't quite enough. If you just do this the button will be positioned but without any positioning constraints. If you try running the program you will find that the button sometimes vanishes on the emulator or real device. The reason is that with no constraints to its positioning applied it rises to the top of the screen and is hidden behind other controls.

This behavior is characteristic of the default ConstraintLayout, more of which later. For the moment we just need to apply some constraints to the button.

The simplest solution is to click on the Infer constraints icon and let Android Studio work out how to position the button:

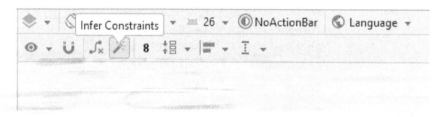

When you click this button constraints are added according to where the Button is positioned. At the moment exactly what constraints you end up applying matters less than the simple fact that there are some. In the screen dump below the button is constrained to be a fixed distance from the top and right-hand side. Notice that you can position the button and then click the Infer constraints button to set the constraints needed to keep the button in its location:

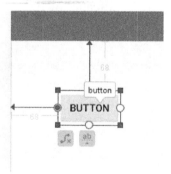

Now you have a button on the UI ready to go, let's add a TextView Widget in exactly the same way – click on its icon in the Palette, position in the Layout Editor and click to set the position. Notice that Android Studio provides positioning information to help you align components of the UI. Again you need to click the Infer constraints icon to position the TextView.

The simplest thing to do is position the TextView where you want it and then click the Infer constraints icon to set the constraints needed for that position:

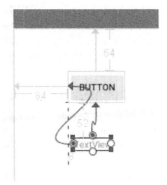

Notice that Android Studio provides positioning information to help you align components of the UI. The simplest approach to creating a layout is to place the components where you want them and then click the Infer constraints icon to apply constraints to fix their position. In practice these constraints may not be exactly what you need but it gives you a starting point. That's about it and in fact creating a complete complex UI is just more of the same, just a matter of picking components from the Palette and positioning them on the design surface.

If you now run the program, by clicking the green Run icon (refer back to Chapter 1 if you don't know how to do this) you will see your new UI:

Of course it doesn't do anything, even if you can click the button. The button does click, but there is no code connected to the button click event to say what should happen, something we will deal with very soon.

## Properties & Attributes

Our next task is to change the caption on the button. Recall that objects have properties and methods. Things like caption text, background color and so on for UI widgets are represented as properties. You can change properties in code, or at design time you can use the Attributes window on the right-hand side of the screen.

What is the difference between a property and an attribute?

The reality is that all of the UI objects are code objects and quantities like text are properties of the object but when you specify a quantity in XML it is known as an attribute. You could say that you set attributes in the XML to set the properties of code objects.

If you select the button and examine the Attributes window on the right you will find the button's text attribute. This currently contains the value "Button". If you change this to "Click Me!" and re-run the app you will see that the Button's caption has changed:

| layout_width | wrap_content | |
| layout_height | wrap_content | |
| **Button** | | |
| style | buttonStyle | |
| background | | |
| backgroundTint | | |
| stateListAnimator | | |
| elevation | | |
| visibility | none | |
| onClick | none | |
| **TextView** | | |
| text | Click Me! | |
| text | | |
| contentDescription | | |
| textAppearance | AppCompat.Widget.Button | |

You can set the initial properties of any of the widgets that you have placed in the UI. There are a great many properties and we need to spend some time looking at some of them. However, for the moment the important thing is that you see how easy it is to change a property using the Attributes window.

As you might guess, the property that you changed results in a change in the XML file defining the layout. Recall that the general principle is that the Layout Editor creates the XML file that you could have created by hand without any help from the Layout Editor. In this sense, the Layout Editor doesn't add anything to the process, other than being much easier.

# Events

Now we want to do something when the button is clicked. Android supports a complete event-driven UI. So what we need to do next is define a method, or function, that is called when the button is clicked.

Java's way of implementing events is complicated but now much simplified in Java 8, Kotlin makes event handlers comparatively easy, but still slightly more difficult than in languages such as C#.

There are a number of different ways to specify an event handler, but the simplest is to use the Layout Editor to generate the XML needed for the system to hookup the event handler to the event. This is not an approach that you can use all of the time. It only works for the click event, but it gets you started.

If you have used something like Visual Studio, it is also worth pointing out that Android Studio doesn't automatically create event handlers for you. In the case of Android Studio you have to create a function and then assign it as the onClick handler.

Using the Layout Editor approach, method click event handlers are simply public methods of the current Activity with the signature:

```
fun buttonOnClick(v: View){
```

Just in case you have missed or forgotten what a function's signature is:

*A function's signature is the number and types of the parameters it accepts. Functions with the same name but different signatures are considered to be different functions. In this case the function takes a single parameter, which is a View, and returns Unit, i.e. nothing.*

You can call the method anything you like, but in most cases it helps to specify exactly what the event it handles is. In this case we want to handle the button's onClick event – which occurs when the user clicks on the button with a mouse or more likely taps on the button using a touch sensitive device.

Load the MainActivity.kt file into the code editor and add the following method:

```
fun buttonOnClick(v: View){
    // do something when the button is clicked
}
```

This needs to be added directly following the onCreate method, or anywhere that makes it a method of the MainActivity class.

With all this code out of the way, now switch back to the Layout Editor, select the button, find the onClick property in the Attributes window and enter buttonOnClick:

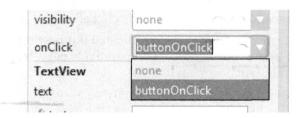

At the moment the IDE doesn't notice Kotlin methods that are suitable event handlers so you have to type them in, but this might well change in the near future. Notice that you don't type in parameters, just the name of the method.

That's all there is to it. You define your event handler with the correct signature and return type and set the appropriate onClick property in the Attributes window.

When it comes to other types of event you have to do the job in code – the XML/Layout Editor method only works for onClick.

## Connecting the Activity to the UI

Now we have an event handler hooked up to the button click event we usually want to do something that affects the UI as a result.

Let's suppose that when the button is clicked we want to change the text displayed in the TextView widget to "I've Been Clicked!".

We can do this by changing the TextView widget's text property to the new text. The only problem is how do we find the TextView widget in code?

This is a fairly standard problem when you use a markup language to define a UI. The markup language defines widgets, or other UI objects, and the code has to have a way of making the connection to those UI objects. For example, in JavaScript you make use of the getElementById method to retrieve a DOM object corresponding to a particular HTML element.

In Android we do something similar.

First make sure you follow the idea that all of the XML generated by the Layout Editor gets converted into a set of objects, one for each component or View placed on the design surface. These objects have the same range of properties as you saw in the Attributes window and have methods to get other things done. All you need to do is find a way to reference one of them.

In the case of the View object that caused the event this is very easy as it is passed to the event handler as the only argument of the call. So if the event handler is:

```
fun buttonOnClick(v: View){
```

and the event handler is only hooked up to the button, then you can be 100% sure that v is the button object when the event occurs.

If you want to change the button's caption you could just use its text property to change its value.

*Note: this is a Java property as all Android classes are Java classes. This means they don't have properties but have get and set methods which retrieve and modify property values. Kotlin automatically converts such get and set properties to properties that can be used without reference to get and set methods. In other words in Java you would have to write v.setText("New Text"); but in Kotlin you can write v .text="New Text". Kotlin automatically converts the assignment to a call to setText.*

*So if you are a Java programmer get out of the habit of calling getter and setters and just use assignment.*

So, in principle, all you have to write is:

```
v.text="I've Been Clicked!"
```

However, this doesn't work because v is declared to be a general View object which doesn't have a text property – not all View objects have any text to display.

To use the Button's text property we have to cast v to its correct type, namely a Button.

*Note: Casting is where you tell the system the type of the object you are working with. If classB is a subclass of classA then you can treat a classB object as a classA - after all it has all of the methods and properties that classA does by inheritance.*

*However, if you want to make use of a property or method that only classB has then you need to cast the reference to the classB object to make its type clear.*

*For example, assuming classB inherits from classA:*

```
val myObject:classA = classB()
```

*creates an instance of classB but myObject is declared to be of type classA. This is fine but you can only access the methods and properties of the classA object.*

*However, if you try:*

```
myObject.classBMethod()
```

*then it will fail if classBMethod only exists in classB.*

*To use the classB method you have to cast myObject to its real type:*

```
myObject as classB
```

*You can store a reference to the cast in a new variable:*

```
val myClassBObject:classB = myObject as classB
```

*and then call the method:*

```
myClassBObject.classBMethod()
```

*or you can just do the cast on the fly at the cost of an extra pair of parentheses:*

```
(myObject as classB).classBMethod()
```

If you simply change the code to cast the v object to a Button object, i.e. (Button) v, you will discover that Android Studio flags an error by showing Button in red. If you hover over the red symbol you will see the exact error message:

```
fun buttonOnClick(v: View){
    val button:Button = v as Button
```

Unresolved reference: Button

This is because you have used a class without importing it. You may see other classes, View for example highlighted in red as which classes are imported by default depends on the exact project template you are using.

Any class that you use has to be listed at the top of the program in an import statement. Whenever you see a "Cannot resolve symbol" error message the most likely cause is that you haven't imported the class.

This can be a tedious business but Android Studio has some help for you. If you click on the error symbol you will see a blue hint message:

```
? android.widget.Button? Alt+Enter
fun buttonOnClick(v: View){
    val button:Button = v as Button
```

*[handwritten note in left margin: Use "." to cast instead!! "as" & Always works!!]*

If you look at the hint message it suggests pressing Alt+Enter which is always good advice because it produces a list of possible fixes for the problem:

```
fun buttonOnClick(v: View){
    val button: Button = v as Button
```

Import
- Create class 'Button'
- Create enum 'Button'
- Create interface 'Button'
- Create type parameter 'Button' in class 'MainActivity'
- Create type parameter 'Button' in function 'buttonOnClick'
- Create annotation 'Button'
- Create type alias 'Button'

You can implement the fix simply by selecting it from the list.

In this case you have to add the class definition to the start of the program.

```
import android.widget.Button
```

You can do this manually, i.e. you can type it in, or just select the first option. The import is added and in a moment the red errors disappear.

If you hover over the corrected Button class name you will also see a light bulb:

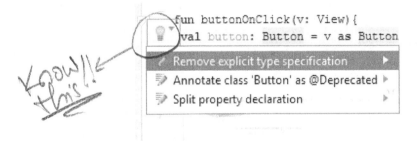

```
fun buttonOnClick(v: View){
    val button: Button = v as Button
```

- Remove explicit type specification
- Annotate class 'Button' as @Deprecated
- Split property declaration

Know this!!

Android Studio offers you hints on improving your code even when there are no errors – look out for the light bulbs. If you click on this one it will offer to remove the explicit type specification which is perfectly reasonable as:

```
val button = v as Button
```

can be considered more idiomatic Kotlin with the use of type inference. However the second option is to add a @Deprecated annotation which is unlikely at best. Android Studio is full of hints and offers to make your code better at every turn – you don't have to accept them.

Now we have the button object we can use its text property:

```
button.text  ="I've Been Clicked"
```

*Remember: No need to use get and set. In Java you would have to write*

```
button.setText("I've Been Clicked");
```

The complete event handler is:

```
fun buttonOnClick(v: View){
  val button = v as Button
  button.text  ="I've Been Clicked"
}
```

Now if you run the program you will see the button's caption change when you click the button.

This is a common pattern in making your UI work – event handlers change the properties of View objects to modify the UI.

Notice that this approach only works if you know the type of the object that caused the event and called the event handler. If your event handler is only connected to a single component then you do know the type of the object that caused the event. If it isn't, or if you want to modify the properties of a View object that isn't the subject of the event, then you have to find it.

This is exactly what we are going to do next.

## Finding View Objects

Now suppose we want to do something to one of the other components in the View. In this case we have to find the object that represents the component without the help of the event handler's argument.

For example how do we find the TextView that we placed below the button?

Kotlin makes this very easy.

Every View object defined in the XML file has an id. You can assign an id manually but the Layout Editor automatically assigns an id to each component you place on the design surface. You can see the id of an object by selecting the object and then looking at the top right of the Attributes window:

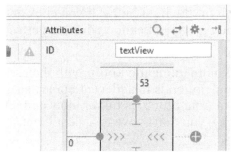

You can also use this window to enter a new value for the id i.e. you can use it to "rename" controls.

In this case you can see that our TextView object has been assigned an id of "textView". In fact this is in reality an integer constant used to identify the View object in the layout but Kotlin makes use of this identifier to create an Activity property of the same name.

The rule is that for every View object defined in the XML file that has an id Kotlin creates an Activity property of the same name. That is, in this case the id of the TextView is textView and so Kotlin automatically creates a property

```
this.textView
```

or, as you can generally drop this, just:

```
textView
```

When the program runs, each of these properties is set to reference the View object created with the same id. That is, the textView property references the TextView object.

This makes working with the UI very much easier. For example, to set the text property of the TextView object all we have to do is:

```
textView.text="You clicked my button"
```

As you type "text" notice that Android Studio will prompt you to import a definition derived from the XML file – accept this and you will be able to refer to all of the components in the XML file by their id.

```
textView
textView from content_main.xml for Activity (Android...   TextView
```

This adds the import:

```
import kotlinx.android.synthetic.main.content_main.*
```

The complete event handler is:

```
fun buttonOnClick(v: View) {
    val button = v as Button
    button.text = "I've Been Clicked"
    textView.text = "You clicked my button"
}
```

Notice that the button variable is a local variable that hides the button property that Kotlin automatically created for you from the XML ids.

If you now run the program you will see that you are informed twice of the fact that this very important button has been clicked:

You may think that this is all very small stuff and nothing like a real app, but this is how building a UI works in Android.

You now know how to design a single screen app using the widgets available in the Layout Editor's Toolbox, how to hook them up to handle their click events, how to find the object that represents them and how to call the methods that modify them.

Apart from the fine detail of how each of the widgets works – radio buttons, checkboxes and so on – you now have the general outline of how to build a single screen app.

# Summary

- An Activity is the unit of the Android app and it roughly corresponds to one screenful of user interface plus the code to make it work.

- In most cases you will create an Activity for each UI screen you want to present to your user.

- Only one Activity from your app is running at any given time.

- An Activity is single-threaded and runs on the UI thread.

- You can set which Activity starts the app in the Manifest. Android Studio sets this to MainActivity by default.

- The Activity has events corresponding to different stages in its lifecycle. The onCreate event is called when the app first starts and this is where you perform all initialization.

- You can also restore the app's state from previous runs at this point.

- The Activity then loads a View or ViewGroup object to create its user interface.

- You can create View/ViewGroup objects in three possible ways: in code, using XML or using the Layout Editor to generate the XML.

- The Layout Editor is far the easiest way to create a UI.

- By opening the XML file you can use the Layout Editor to place widgets corresponding to View objects on the design surface.

- You can use the Attribute window to set the attributes of each widget.

- The XML file that the Layout Editor creates is used by the Activity to set its UI by creating objects that correspond to each of the View objects placed using the Layout Editor.

- When you reference a class that isn't defined in the file, i.e. most of them, then you need to add an import statement to the start of the code.

- If you use Alt+Enter when the cursor is positioned within any word that is displayed in red then Android Studio will help you fix the problem.

- You can hook up onClick event handlers defined within the current Activity to the widgets using the Attributes window.

- An onClick event handler is just a public function with the signature myEventHandler(v:View):Unit.

- The View object parameter is sent to the View object that raised the event. This can be used to access the properties/methods of the View object that the user interacted with.

- To access other View objects directly you can make use of the fact that Kotlin converts all of the id attributes assigned by the Layout editor into Activity property initialized to reference the corresponding View object.

# Chapter 3

# Building a Simple UI

By this point in you understand how the Activity and the View fit together to create a simple application, but the Android UI is more complicated than most because of its need to cope with a range of very different screen sizes and orientations. In this chapter we look at the problem of layout and working with the UI framework and on the way we'll build a calculator app.

When building an Android app you will spend far more time than you could possibly imagine on perfecting the UI. So it is important that you master the basics so that you can move on to code that does more interesting things.

The learning curve with any UI framework is more or less the same. First you have to find out what constitutes an application that you can run i.e. where is the code? In Android's case this is an Activity.

Next you have to work out how UI components are represented, how you can create them and how to hook up the UI with the code. In Android's case this is a matter of a hierarchy of View objects and hooking up with the code is a matter of finding the objects representing each UI component and adding event handlers.

Once you have the basics you have to start exploring what components you have been provided with to build a UI. In general this varies from the extremely simple - the Button, for example - to almost complete applications in themselves - the Listview, for example. It would take a long time to master all of them, but what most programmers do is make sure that they can use the basic components and then find out about the bigger more sophisticated components when needed. The good news is that once you know how one component, even the simplest, works then most of it generalizes to bigger more complicated things.

We also have to worry about how to lay out the UI – how to size and position sets of components. Android is particularly sophisticated in this respect because being a mobile operating system it has to contend with a wide range of screen sizes and even orientation changes while an app is running. This is not a simple topic and we will have to consider it in more detail later, but for the moment let's just take a look at the easier aspects of screen layout.

Using the Layout Editor is the simplest and most productive way to work so let's continue to concentrate on this method of creating a UI. This chapter is mostly about how to use the Layout Editor with the default layout and the challenges of creating a UI.

## What's in the Palette

Start Android Studio and create a new simple basic activity project called **UItest**. This is going to be our UI playground for the rest of this chapter. Accept all the defaults, apart from selecting a Basic Activity, and wait while the project is created. Make sure you have checked Include Kotlin support on the first dialog page.

If you now open the file content_main.xml in the app/res/layout folder then the Layout Editor will open and you will see the familiar rendering of the default layout.

Now it is time to look at the Palette in more detail:

The top four sections of the Palette hold the most important UI components with a further five sections with more specialized ones.

1. The Widgets section contains the most frequently used components – Buttons, Checkboxes and so on. This is the set of components you need to learn to use first.

2. Text Fields are a set of text input components which all work in more or less the same way.

3. Layouts are containers for other components that provide different layout rules.

4. Containers are like mini-layouts in that you generally put other components inside them and the container "looks after" them:

5. Images and media are containers for specific types of resources such as images and videos.

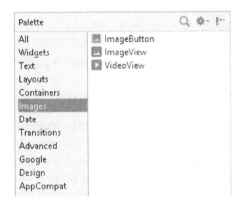

6. Date and time are widgets concerned with date and time entry and display.

7. Transitions perform limited animation between different components.

8. Advanced doesn't really mean advanced – more bigger and complex components such as the number picker.

9. Google is for services provided by Google and consists of MapView and AdView at the moment.

10. Design is a collection of more advanced controls such as tabbed pages.

11. AppCompat are controls that provide up-to-date controls for older versions of Android.

## The Button an Example

Where else should we start – the Button is almost the "Hello World" of UI construction. If you know how to work with a Button you are well on your way to understanding all of the possible components. The good news is that we have already met and used the Button in Chapter 2 and discovered how to work with it in code. However, there is still a lot to find out.

Generally there are three things you need to discover about using any component.

1. How to make it initially look like you want it to. This is a matter of discovering and setting properties using the attributes provided in the Layout Editor.

2. How to modify the way a component looks at runtime. This is a matter of finding out how to work with properties in code.

3. How to hook up the events generated by the component to the code.

Setting properties sounds easy, but there are different types of properties and these have different appropriate ways of allowing you to interact with them.

The first thing we have to find out about is how to position a component.

## Positioning – the ConstraintLayout

Before you continue with the project select and delete the default "hello world" text – it makes trying things out easier to have a clean design surface.

There are two views of your layout you can opt for – design and blueprint. The design view looks like your UI when it runs on a real device. It is useful for getting an overall feel and impression of what the UI really looks like. The blueprint view shows you the UI in skeleton form. This makes it quicker and easier to work with when you are positioning things.

You can view both at the same time but this is mostly a waste of screen space.

Some users prefer the blueprint view because it seems to be light weight others prefer the design view because it is complete. Use whichever you find workable but there is no doubt that the blueprint view is faster and suffers from less lag as you try to position components.

Next click on the Button in the palette and drag it onto the layout.

Notice the way the layout information changes as you move the button around the design surface:

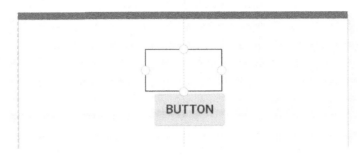

It is important to realize that this positioning information is only to help you locate UI components relative to the existing layout. With the new constraint layout where you drop a component has no effect on where is will show when the app is run. In fact if you simply drop a UI component on the design surface without applying any constraints then when you run the app the component will drift up to the top left-hand corner. In fact things are slightly more complicated because there is a facility that will automatically add constraints when you drop the component that realizes the alignments shown at the moment you drop. However this can be turned off as we will see. The key thing to realize is that the alignments displayed are not constraints.

Using the constraint layout the only thing that affects where a component is displayed are the constraints you apply.

So how do you apply a constraint?

You can have the Layout Editor suggest them for you automatically or you can apply them manually.

Automatic constraints are the easiest to use and there are two ways to get the editor to apply constraints dynamically:

1. Autoconnect mode
2. Infer Constraints

They do slightly different things and you need to learn to make them work together.

The Autoconnect mode seems the most useful when you first meet it but in practice it can be confusing and error prone. However, it is worth trying out. To turn Autoconnect on simply click the Autoconnect icon on at the top of the Layout Editor:

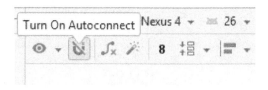

With Autoconnect on, when you place a component on the design surface the editor attempts to work out suitable constraints based on where you drop the component. If it fails to apply any constraints then it will try again if you drag the component to another location. It will only apply constraints to satisfy the alignments that are indicated in the Layout Editor. If you drop a component at an arbitrary point on the screen with no alignments indicated then no constraints will be applied.

Once it has applied constraints, these are not altered if you modify the component. For example if you drop a component in the middle of the screen then constraints are applied to place the component 50% of the way down the screen and 50% from the left. If you then move the component the percentages are changed to position it but the actual constraint use wont change to anything more appropriate if you move it to say the top left hand corner. Once a constraint has been applied its type will not change.

The Infer Constraints option is actually easier to use and reasonably effective. All you have to do is position all the components where you want them and then click the Infer Constraints button:

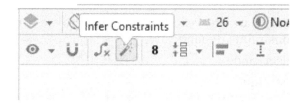

When you do this constraints will be calculated based on where each component is. This gives you more time to position the components and you can always delete all the constraints and click Infer Constraints again to recompute them. Only constraints that are necessary to fix the position of a component are added – existing constraints are not modified. This means you can use Infer Constraints to make sure that your layout has enough constraints to make it work – if none are added it was OK.

Also notice that once Infer Constraints has added a constraint the type of constraint wont change if you drag the component.

A good strategy is to switch off Autoconnect and use Infer Constraints every time you place a new component on the design surface. This allows you to build up a layout one component at a time and check each new set of constraints. You can then modify the newly added constraints and move on to the next component.

Where things get difficult is when you have a multi component layout and need to make radical changes. Often it is easier in this case to delete all of the constraints using the Clear All Constraints icon, and start again:

For a component that has been placed on its own close to the top and left-hand edge of the screen, constraints will be added that fix its distance from the left and top:

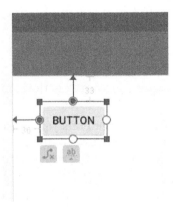

From now on when the button is displayed it will position itself at 36 from the left and 33 from the top. These constraints are applied no matter what the size of the physical screen is. This is the sense in which they are constraints rather than absolute positioning.

It is worth knowing that the actually positioning is achieved by setting the button's margin properties to 36 and 33. The constraint layout may be the most sophisticated of the layout components but it positions other components using properties that have been in use from the start of Android.

You can see that things aren't quite as simple as positioning relative to the edge of the screen if you place a second button on the surface and move it close to the first. Now if you click the Infer Constraints button the constraints that are applied are taken relative to the first button:

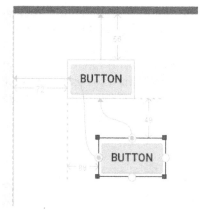

You can see that in this case the second button is positioned 88 from the left edge of the first button and 49 below it. Once again these constraints will be obeyed no matter how large or small the physical screen the UI is displayed on. What is more if you move the first button the second button will keep its position relative to the first. In fact if you click and drag the first button, the second will move with it.

If you play with the positioning in the Layout Editor you will quickly get the idea.

The big problem with inferring constraints is that the system sometimes gets it wrong.

Rather than let the Layout Editor infer constraints incorrectly you can place them manually. All you have to do is drag a line from the constraint circles on the component to the edge you want to use as a reference point.

For example to position the button relative to the right side of the screen simply drag the circle on the right of the button to the right side of the screen and then move the button where you want it:

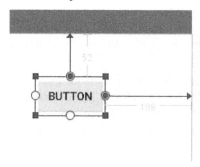

There are quite a few different types of constraint that you can apply and we will go into these in detail in Chapter 5 where we examine layouts in depth. For the moment this almost all you need to know.

Constraints can be applied automatically or manually and they often set the distance from some point on the component to a point on some other component.

For example, if you want to place a component relative to another then simply drag the constraint point on the first to an edge of the second.

In the case shown below manual constraints have been applied because constraint inference would have placed constraints on the left-hand edge of the screen:

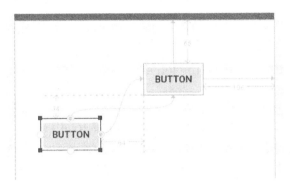

It is also worth knowing at this early stage that the Attributes window can help you in a number of ways. The first is that it has a diagram that shows you the currently applied constraints, and lets you modify them and set distances exactly:

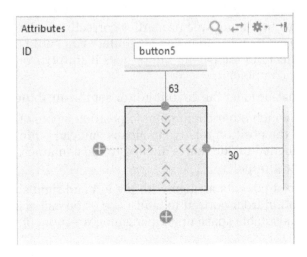

If you click on one of the constraint lines then you can enter a value for the distance. You can also click on the dot and delete the constraint completely or on the + and add a constraint.

As you might guess, there are attributes which let you set the location and margins for each position using the editor.

To see all of the attributes you have to click on the View all attributes icon at the top right of the Attributes window – the double arrow.

The attributes listed in the window are not a simple representation of the properties that you might set in code to achieve the same results. They are organized and simplified to make using the Layout Editor easier.

For example, if you look in the fully expanded Attributes window you will see:

```
Layout
  Top
```

which gives the distance from the top edge and

```
Contraints
  top_toTopOf
```

which specifies the object that the positioning is relative to.

If you look in the XML file you will see:

```
app:layout_constraintTop_toTopOf="parent"
android:layout_marginTop="348dp"
```

All layout attributes start with layout_*name* where the *name* gives the positioning affected. The mapping from the Attributes window to the XML properties is fairly obvious.

It is also worth understanding that in allowing you to set the position of a component by simply dragging it to the location you want, the Layout Editor is working out how to set multiple properties correctly. In the example above it sets the top_toTopOf and MarginTop attributes. You could do this manually to get the same effect but the Layout Editor does it simply from where you have positioned a component.

This is why it is easier to let the Layout Editor set the attributes for you.

The ability to set which other component to position against i.e. which component to set the position relative to means you can build sets of components all aligned to one that is aligned to the container, so that they all move together as a group.

You can also set components to align with the left and right side of the screen and allow for rotation from portrait to landscape. You can also set constraints which divide the available space up by percentages – more of this in Chapter 5.

The constraint layout is the preferred layout component. The reason is that it is fast and efficient compared to the usual alternative of putting one layout inside another. Unless you have a good reason not to, it is the one to use.

However, all this said it is very easy to get into a complete mess with the layout in the Layout Editor. If components go missing then chances are they are on top of each other. The easiest way to sort this problem out is to go to the Attributes window and manually reset one of the positioning properties.

It is helpful to notice the following:

- Use positioning relative to another component if it makes logical sense. That is if you have a text entry component then it make sense to position its Accept Button relative to its right-hand side.

- If you position everything relative to the container parent then you effectively have an absolute layout.

- If the screen size changes then it is possible that components will overlap one another if there isn't enough space. Always make sure your layouts have plenty of unnecessary space.

- A good strategy when working with a group of components is to pick one that you position relative to the container, then position all other components relative to it to ensure that you can move the group and keep alignments.

- Remember that some components can change their size as well as location and this can modify the position of components positioned relative to them.

The Constraint Layout component is used by default but you can change this for any of the other layout components – Relative, Linear, Table, Grid and Frame. There are also other container components which can be used in place of these standard layout components.

One thing worth knowing at this early stage is that components have layout properties that are provided by their container, so the set of properties that we have looked at in connection with the Constraint layout component are unique to it. That is if you use another Layout then you have to learn its layout properties from scratch.

Again this is another topic we have to return to.

## Sizing

In comparison to positioning, sizing a component is almost trivial.

All components have a Height and Width property and these correspond to their drawn height and width when the component is actually rendered on the screen.

You may have noticed that there are what look like sizing handles in the corners of the components that you place in the Layout Editor. If you drag any of these, the component will change its size. However, the components content will not be resized. All that happens is that the content has some space around it. If the content gets bigger or smaller the component stays the same size. If the content it too big then it won't fit in the component.

You can see the space is fixed in the Attributes window. The lines shown inside the component relate to the size of the component and its relation to its content. Straight lines indicate a fixed size:

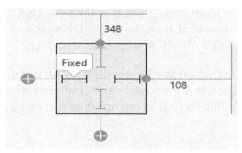

An alternative to fixed size components is to allow them to automatically resize to fit or wrap their contents. To set this all you have to do is click on the inner straight lines which change to $<<<$ to suggest springs which allow the component to change its size:

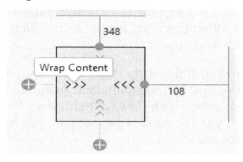

The third option is Match Constraints which lets the component change it size to fill the available space.

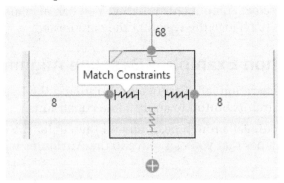

This auto-sizing behavior is set by the layout_width and layout_height properties. You can modify this by typing in an exact size e.g. 100dp into the value box next to the property.

Also notice that you can set a maximum and a minimum size for most components.

Setting a maximum will result in the content being truncated if it doesn't fit. Setting a minimum is often the best plan because then the component will increase in size when necessary.

## The Component Tree

If you look to the bottom left corner of Android Studio in Design mode you will see a window called Component Tree. This is almost self explanatory and hardly needs explanation other than to draw your attention to it. Notice that you can see the tree structure of the layout starting at the Layout container. You can see that the default layout is ConstraintLayout   and you can see all of the other components correctly nested within their parent containers:

Notice that you can select and delete layout elements directly in the tree. This is useful when you have a complex layout that has gone so wrong that you are finding it hard to select components reliably. You can also move elements around in the tree to change the way that they are nested.

## A Simple Button Example – Baseline Alignment

As a simple demonstration let's first place a Button on the Layout Editor and use the Infer Constraints button to apply some constraints.

If you find it difficult get a rough position and then enter the exact margins then always remember that you can move to the Attributes window and enter them directly.

Next place a TextView widget on the Layout Editor.

In this case the alignment we want is for the text to be on the same line as the text in the Button. This is a baseline alignment and one of the more sophisticated alignments but if you have the Layout Editor zoomed so that you can see the full area of the screen the chances are all you will be able to do is align to the top or bottom of the Button.

If you look at the TextView's representation in the Layout Editor you will see that there are two small icons below it. The first removes all of the constraints from the component, and the second makes the text baseline, a small elliptical box, appear inside it:

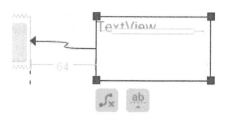

This represents the text in the TextView and you can use it to set up a baseline constraint.

All you have to do is select the TextView and hover the cursor over the elliptical box until is highlighted. Next drag from the elliptical box to the baseline of the text in the button, or any component that you want to align the baseline with:

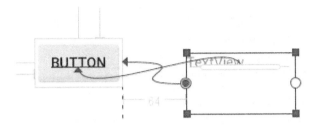

That's all you have to do. After this the text in the button and the text in the TextView will share a common baseline. If you move the Button then the TextView will move with it. If you want to remove the baseline alignment then all you have to do is select the TextView, hover over the elliptical box, and click when the remove baseline constraint appears.

## Orientation and Resolution

One of the biggest challenges in creating apps for Android is allowing for the range of screen sizes and orientations. Mobile app development is distinctly different from desktop development because of this need to deal with differing screen sizes. Even when your app is running on a fixed device, the user can still turn it though 90 degrees and change the screen dimensions in a moment and then turn it back again. So your app has to respond to these changes. Fortunately Android makes is easier for you by providing facilities that specifically deal with resolution and orientation changes, but you need to come to terms with this situation as early as possible in your progress to master Android programming.

Android Studio has lots of tools to help with the problem of variable layout. For example, it lets you see your layout in a range of devices, orientations and resolutions. This makes it so much easier.

We can test our layout in landscape mode simply by selecting the Landscape option:

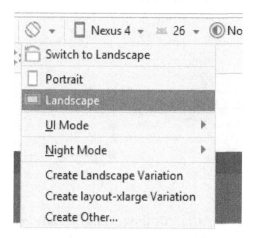

The relative positions that you set in portrait mode are applied in landscape mode without modification and so it is important that you work on their specification so that the UI looks good in either orientation. If this isn't possible then you can provide a separate layout for each orientation.

You can also see what your UI looks like on the range of supported screen sizes by selecting from the list of devices that appears when you click on the **Device In Editor** button:

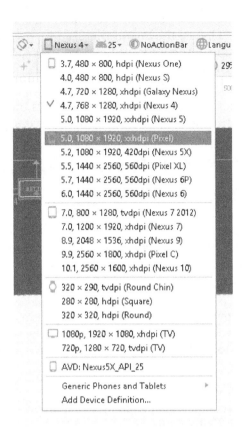

For simple layouts this is probably enough but Android has more up its sleeve to help you work with different sized screens. In particular you can make use of "fragments" and create a separate layout for each screen orientation and resolution. Fragments are advanced and the subject of a separate book, **Android Programming: Mastering Fragments & Dialogs.** On the other hand, using different layouts for each orientation and resolution is fundamental to Android UI design and you need to at least know it exists at this early stage.

The idea is quite simple – provide a layout resource for each orientation and resolution you want to support. The system will automatically select the resource layout needed when the app is run on a real device.

How this works is simple, but Android Studio has some helpful features that shield you from the underlying implementation. It is a good idea to first discover how it works and then move on to see how Android Studio does it for you.

If you create a new layout file called activity_main.xml, i.e. exactly the same name as the portrait layout file you have already created, but in the folder layout-land this will be used automatically when the user rotates the device into landscape mode. That is, the layout file used in any situation is determined by the name of the folder it is stored in. With this new layout which applies only to a landscape orientation you can now create a layout that will only be used in this orientation.

What happens in general is that when your app starts the system picks the best available layout file for the screen according to what has been stored in the resource folders, i.e. layout for portrait and layout-land for landscape..

When the device is rotated the system restarts your app and loads the best available layout. If you only have a portrait layout then it is used for all orientations, but if you also have a landscape layout file then it will be used for landscape mode.

What has just been described is exactly what happens. To recap, there are folders for each resolution and orientation and you can create multiple versions of layout resources all with the same name. The system automatically picks the folder to use to load the layout appropriate to the hardware at runtime.

Android Studio, however, tries to present this to you in a simpler way. The project view hides the fact that different folders are used and simply shows you the different versions of the resource files with a qualifier appended - (land) for a landscape file etc.

Let's see how this works.

To add a landscape layout to the button and text layout given above simply use the Orientation in Editor button:

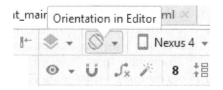

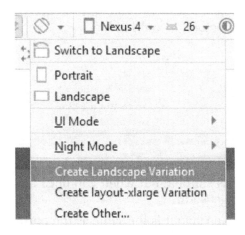

Initially the portrait layout is used as the template for the landscape layout. Make sure you are editing the content_main.xml file before you create the landscape layout based on it. This ensures that this is the file that is used as the template for the landscape version of the file.

The landscape version of the file will contain all of the UI components that the template file does. This means that your code can interact with it in the usual way without knowing that it is working with a different layout. All the code cares about is that there is a button or there is a textView – not where they are placed or what orientation is in use.

If you examine the Project window you will see the new layout file listed:

You can see that there are now two content_main.xml files and one has (land) added after its name. As already explained this is a simplification that Android Studio offers you.

If you switch to the Project Files view you will see that in fact the new layout resource is in a new directory, layout-land:

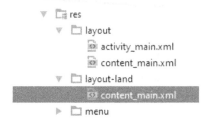

Android Studio's view is simpler, but when you need to know where files are really stored this view is useful.

At first the new landscape layout is the same as the portrait layout, but you can edit it to make it more suitable for the orientation. For example, we might want to place the text under the button in landscape mode:

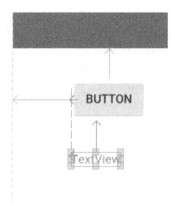

Now if you run the app using the simulator you will initially see the portrait screen, but if you rotate the simulator to landscape mode using the menu to the right, you will notice a pause where the portrait layout is visible and then it will change to the landscape layout.

If you view the app on a range of devices you can rotate to landscape and see your custom landscape layout.

In general the best plan is to create a complete portrait layout and generate a landscape layout as late as possible in the development so you don't have to repeat UI tweaks.

Also notice that the auto-switching of layouts causes a potential problem. When the layout is switched your app is restarted and this means that it can lose its current state. It is as if your app has just been started by the user. To solve this problem we need to look into the app lifecycle and discover how to preserve state, which is covered in Chapter 13.

You can also use the same approach to supporting different screen resolutions. The idea is the same – multiple layout XML files are provided, one for each resolution, and the system automatically picks which one to use. This is slightly more complicated than dealing with orientation because you might well have to provide different resolution images to make the layout look good. More on this after we have looked at resources and resource management.

This is just our first look at a particular aspect of app development that makes Android more complicated than developing for a fixed screen size and it turns out not to be so difficult as it might first appear.

## A First App – Simple Calculator

As an example of building a simple app using the ConstraintLayout and the Layout Editor, let's build a Calculator App. Some of the techniques used in this app are a little beyond what we have covered so far but you should be able to follow and it is time to show what something more than a single button app looks like.

This is a very simple calculator - all it does is form a running sum. It has just ten numeric buttons and a display. It takes the values on each of the buttons and adds them to a running total. There are no operator buttons, add, subtract or clear – but you could add them to extend its functionality.

Start a new Basic Activity project called ICalc or whatever you want to call it. Accept all of the defaults.

The principle of operation is that we are going to set up a grid of ten buttons. Set each button to 0 through 9 as a text label. We are then going to assign the same onClick handler to each of the buttons. All it is going to do is retrieve the text caption showing on the button, convert it to an integer, add it to the running sum, and then store it back in the TextView after converting it back to a String.

Put simply, when a button is clicked the event handler is called which retrieves the button's label as a digit and adds it to the running total on display.

### Code

So the code is fairly easy.

We need a private property to keep the running total in:

```
private var total = 0
```

Next we need an onButtonClick function which is going to be used to handle the onClick event for all of the buttons. Refer back to Chapter 2 if you don't know about simple event handling.

73

The button that the user clicks is passed as a View object as the only argument to the function and we can use this to get its text caption:

```
fun onButtonClick(v: View) {
    val button = v as Button
    val bText = button.text.toString()
```

Now that we have the button's caption, 0, 1, 2 and so on, we can convert it to an integer and add it to the running total:

```
val value = bText.toInt()
total += value
```

Finally we set the TextView's text property to the total converted to a String:

```
    textView.text= total.toString()
}
```

The complete event handler is:

```
private var total = 0
fun onButtonClick(v: View){
    val button=v as Button
    val bText=button.text.toString()
    val value=bText.toInt()
    total+=value
    textView.text= total.toString()
}
```

Put this code within the MainActivity class as one of its methods, for example right at the end just before the final closing }.

When you enter this code you will see many of the classes and methods in red:

```
fun onButtonClick(v: View) {
    val button = v as Button
    val bText = button.text.toString()
    val value = bText.toInt()
    total += value
    textView.text = total.toString()
}
```

This is because they need to be imported to be used by the project. You can do this manually, adding the necessary import statements at the start of the file, but it is much easier to place the cursor into each one of the symbols in red and press Alt+Enter and select **Import Class** if necessary. This should be becoming second nature by now.

Notice that the error flagged in textView cannot be cleared – it is a real error. We haven't as yet defined the UI and textView doesn't exist. It will once we create the UI, so for the moment ignore the error.

## Layout

Now we turn our attention to the layout. Open the layout file, delete the default text and place a single button on the design surface at the top right of the screen with a little space. We need to modify its text attribute and we can use a shortcut to get to it. If you double click on it you will be transferred to the text property window where you can enter 7 as its text attribute.

While in the Attributes window find the onClick attribute. Set this to onButtonClick, the event handler you have just written:

To create a grid of buttons you have to repeat this process nine more times. You could do this by dragging each button onto the design surface and manually set the constraints needed to locate each one relative to the buttons already placed. However, we can use the one Button we have already created to make the rest using copy and paste.

Select the button in the Component Tree and use the Copy command and then paste two more Buttons onto the design surface. The copies will be placed on top of the first Button so drag them to form a rough line of three Buttons. Don't worry at this stage about exact positioning, we only need to do this after the constraints are in place. Change the text attribute of each button to read 7, 8 and 9 respectively:

If you try to use Infer Constraints you will discover that it works but the constraints applied are not necessarily as logical as you might wish for. In this case the constraints are reasonable but notice that the vertical position of the row is set by the middle button and the horizontal position by the first button:

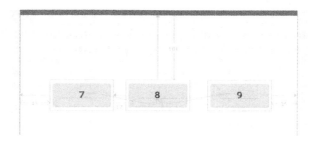

There are many ways to set the constraints but it is convenient to be able to position the entire array of buttons using the top left-hand button. So position it with constraints to the top and left of the screen.

The second button in its row can have a constraint set to position it to the right of the first button and align its bottom with the bottom of the first button.

The third button in the row has the same constraints as the button on its left:

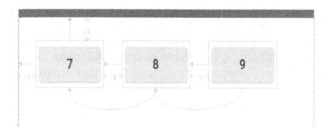

Now is also a good time to position the buttons accurately either by dragging or by using the Attributes window.

Continue this pattern with the next row, don't try and copy and paste an entire row because the constraints become complicated. Copy and paste three more buttons. Apply constraints as for the first row, but in this case position the first button in the row relative to the top left button:

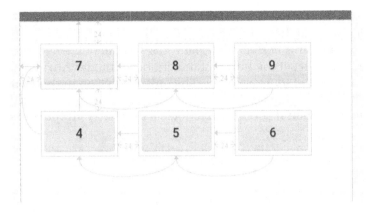

Change the text in the buttons to 4, 5 and 6 as shown.

The final row is the same but its first button is positioned relative to the first button in the second row. Finally add the lone zero button and position it relative to the first button in the third row:

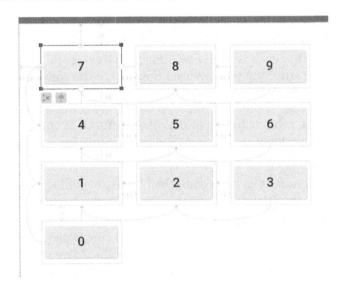

Make sure that you change the text of the last four buttons to 1, 2, 3 and 0 respectively.

Check the constraints carefully as it is very easy to make a mistake. The principle is that the first button in each row is positioned vertically by the button above and the other buttons in the row are positioned relative to the first button.

This is a lot of work!

Now we need to make the grid more regular. Select each button in turn and make sure its caption is correct and that it has the onclick event handler set. Then for each button set the horizontal margins using the Attributes window to 16 horizontally and to 0 vertically. The only exception to this is the first button in each row that needs to be set to 0 horizontally and 16 vertically - if you think about it then it should make logical and fairly simple sense:

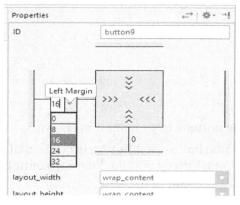

Now you have a grid of buttons correctly positioned.

Try to make sure that each Button you add is relative to one of the other Buttons and make sure that you have set them all to the same onClick handler. You can check that you have done this successfully by dragging one of the Buttons and see if they all follow! If one or two don't then try repositioning them relative to one of the other Buttons. If you find any positioning difficult zoom in.

If you get into a mess delete all the constraints and start over.

To make this look more like a keypad select the 0 key and size it so that it occupies a double width.

Finally add a TextView at the top. You can position it relative to the top row and the 7 key and then size it so that it spans the complete set of buttons. To do this you will have to delete the constraints on the 7 key and set its top relative to the bottom of the TextView and its left to line up with the left of the TextView.

Don't forget to position the TextView relative to the top of the screen:

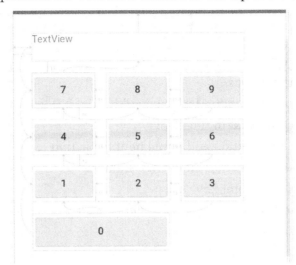

Now you should be able to move the entire block when you move just the TextView to a new location.

It is good to know that you can undo an action by using Ctrl-Z. If you find the Layout Editor too difficult to work with to create this layout, and it can be difficult, you might prefer to set the layout attributes using the Attributes window.

Select the TextView and use the Attributes window to change the font size to 18p or more – you will find it under the textAppearance field.

Finally run the program in the usual way and you will be please to discover your first app does actually calculate things!

Try rotating the emulator to see what it looks like in landscape mode.

Not bad but as forewarned, as the app restarts you lose any calculation you were performing since the app is restarted when the orientation changes.

If you can, try it out on a real Android device. This lets you find out what it really feels like. Also do have a look at what the layout looks like on a range of screens and orientations.

This isn't much of a calculator, but you could make it into a really good one.

- Right align the text in the display
- Add a + and – button and implement the action
- Allow the user to enter multi-digit numbers
- Add a decimal point key
- Add * and / keys
- Add a clear key

# Summary

- You can create the XML layout file by hand, but using the Layout Editor is easier.

- It is still useful to know how the XML file works so that you can edit it when the Layout Editor lets you down in some way.

- The Layout Editor modifies the way components look in the Layout mode by changing a component's attributes.

- How you position a component depends on the Layout you are using.

- ConstraintLayout lets you position components relative to each other or to the container.

- The Layout Editor may change multiple attributes to position the component where you want it.

- Use the Component Tree to select components that are difficult to select in the Layout Editor.

- You can use the Attributes window to select and directly set any attribute.

- If you find positioning or sizing difficult in the Layout Editor try zooming in.

- You can use Android Studio to view what your app looks like on various screen sizes and orientations.

- Different orientations and resolutions can be accommodated by creating additional layout files all with the same name. The system will pick which one to use at runtime.

- You can copy and paste components in the Layout Editor to quickly build up repeated UI designs.

- A single event handler can be attached to many components.

Working with Android Studio makes building the UI easy with an interactive editor, but you still need to find out how to handle the things it isn't quite so good at. We now need to find out how to work with any event, not just onClick. Even though most controls can be used very successfully using just the onClick event, there are other types of event that cannot be handled simply by setting an onEvent attribute in the Attribute Window.

In this chapter we look in depth at Android event handling. As before, the emphasis will be on using Android Studio and the Layout Editor to get as much of the work done as possible.

The good news is that Kotlin's support for passing functions as parameters makes it all much easier. However, this doesn't mean that you can completely ignore the way that Java handles the problem. Kotlin has to work with libraries written in Java and are based on Java's way of implementing event handlers. You don't have to go too deep, but you do need to know how Kotlin makes use of the Java object-oriented event mechanism.

## How Java Passes Functions

If you don't want to know how things work you can skip this section until you get stuck with an event handler and then come back and read it.

Events in Java are slightly more complicated than other languages because originally everything in Java was an object and the only way a function can exist is as a method, i.e. as part of an object. When you need to set up an event handler you need to specify the function to be called when the event happens. You can't pass a function as a parameter to another function as Java doesn't support function types.

The solution is to define an Interface that has one abstract method – a SAM or Single Abstract Method. The abstract method is the function that will be used as the event handler. To pass it you have to create an instance of the Interface, i.e. an object that has the method defined, and pass it.

*An interface is like a class but it simply defines the functions that a class has to support. If a class inherits or implements an interface then you have to write code for each function defined in the interface. You can think of an interface as a specification for a list of functions you have to write to implement the interface. Both Kotlin and Java support interfaces.*

It is worth saying at this early stage that not all event handlers in the Android SDK are implemented as SAMs.

Some are classes or interfaces that have more than one abstract method. That is they are objects that bundle up a set of related events. Both Java and Kotlin have provided easier ways of working with SAMs, but these don't work when the object in question has multiple abstract methods. When you encounter this situation you have to create a full instance of the class in question – the good news is that there are easy ways of doing this as well.

## Android Events

The way that events are implemented in Android follow a standard pattern.

Any object that can generate an event will have a set*event*Listener method which can be used to attach an on*Event*Listener object to the event handler list.

The name of the method and the object includes the name of the event. So there is a setOnClickListener method which takes an OnClickListener object as its only parameter.

Notice that this naming system is entirely convention and not part of the Java language.

The On*Event*Listener objects are all derived from an interface of the same name which defines a single abstract method which acts as the event handler.

For example, OnClickListener is an interface which has the single method onClick(View v) defined.

To use it as an event handler you have to create an instance that implements onClick and then add it to the event handler list using setOnClickListener.

In Java this is a simple but tedious process, if you use the fundamental way of implementing an event handler, that involves a lot of boilerplate code. First you would have to create a new class that implemented the Interface. Then you would have to create a new instance of this class and pass it to setOnClickListener.

## The Kotlin Object

In Kotlin you don't have to first create a class and then create an instance, you can go directly to the new object you require using the ability to declare objects directly.

You can declare an object using very similar syntax to declaring a class. For example:

```kotlin
object myObject {
    fun myMethod() {
        . . .
    }
}
```

creates an object instance called myObject with a single method. Notice that this gives you an object without having to define a class. Objects declared in this way can implement an interface in the same way as a Class.

```kotlin
object myObject:myInterface {
    . . .
}
```

So to create an instance that implements OnClickListener all we have to do is start the declaration of the object with:

```kotlin
object MyOnClick:View.OnClickListener{
}
```

Android Studio will implement the methods defined in the interface for you. All you have to do is place the cursor in the red line that signals that you haven't implemented the interface and then press Alt and Enter. Select Implement members from the menu that appears:

The generated code is easy to understand:

```kotlin
object MyOnClick: View.OnClickListener {
    override fun onClick(p0: View?) {
        TODO("not implemented")
    }

}
```

The question mark at the end of View is the only thing that might confuse you. This declares p0 to be a nullable type. Java doesn't use Kotlin's non-nullable types and rules and hence anything passed into a Kotlin function that is a Java object has to be treated as a nullable type – hence the question mark. It is good practice not to convert nullable types to non-nullable types without checking that it isn't actually null – see Chapter 17 for more information.

In this case there is no way that p0 can be null so we can cast it "unsafely" to Button which is non-nullable:

```kotlin
object MyOnClick:View.OnClickListener{
    override fun onClick(v: View?) {
        (v as Button).text = "You Clicked Me"
    }
}
```

If, for any reason v is null, an exception will be thrown.

Now that we have our instance of OnClickListener we can set it as an event handler for the Button b:

```kotlin
b.setOnClickListener(MyOnClick)
```

You can also make use of an object expression to create and pass the object in one step.

An object expression is an anonymous object that you create in the usual way, but without supplying a name

```kotlin
object {
    fun myMethod() {
        . . .
    }
}
```

An object created in this way can implement an interface or inherit from a class:

```kotlin
object:myInterface{
}
```

So you can write the previous example as:

```kotlin
b.setOnClickListener(object: View.OnClickListener {
        override fun onClick(p0: View?) {
            (p0 as Button).text = "You Clicked Me"
        }
})
```

This is the simplest way of doing the job, but sometimes it is useful to define the object so that it can be reused. There is also a subtle difference in what variables are accessible depending on where the object is created – see the section on closure later in this chapter.

This method of creating event handlers works for any type of event. All you have to do is:

1.  create an instance of the On*Event*Listener object and provide implementations for all of the abstract methods.

2.  Use the setOn*Event*Listener function to add the On*Event*Listener you have just created to the list of event handlers.

If there are multiple event handlers defined in the On*Event*Listener you simply implement them all and pass the entire object.

In most cases, however, there is only a single abstract method (SAM) and in this case there are even simpler ways of achieving the same result.

## Passing Functions In Kotlin

We have examined the fundamental way of passing an object that hosts event handlers as methods, but there are three different, although related, ways of passing an event handler when the event object is a SAM, i.e. only defines a single event handler:

◆   Function References

◆   Anonymous Functions

◆   Lambda Expressions

Of the three, the lambda expression is the most commonly used and encountered.

Notice that Kotlin provides other ways to define and work with functions including function types, extension function, infix functions and more.

## Function References

Kotlin supports functions that don't belong to an object. In fact, the flexibility of Kotlin's approach to functions is one the reasons for wanting to use it.

So in Kotlin it is perfectly valid to write:

```
fun myFunction(){
    ...
}
```

outside of a class definition. Of course, to stay compatible with Java this top-level function is in fact a method of a class, but one that is generated by the compiler to have a name that is derived from the package and the file name.

You can explicitly set the name of the class used to contain top-level functions with the

```
@file:JvmName("class name")
```

annotation. Notice also that Kotlin lets you call the top-level or package level function without having to give the class name.

That is:

```
myFunction()
```

is legal.

Kotlin also has a function reference operator :: which can be used to pass almost any function as a parameter in another function or store a reference to the function in a variable. This makes it possible to use any function as an event handler.

For example, if you define the function at the package level:

```
fun clickEvent(v: View?) {
        (v as Button).text = "You Clicked Me"
}
```

then you can write:

```
b.setOnClickListener(::clickEvent)
```

If the function is defined as a method within a class you have to write:

```
b.setOnClickListener(this::clickEvent)
```

The latest version of Kotlin will allow you to drop the this for method references.

Notice that even though this looks as if you are using and passing a reference to a function, what is happening is that the function is being converted into an instance of the SAM that is specified by the parameter's type. That is, it is not a reference to a function that is passed, but an object constructed using the function. Each time you pass the function, a new object is constructed from the function. Most of the time this doesn't make any difference but you need to be aware of it if you are using the function reference operator to pass a function multiple times. Each time you use it another object implementing the SAM is created and this uses memory faster than you might expect.

## Anonymous Functions

An anonymous function is exactly what its name suggests – a function with no name defined. You simply write:

```
fun(parameters){body of function}
```

You can store a reference to an anonymous function in a variable of the correct type and pass it to another function. For example:

```
b.setOnClickListener(fun(v: View?) {
        (v as Button).text = "You Clicked Me"
})
```

You don't have to use the reference operator because the compiler understands that you want to pass the anonymous function. It converts the anonymous function to an instance of the SAM specified by the parameter's type. You could save the anonymous function in a variable and then pass the variable.

For example:

```
val clickEvent=fun(v: View?) {
        (v as Button).text = "You Clicked Me"
}
b.setOnClickListener(clickEvent)
```

It is difficult to see any advantage of doing this, however, other than if you are using the same function more than once.

## The Lambda

First, what is a lambda?

**A lambda is a function that you can define using special notation**.

From this point of view, you don't really need lambda as you can do everything you want to using the reference operator and anonymous functions.

In fact, a lambda is much like an anonymous function that you can define more easily. As the function doesn't have a name, it is an anonymous function and it can also be stored in a suitable variable and passed to another function.

You define a lambda by supplying parameters and some code:

```
{parameter list ->   code... }
```

For example:

```
{a:Int,b:Int -> a+b}
```

is a lambda that will add its two parameters together.

Note that a lambda cannot have a return statement – the final value that the lambda computes is automatically returned. In the previous example the lambda automatically returns an Int which is a+b.

A lambda behaves like an expression and you can store a lambda in a variable:

```
var sum={a:Int,b:Int -> a+b}
```

You can use the lambda by calling it as a function:

```
sum(1,2)
```

which returns 3.

There are a few simplifications of the lambda syntax that can make them look mysterious until you get used to them.

If a lambda has no parameters then you can leave them out and the arrow. So:

```
{1+2}
```

is a lambda that returns 3.

At its most extreme a lambda can simply return a value:

```
{0}
```

These rules can make lambda expressions look very strange in your code and this might make it harder to read. Don't go for the shortest and most compact expression make sure your code is easy to understand.

## Events Using Lambdas

To define an event handler for an event all you have to do is to use the Set*Event*Listener method with a lambda as its parameter. The lambda is the event handling function.

For example:

```
button.setOnClickListener({ view ->
            (view as Button).text = "You Clicked Me"
})
```

sets the lambda:

```
{view -> (view as Button).text = "You Clicked Me"}
```

as the event handler. Notice that you don't have to specify the type of the parameter because the compiler can deduce it from the type of the parameter that the setOnClickListener takes.

There is one last syntactic simplification. If a function accepts a single function as its only parameter you can omit the parentheses:

```
b.setOnClickListener {view->(view as Button).text ="You Clicked Me"}
```

This is the form Android Studio uses for any events it generates in templates. Its only advantage is that it looks more as if the code of the event handler is part of the method it is being defined in.

You can also store the lambda in a variable and use it later, but in this case the compiler cannot work out what the parameter and return types are and so you have to specify them.

For example:

```
val clickEvent=
        {view:View -> (view as Button).text = "You Clicked Me"}
b.setOnClickListener(clickEvent)
```

Notice that, as with the other methods, the lambda is converted to an instance of the event object before it is passed to the setOnEventListener method.

Lambdas are used for all Android Studio generated event handlers and it is the standard way of doing the job. Where possible it is the method used in all further examples in this book.

## Closure

Closure is one of those topics that sounds as if it is going to be difficult. Lambda expressions are different from most functions in that they have access to all of the variables that belong to the method that they are declared in.

The fact that the lambda has access to the variables in the enclosing method has the strange consequence that you could write the event handler as:

```
val message="You Clicked Me"
button.setOnClickListener {view -> button.text = message}
```

This may look odd but it works. If you don't think that it is odd then you haven't noticed that the event handler, the lambda, will be executed when the Button is clicked and this is likely to be well after the enclosing method has finished and all its variables not longer exist – and yet the lambda can still use message to set the Button's text.

The system will keep the value of message so that the lambda can make use of it. This is the essence of a closure – the preserving of variables that have gone out of scope so that a lambda can still access them.

Unlike Java the variables captured by the Kotlin closure do not have to be final.

Notice that accessing message within the lambda makes it look as if the lambda is naturally still part of the code it is being defined in and not a "detached" functional entity that runs at some time in the distant future – which is what it really is.

Now we come to a subtle point.

The variables captured by a Kotlin closure are shared between all entities that capture them. That is, they are captured as references to the variable. This only matters when more than one lambda is in use.

For example place two Buttons on the design surface and in the onCreate event handler add:

```
var i=0
button.setOnClickListener {view -> button.text = (++i).toString()}
button2.setOnClickListener {view -> button2.text = (++i).toString()}
```

Notice that the click event handler for each button captures the variable i within its closure and both share the same variable. If you click the first button you will see 1 as its caption and if you then click the other button you will see 2 as its caption. The lambdas are sharing a single captured variable.

Lambdas are not the only entity that you can use to define a function complete with a closure. Local functions passed by reference, objects that implement SAMs and anonymous functions all have closures that work in the same way. Function references don't have closure because they are defined away from where they are used.

For example, using a local named function:

```
var i=0
fun eventHandler(v:View){
        button.text = (++i).toString()
}
button.setOnClickListener(::eventHandler)
```

Notice that this doesn't work for a general named function or method. It has to be a local function.

Similarly for an anonymous function:

```
var i=0
button.setOnClickListener(fun (v:View){
                      button.text = (++i).toString()
})
```

This works because of the same closure.

For example, using an object:

```
var i=0
button.setOnClickListener(object: View.OnClickListener {
        override fun onClick(p0: View?) {
                button.text = (++i).toString()
        }
    })
```

the function defined in the object has access to i via a closure.

When you first meet the idea of a closure it can seem very strange and even unnecessary. However, when a function is defined within a method the method forms its local context and it is very natural that it should have access to the local variables that are in scope when it is defined.

Closure is useful for event handlers but it is particularly useful when used with callbacks supplied to long running function. The callback usually has to process the result of the long running function and having access to the data that was current when it was created is natural and useful.

There are dangers, however, to relying on a closure. Not everything that was in scope at the time the function was declared can be guaranteed to still exist. If a local variable is set to reference an object then it will be included in the closure and the variable will exist, but there is no guarantee that the object it referenced will still exist at the time that event handler is executed.

## Using Breakpoints

The easiest way to check that the event handler is called is to insert a breakpoint on the first line of the onClick method.

Breakpoints are a fundamental debugging tool and you need to learn to use them as early as possible.

To place a breakpoint simply click in the "margin" next to the line of code. A red blob appears:

```
19          setSupportActionBar(toolbar)
20          setContentView(R.layout.activity_main)
21  ⊘       val message="You Clicked Me"
22          button.setOnClickListener {view -> button.text = message}
23
```

Now when you run the program using the Debug icon or the Run, Debug command the program will stop when it reaches any line of code with a breakpoint set.

Once the program pauses you can see where it has reached in its execution and you can examine what is stored in all of the variables in use:

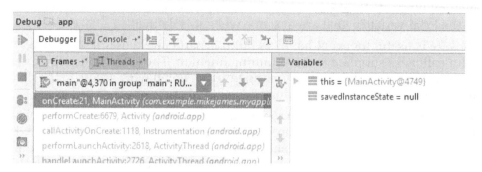

You can also restart the program or step through it – see the icons at the top of the debug window. As you step through you will see the values in the variables change. Any bug will be found at the first place you find a discrepancy between what you expect to find and what you actually find.

Lambdas pose a particular problem for breakpoints because you often only have a single line to work with:

```
button.setOnClickListener {view -> button.text = (++i).toString()}
```

If you try to set a breakpoint on this Android Studio pops up a message that lets you select where you want to set the breakpoint – on the setOnClickListener or the lambda:

There is much more to learn about debugging but for now this small introduction is enough to save you a lot of time.

## Modern Java Event Handling

If you keep to Kotlin code then you now know all you need to about how to define an event handler. However, if you need to work with existing Java code you will encounter a number of other ways of doing the job.

Java 8 now has lambdas and these are used to define event handlers.

Before Java 8 there were two main ways of creating an event handler. One way was to get the Activity to implement the interface. This turned the

Activity into an event handling object and it had to implement the event handling function as a method. The even handler was then set using:

```
setOnClickListener(this);
```

Which passes the Activity to the component's event handler list. When the even occurs the event handling function within the Activity is called.

Although using the Activity as the event handling object is encountered the most common way of doing the job is to use a local anonymous class:

```
Button button= (Button)findViewById(R.id.button);
button.setOnClickListener(new View.OnClickListener() {
 @Override
 public void onClick(View view) {
   Button b=(Button) view;
   b.setText("you clicked me");
 }
});
```

You can see that the OnClickListener object is created in one step and the onCLick event handler defined in much the same way as using a Kotlin object. In fact the two are directly equivalent and the Kotlin object is complied into an anonymous class.

The good news is that you only need to worry about these things is if you stray from Kotlin.

# Summary

- In Java you can't pass a function to set up an event handler you have to pass an object that contains the function as a method.

- Events are mostly handled by Single Abstract Method SAM interfaces. The method declared in the SAM is the function that does the event handling.

- For each event and each control that can generate that event there is a SAM of the form on*Event*Listener and the object has a set*event*Listener method which can be used to attach the event handler.

- You can create a SAM in a number of ways the most general of which is to use a Kotlin object. This can be used even when the event isn't implemented as a SAM.

- There are three alternative ways of implementing a SAM other than using an object:

    1. Function References
    2. Anonymous Functions
    3. Lambda Expressions

- Function references can be used to pass a package or local level function or a method.

- An anonymous function works in the same way but you don't need the reference operator.

- A lambda is a shorter way of writing an anonymous function and it is the standard way of implementing event handlers.

- The final syntactic simplification is that if the setListener function has a single function parameter then you can drop the parentheses.

- Local objects, local function references, anonymous functions and lambda are all subject to closures which make the variables that are accessible to them at the time of their declaration accessible when they are run.

- Breakpoints are the best way to debug your program and they become essential as soon as you start to implement several event handlers. When run in debug mode a breakpoint will pause your program so that you can examine the contents of variables.

- If you can restrict your attention to Kotlin you can create event handlers using nothing but objects and lambdas. If you need to understand Java code then there are a number of other ways of doing the job including implementing the interface in the Activity and using anonymous local classes.

# Chapter 5

# Basic Controls

We have already used some UI controls in previous chapters, but now we have discovered how events work it is time to examine how they work and how you can change the way they look.

## Basic Input Controls

The term control comes from the idea that the user "controls" your program using them. Widget or component are also terms that are used to mean the same thing. The Android community seems very sloppy about terminology.

The basic input controls are:

- ◆ Buttons
- ◆ Text Fields
- ◆ Checkboxes
- ◆ Radio Buttons
- ◆ Toggle Buttons
- ◆ Switches

If you have used other UI frameworks many of these will be known to you and you can probably skip to just the ones that interest you.

TextView also has to be included in the full list of basic controls, but unlike the Text Field it cannot be modified by the user, i.e. it is an output control only.

Starting right at the beginning, let's revisit the Button in a little more detail.

## Button Styles and Properties

There are two basic types of button, Button and ImageButton. The ImageButton is much the same as the Button but it has a src (source) property which can be set to an image which will be displayed as the button icon and it doesn't display any text.

The main attributes that you work with in the case of a button are things like background, which can be set to a color or a graphic. You can spend a long time changing the way buttons look, but in the main the only important attribute of a button is its onClick handler. A button is in your UI to be clicked.

If you place a Button on the design surface you can use the Attributes window to customize it. There are two distinct ways you can change the way a control looks. You can set a style or modify an attribute.

Setting the style modifies a set of attributes to given standard values. You can set a style and then modify individual attributes to tweak it. Often when you first start work on a UI you will set individual attributes only later to formulate a coherent style to be applied to the entire UI.

Set the background of the Button to dark gray by clicking on the ellipsis at the right of the attribute:

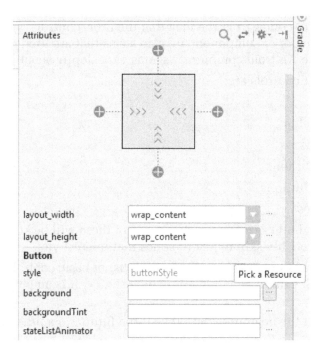

The Resources window that appears gives you access to all of the resources that your program can make use of. Resources are a big part of programming in Android and we cover them in detail in later chapters.

You could enter a color for the background directly by specifying the value of RGB and optionally Alpha, its transparency. Using a resource, however, means that if you change the resource value in the future all of the UI components that make use of it change.

There are different types of resource you can select from, and there are resources defined by the project, the Android system and any Themes you might be using. Sometimes you can't see these three categories because they are expanded into long lists:

In this case you want to select a color so select the Color tab and then the android list. Scroll down and you will see a set of predefined colors that you can use. Find background_dark and select it:

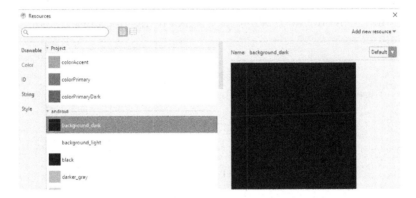

Of course, you now cannot see the text in the Button. To modify its color scroll down in the Attributes window until you can see TextView. The Button is a composite object and it has a TextView object inside of it that displays the Button's text. If you drop down the textAppearance menu you will see textColor.

Simply select an alternative light color to use:

If you now place an ImageButton, located lower in the palette in Images, on the design surface, the Resources window opens at once. This is to allow you to select a "drawable", or icon, for the ImageButton to display. Scroll down until you find ic_menu_add. When you select it this becomes the src property for the button:

The result is two buttons that look something like:

You can spend a great deal of time exploring ways to make use of a button's attributes to style it just as you want it to look.

To attach a click event handler on both buttons you can simply define a function in the Activity and set the `onClick` property on each button. You can find examples of using buttons this way in earlier chapters.

Now that we know how to handle events using lambdas it is worth applying this more sophisticated technique. As we want to assign the same event handler to all three buttons we need to create an instance of OnClickListener using a lambda.

All you have to do is enter:

```
val myOnClickListener = { view: View? ->
            val b = (view as Button)
            b.text = "You Clicked Me"
        }
```

Notice that you now have to supply the type of the parameter as the system cannot infer it. All that remains to be done is to set an instance on each of the buttons:

```
button.setOnClickListener(myOnClickListener)
imageButton.setOnClickListener(myOnClickListener)
```

Now when you click on either of the buttons `myonClickListener` is called.

Note that saving the lambda in a variable for reuse isn't more efficient than copying out the lambda each time it is required – a new instance of onClickListener is created for each Button. Its only advantage is that there is a single function that you need to modify and maintain rather than two.

It is also worth noting that, while a button has no function in life other than to be clicked, all of the other controls can also respond to an `onClick` event. That is you can use anything as a button if you want to.

## All Attributes

If you have looked at any example of using Buttons in the documentation, or if you look at slightly older Android code, you may discover some attributes that you can't seem to access using Android Studio. This is because the Attributes window only shows you the most used attributes. To see them all you need to click on the double-arrow icon at the top or bottom of the window.

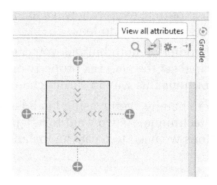

The big problem with it is that you go from a very small subset to an overwhelming list.

The best way to deal with this is to know what you want to change and find the exact name of the attribute that does the job. This is easier to say than to do in many cases. For example, suppose you want to set an icon within a standard text button so that it displays to the left of the text that the button contains. This appears to be impossible if you restrict yourself to the attributes presented in the initial property window.

If you look up the details of the attributes that Button inherits you will find:

- drawableLeft
- drawableRight
- drawableStart
- drawableEnd
- drawableBottom
- drawableTop

which are not in the Attributes window list. These allow you to display a drawable, i.e. a graphic or icon, at the location specified relative to the text.

Once you know the name of the attribute you can find it in the list of all attributes:

Click on the ellipsis button next to it and select a drawable of your choice to display the graphic to the left of the text:

## Text Fields

Text Fields are the way you get the user to enter some text for you to process and as you can guess they form an important part of most UIs.

There are a lot of Text Fields provided in the Toolbox, but they all work in the same way differing only in the type of input they expect the user to type. In the course of developing apps you will encounter most of them sooner or later, but you really only need to know how to use one of them to understand how they all work.

If you have used another UI Framework then you will have encountered some form of the Text Field before, but the Android control is slightly different in that it generally offers the user a customized virtual keyboard referred to as an IME (Input Method Editor). You can build your own IMEs, but for the moment let's just use the ones provided by the system.

If you want the Android emulator to make use of the IME that a real Android device would use then you need to deselect the Hardware Keyboard Present option when you are creating the AVD (Android Virtual Device). If the emulator makes use of the host machine's keyboard you don't see the IME at all.

The first thing to clear up is that even though there appear to be a lot of different types of Text Field controls in the Toolbox, they are all examples of the EditText control with its inputType property set to a particular value. When you place one on the design surface you will see that it is of type EditText and if you scroll down to its inputType property you can change the type of input the Text Field will handle.

When you use a particular inputType the user is presented with a virtual keyboard that is suitable for typing a value:

For example if you select a numeric type you will present the user with a simplified IME that only shows numeric keys:

You also get an action key at the bottom right of the keyboard that the user can press to complete the action - Send in the case of an SMS message, for example. To select the action button for a particular keyboard you will need to use the All Attributes view and select a setting for the imeOptions property:

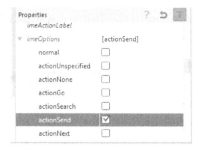

For example setting it to actionSend forces a Send button, the green paper dart button, to be displayed:

There are many other properties that you can use to customize a Text Field, but there is one standard task worth explaining in detail – writing a handler for the onEditorAction event.

# The onEditorAction Event

Returning to the EditText control, let's add a handler for the Send button. This provides another opportunity for an example of the general process of adding an event handler.

First place an EditText for an email on the design surface and use the Attributes window as described in the last section to add a Send button to the IME that pops up when the user enters text, that is find imeOptions and select actionSend.

Before you can handle any new event you have to discover the name of the event listener interface and the setOn method for that event. For the EditorAction event the listener interface is called OnEditorActionListener and the setOn method is setOnEditorActionListener.

With this information we can proceed as before and use a lambda to implement the event handler. In this case we might as well do the job within the setOnEditorActionListener as the event handler will only be needed by this one control:

```
editText.setOnEditorActionListener {v, actionId, event->
                                    process the event
                                    true
                                    }
```

Notice that now our event handler has three parameters but we still don't have to supply their type as the compiler can infer them. The final value true is the return value.

Now all that remains is to write the event handler, onEditorAction. You can look up the details of the event handler in the documentation:

```
@Override
public boolean onEditorAction(
        TextView textView,
        int i,
        KeyEvent keyEvent)
```

In this case textView is the control that the event is associated with, i is the action id and keyEvent is null unless the enter key was used.

If the action has been "consumed", i.e. acted upon, then the routine should return true and no other handlers will get a chance to process it. In general, events can be passed on to other controls that contain the source of the event.

For a simple example let's add a TextView and transfer the text that the user enters when they select the send button. Imagine that the scenario is actually sending an email or sms.

We test to see if the user selected the send button or some other button and if they did we transfer the text:

```
editText.setOnEditorActionListener { v, actionId, event ->
        if (actionId == EditorInfo.IME_ACTION_SEND) {
            textView.text = editText.text
        }
        true
}
```

Notice the use of the EditorInfo static class to obtain the integer id corresponding to the send action. The EditorInfo class has lots of useful constants and methods.

If you run the app you will discover that you can enter an email address into the EditText field with the help of the keyboard and when you press the Send button the address is transferred to the TextView.

## CheckBoxes

A CheckBox is a fairly obvious UI element. It displays a small label, controlled by the text property with or without a tick mark next to it. The user can select or deselect as many checkboxes as desired.

In most cases you don't bother to deal with the state of a CheckBox until the user presses some other control, usually a big button marked Done or similar. Then you can discover the state of each CheckBox by simply using the isChecked method which returns true or false:

For example, if you have a CheckBox with id checkBox then you can discover its state when a button somewhere on the view is clicked using:

```
var checked = checkBox.isChecked
```

*Notice that you can use the isChecked method as if it was a Kotlin property as not only are get and set methods converted to a property but also methods starting with is returning a boolean.*

The CheckBox also supports the onClick event which can be used to process changes to its state, and you can set up the onClick event handler using the Attributes window as in the case of a Button.

So to handle the CheckBox change of state all you have to do is set its onClick event handler to:

```
checkBox.setOnClickListener { v -> checked = checkBox.isChecked }
```

Of course the event handler would typically do more than just store the state in a variable.

If you need to modify a CheckBox value then use the setChecked or the toggle methods.

## Switches and Toggle buttons

Switches and Toggle buttons are just CheckBoxes in another format. They store one of two states and they change state when the user clicks on them, just like a CheckBox:

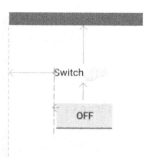

You can check the state of a Switch/Toggle button using the isChecked method and you can use its onClick event to monitor when its state changes. The only real difference is that you can use the textOn and textOff to set what is displayed when the switch/toggle is on or off.

## Radio Buttons

The final "simple" input control is the RadioButton. This works like a CheckBox in that it can be in one of two states, but the big difference is that a set of RadioButtons works in a group and only one of them can be selected at a time.

*The reason for the term "radio button" is that, in the early days of electronics, car radios had mechanical tuning buttons arranged in a line which let the driver quickly select a station by pressing a button. When you pressed a new button the current button popped up so that only one button was pressed at any given moment, making sure that you only listened to one station at a time.*

The only complication in using RadioButtons is making sure you group them together correctly. To do this we have to make use of a RadioGroup container which is used to hold all of the buttons that work together. There are a number of different containers used to group controls, but the most basic of these is the RadioGroup.

Using Android Studio you can create a group of RadioButtons by first placing a RadioGroup container on the design surface and then placing as many RadioButtons inside the container as you require. If a group of RadioButtons doesn't work as you expect, the chances are that not all the buttons are within the RadioGroup.

The easiest way to check, create and edit a group of RadioButtons is to use the Component Tree window where you will be able to see exactly how they are nested. You can also add RadioButtons to the container by dragging to the Component Tree window.

All the RadioButtons within a RadioGroup automatically work so that only one button can be selected at a time and you don't have to do any extra work to implement this behavior.

To find out which button is selected you can use the isChecked method as in the case of the CheckBox. In fact you can work with a set of RadioButtons in exactly the same way as a set of CheckBoxes, with the only differences being the use of the RadioGroup and the fact that only one button can be selected at any one time.

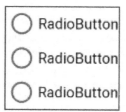

You can use the onClick event to detect when any button has been modified and the setChecked or the toggle methods to modify the state of a button.

## Summary

- The basic controls that make up most of the simple Android UI are:

    Buttons
    Text Fields
    CheckBoxes
    Radio Buttons
    Toggle Buttons
    Switches

- Each control is customized using its attributes and event handlers.

- Some attributes are hidden from you by Android Studio unless you select the All Attributes button.

# Chapter 6

## Working With Layouts

The choice of Layout is vital to an Android UI. The Layout is what allows you to position and generally arrange other components. A good understanding of what is on offer in each of the available Layouts can make the difference between an easy and a difficult UI, from both the point of view of the programmer and the user. This is especially the case if you want to support a range of devices.

All of the classes and objects that make up the Android UI are derived from the same base class, the View. That is, a Button is a View and so are the Layout classes. However, Layouts seem to behave in very different ways to the simple Button and this raises the question what exactly is a Layout?

## Understanding Layouts

A Layout is a container for other View-derived objects. When the Layout is asked to render itself, it renders all of the View objects it contains and arranges them inside the area of the display it occupies.

The default Layout used by Android Studio is the ConstraintLayout and we have already looked at using it in earlier chapters, but it is not the only Layout you can use with the Layout Editor.

There are six currently supported Layouts:

- ConstraintLayout
- GridLayout
- FrameLayout
- LinearLayout
- RelativeLayout
- TableLayout

The ConstraintLayout was new in Android Studio 2.2. It is currently the recommended layout to use, and it is the default in Android Studio 3. It can be thought of as a development on the RelativeLayout. In principle, it can be used to create any layout that you can implement using a combination of the other layouts. It is claimed that ConstraintLayout based UIs are easier to construct and faster because they are "flat" i.e. do not use multiple layouts nested inside one another.

Android Studio really doesn't want you to use any layout other than ConstraintLayout as the initial container and so it doesn't let you delete the default layout. It will let you replace a RelativeLayout in an existing project with a ConstraintLayout, but you cannot delete or replace it by any other layout. The reason is that replacing one layout by another is difficult because of all of the changes in the supported properties.

You can edit the XML file directly to replace one layout by another, but you will have to re-edit all of the layout properties. You can replace an empty layout by another by editing the XML file and this is currently the only way to do the job.

Despite the fact that ConstraintLayout is the recommended layout to use there are still many Android projects that use the original layouts and some programmers simply don't like the ConstraintLayout. Hence it is worth knowing how the simpler layouts work.

Among the original layouts, RelativeLayout and LinearLayout are the most used, with FrameLayout coming a distant third. The final two, TableLayout and GridLayout, are suitable for specialized types of UI and in Android Studio 3 are more or less unsupported in the Layout Editor so you have to work directly with their properties. For this reason they are best avoided.

Before looking at these alternatives and how to work with them, it is worth getting to grips with the basic ideas of layouts and the principles they share in common. Then we will look at the Frame, Linear and Relative layouts because they are still important. ConstraintLayout, however, is so important because it is the preferred layout type for the future that it gets a chapter all to itself.

## Layout Properties

Mostly you tend to think of the properties that are relevant to a control as belonging to the control, but a layout can do its job in many ways and requires the control to have lots of very specific properties to determine how it is positioned. In other words, the properties that a control needs to work with a layout depend on the layout chosen and this makes things difficult to organize.

The simplest but unworkable way of implementing this would be to insist that every control implemented every property used by every layout, even the ones not currently being used. This is clearly inefficient.

The solution to the problem actually used is that each layout defines a nested class, derived from LayoutParams, that has all of the properties it needs the control to define. The control that is to be placed inside the layout creates an instance of the appropriate LayoutParams class and so varies the parameters it has access to depending on the layout container it finds itself in.

That is, instead of defining every possible property that any layout could want, a UI component that can be placed in a layout uses the appropriate LayoutParams class to "import" the properties it needs for the layout it finds itself in. This means that a control has two types of property – its own and those that it gets from LayoutParams.

Thus in the Layout Editor where the properties are represented by XML attributes a control's attributes are shown in two groups:

- Attributes that belong to the object.
- Attributes that are required by the Layout object.

You can tell Layout attributes because they are of the form layout_*name* in the XML file. You can see them in the Attributes window in the Layout Editor:

So in the screen dump the layout_margin attributes are supplied by the ConstraintLayout.LayoutParams object, but the Padding attribute is something that the Button supports. In other words, which layout attributes you see depends on what sort of layout the control is, but the other attributes belong to the control and are always listed. It is also worth knowing at this early stage that the Layout Editor often presents a simplified set of layout attributes which it then maps onto a larger and more confusing set of layout_ attributes in the XML.

## Width and Height

The exact set of Layout attributes that you see depends on the Layout you use. However, there are two that all Layouts support:

- layout_width
- layout_height

You might think that the width and height of a control were attributes that should belong to a control, but here things are more subtle. A control doesn't necessarily have a fixed size. It can, for example, ask the Layout to give it as much space as possible, in which case the Layout sets the size of the control. This is the reason why controls have layout_width and layout_height and not just width and height.

You can set these properties to any one of three possible values:

- a fixed size, e.g. 24px
- wrap_content, which sets the size so that it just fits the control's content without clipping
- match_parent, which lets the control become as big as the parent Layout can allow

If you use the mouse to drag the frame of a control in the Layout Editor then what happens depends on the control and the Layout.

In most cases the default set by the Layout Editor is wrap_content and it will ignore any attempts you make to interactively size a control. Indeed, in most cases trying to interactively resize a control doesn't change the layout_width or layout_height properties. However, depending on the Layout in use you might appear to change the size of the control due to the setting of other layout properties. More of this when we deal with particular Layout types.

The point is that the layout_width and layout_height are not necessarily the only attributes that control the final displayed size of a control. One thing is fairly certain, if you want to set a fixed size for a control then you need to type the values into the Property window.

## Units

If you are going to enter a fixed size or a location you need to know how to do it. Android supports six units but only two, both pixel-based units, are used routinely:

- px – pixel
- dp – density-independent pixel

The unit that it is most tempting to use when you first start creating an app is px, the pixel, because you generally have one testing device in mind with a particular screen size and resolution. This is not a good idea if you want your app to look roughly the same as screen resolution changes. For this you need the density-independent unit, dp, because it adjusts for the screen resolution. If the device has a screen with 160 pixels per inch then 1dp is the same as 1px. If the number of pixels per inch changes then dp to px changes in the same ratio. For example, at 320 pixels per inch 1dp is the same as 2px.

- By using density-independent pixels you can keep controls the same size as the resolution changes.

Notice that this does not compensate for the screen size. If you keep the number of pixels fixed and double the resolution then the screen size halves. A control on the screen specified in px would then display at half its original size. A control specified in dp would display at its original size but take up twice the screen real-estate.

- Using dp protects you against screens changing their resolution, not their physical size.

If you specify sizes in dp then your layout will look the same on a 7-inch tablet, no matter what resolution it has.

As well as pixel-based measures there are also three real world units:

- mm – millimeters
- in – inches
- pt – points 1/72 of an inch

All three work in terms of the size of the screen, and the number of pixels a control uses is related to the screen resolution. If the screen has 160 pixels per inch then 1/160 in=1 px and so on. Notice that once again these units protect you against resolution changes, but not changes to the actual screen size. Your button may be 1 inch across on all devices, but how much of the screen this uses up depends on the size of the screen the device has. The danger in using real world units is that you might well specify a fractional number of pixels and end up with an untidy looking display.

The final unit is also related to pixels but is tied to the user's font size preference:

- sp – scale-independent pixel

This works like the dp unit in that it is scaled with the device's resolution but it is also scaled by the user's default font size preference. If the user sets a larger font size preference then all sp values are scaled up to match.

**Which unit should you use?** The simple answer is that you should use dp unless you have a good reason not to, because this at least means that if you have tested your UI on a device of size x it should work reasonably on all devices of size x, no matter what the resolution.

Android Studio defaults to working in dp whenever you enter a value without a unit or when you interactively size or move a control.

## A Control is Just a Box

As far as a Layout is concerned, a control is just a rectangle. Its size is given by layout_width and layout_height and these can be set by the control or, more often, by the Layout. Once the Layout knows the size of the control it can position it according to the rules you have established using the Layout's properties.

If you want to know the position that a control has been assigned then you can use its Top and Left properties. This gives you the position of the top left-hand corner of the control's rectangle. You can work out where the other corners are by using Width and Height properties, but to make things easier there is also Right and Bottom property. Notice that the position of the top left-hand corner of the rectangle is always relative to the Layout it is in. That is, the position is not an absolute screen position.

It is also worth knowing that controls also support padding, dead-space inside the control. This is space left between the outside edge and the content. In addition some, but not all, layouts support margins, dead-space outside a control that can be used to add space between controls:

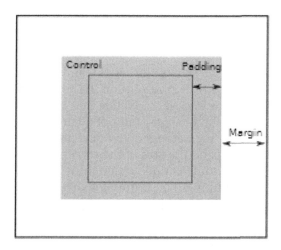

Notice that padding is a property of the control and margin is a layout property. You can set each margin or padding on the left, right, top or bottom individually or specify a single value to be used for all of them.

In theory, padding is used to put space around the content of a control, but it can also be used simply to make the control bigger when its dimensions are set to wrap its contents. For example, the Button on the left has zero padding and the one on the right has a padding of 30dp all round:

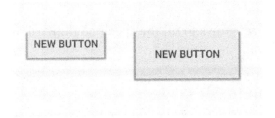

Similarly, margins are used to put space around a control, but they can be used to position one control relative to another or to its container. This is how RelativeLayout and ConstraintLayout work.

## Gravity

Gravity is often regarded as mysterious, partly because of its name and partly because there are often two gravity properties in play. Basically, gravity just sets where in a dynamic layout something is positioned.

Simple gravity settings are:

- top
- bottom
- left
- right
- center
- center_vertical
- center_horizontal

The meaning of all of these is obvious in that the object just moves to the specified position. However, things get a little complicated if you try to set an object to display at the left when the size of its container has been adjusted to fit, i.e. it is already as far to the left and the right as it can be. You can also set multiple gravity options. For example, you can set left and right at the same time and this just centers the object horizontally.

What makes gravity even more complicated is that there are settings that change the size of the object affected:

- fill
- fill_vertical
- fill_horizontal

In each case the object grows to fill the specified dimension.

There are also two clipping settings:

- clip_vertical
- clip_horizontal

These work with the top, bottom, left and right to clip an object to fit the container. For example, if you set gravity to top and clip_vertical then the object will be positioned at the top of the container and its bottom edge will be clipped.

Most of the time you will simply use gravity settings like center or top. If you try to use complicated combinations then things tend not to work as you might expect.

The final complication, which in fact turns out to be quite straightforward, is that controls have a gravity property and Layouts provide a layout_gravity property. The difference is very simple. The gravity property sets what happens to the contents of a control and the layout_gravity sets how the control is positioned in the Layout container. For example, if you have a Button and you set its gravity property to top then the text within the button will be moved to align with the top. If, on the other hand, you set the Button's layout_gravity to top the whole Button moves to the top of the Layout container. Notice that not all Layouts provide a layout_gravity property to their child controls.

## The FrameLayout

The FrameLayout is the simplest of all the Layouts. It really doesn't do very much to position the controls it contains and its intended use is to host a single control, i.e. it really does just act as a frame around a control.

The Layout Editor no longer provides as much help with FrameLayout as it did and if you have used an earlier version you may well find the new behavior frustrating. Indeed, the only way you can make a FrameLayout the main layout control is to edit the XML file and replace ConstraintLayout by FrameLayout. If you want to try out a FrameLayout, simply drag and drop it onto the default ConstraintLayout and use it there.

When you drop a control in a FrameLayout it is positioned at the top left and you cannot drag it to a new position within the layout. To set a control's position you have to find the layout_gravity attribute, not the gravity attribute, and set one or more of top, bottom, left, right, center_horizontal, and center_vertical.

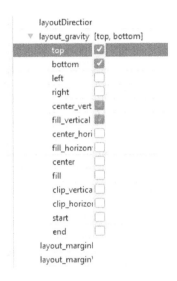

You can use this to position multiple controls in the same FrameLayout, but notice that if the total size of the FrameLayout changes the different controls may well overlap:

If two controls overlap in a FrameLayout, they are drawn in the order in which they were added. In other words, the last one added is drawn on top of the others. This aspect of the FrameLayout makes it useful if you want to display multiple controls and switch which one is visible. Simply put all the controls into the FrameLayout and select one to be visible using its Visible property.

More commonly a FrameLayout is used simply as a placeholder for a component of a layout that isn't specified until some time later. For example, if you make use of a Fragment, see the companion book *Android Programming: Mastering Fragments & Dialogs*, to create part of a UI or read in a list of things to display, then often you need a container for the new component to be present in your static layout. A FrameLayout does the job very efficiently.

- Use a FrameLayout when you need the simplest Layout that will hold one or a small number of components without the need for much in the way of positioning or sizing.

## LinearLayout

The next layout we need to consider is the LinearLayout. This is a simple layout that can be used to do a great deal of the basic work of organizing a UI. In fact once you start using LinearLayout, it tends to be the one you think of using far too often. You can use a LinearLayout as the base Layout, replacing the default ConstraintLayout that Android Studio provides, or you can place a LinearLayout within the ConstraintLayout.

In Android Studio LinearLayout occurs twice in the Palette – once as a vertical and once as a horizontal LinearLayout. The difference, however, is just the setting of the orientation property to horizontal or vertical. In other words, you can swap a horizontal and vertical linear layout with a simple property change.

The horizontal LinearLayout acts as a row container and a vertical LinearLayout acts as a column container. You can use nested LinearLayouts to build up something that looks like a table, but if this gets very complicated it is better to use ConstraintLayout. Nesting layouts like this is also inefficient as the rendering engine has to compute the layout multiple times to get it right. The advice is to use a ConstraintLayout and avoid nesting.

If you place a LinearLayout on the ConstraintLayout then you can position it like any other control. If you then place other controls inside it then they will stack up horizontally to form a row or vertically to form a column.

This sounds easy but there are lots of ways to use a LinearLayout.

For example, if you put a horizontal and a vertical LinearLayout in the ConstraintLayout then how they behave depends on what you set their layout_width and layout_height to. If you set it to wrap_content then the two Layouts act like a horizontal and vertical panel of controls, i.e. you can move all of the controls as a block:

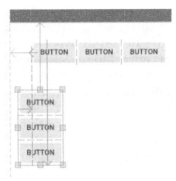

It can be very difficult to be sure what you are dragging in the Layout Editor as it is easy to pick up one of the Buttons rather than the layout. Make use of the Component Tree window to select the layout and to make sure that the Buttons are in the layout you think they are.

Things get more interesting when you nest one LinearLayout inside another to create a table. For example, you can create a calculator style keypad by nesting three horizontal LinearLayouts inside a single vertical LinearLayout. That is, place a vertical LinearLayout on the screen and then place three horizontal LinearLayouts within it. Within each horizontal LinearLayout place three buttons. If you have difficulty doing this, use the Component Tree to make sure that the components are correctly nested. Make sure that you set the layout_width and layout_height to wrap_content, otherwise the LinearLayouts will overlap:

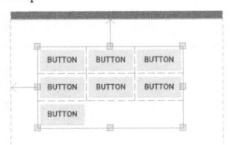

This is easier to arrange than using the ConstraintLayout. The final Button is just placed into the vertical LinearLayout and it forms a row all of its own.

- LinearLayout is a useful grouping device whenever you need a row or column of controls.

125

## Layout_weight

There's one last mystery of the LinearLayout to discuss, layout_weight, a layout property that only the LinearLayout supports. If you assign a layout_weight to any of the controls in a LinearLayout then the controls are adjusted in size to fill any unused space in proportion to their weights.

The really important part of this description is "unused space". What happens is that Android first computes the layout ignoring any weight assignments. This means that the controls are set to the sizes you specified. Next the system determines what space remains unused in the containing LinearLayout. This is then distributed between the controls that have non-zero values of layout_weight in proportion to their weights. For example, suppose we have a horizontal LinearLayout with three Buttons all set to wrap_content. The screen has been rotated to provide a lot of unused space for the example:

You can see that there is a lot of unused space over to the right. If we now set the first Button's layout_weight to 1 it will be allocated all of that unused space:

126

If you now set the second Button's layout_weight to 1 then the unused space will be shared between the first two Buttons equally:

You can guess what would happen if we now set the third Button's layout_weight to 1, the space would be shared equally and all three buttons would be the same size. If, however, the first button was given a weight of 2 then the unused space would be shared out in the ratio 2:1:1 and so on.

More interestingly what do you think would happen if you assigned a fixed width to the third Button? The answer is simple. If the third Button's layout_weight is zero then it is set to the width specified and the other two buttons get the unused space. For example setting the third Button to 350dp gives:

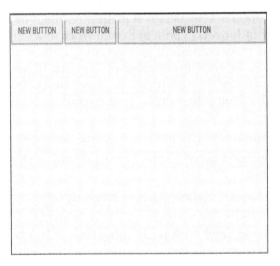

However, if the third button has a layout_weight set then it will probably change its width because it gets a share of the unused space just like the other buttons. In other words, when you set a non-zero layout_weight a control can change its size even though you have set a specific size for it. This leads to the idea of "measured size" and "actual size".

In the case of the third Button its measured size is 350dp but if its layout_weight is non-zero then its actual size on the screen will be different – it will be allocated some of the unused space.

When you are working with components in code the Width and Height properties will give you the actual width and height of the control. The MeasuredWidth and MeasuredHeight properties will give you the measured width and height before any adjustment by the Layout has been performed.

Finally, it is worth pointing out that if you want to be sure that the three Buttons are the same size you have to set their widths to 0dp and weight to 1 (or the same value). Why is this necessary? When you set the widths to zero all of the space is unused and the system will divided it equally between each one. You can also set their widths to some constant minimum value and then let the weight mechanism share out the unused space.

## RelativeLayout

The RelativeLayout was the most used in the past and it is still worth knowing about because you will meet it in existing apps and you might have to use it if ConstraintLayout doesn't work for you. It was the one that was favored by Android Studio until the ConstraintLayout was introduced.

It is a complex and sophisticated layout component and you might think that you should prefer simpler alternatives if at all possible. For example, you can often use a number of LinearLayouts to do the work of a single RelativeLayout. The most commonly quoted rule is that you should try to design your UI using the smallest number of Layouts. In particular, deep nesting of Layouts, i.e. one Layout inside another, slows things down because the system has to dig deep into each layer of Layout and this can take a lot of work. The rule is:

- Prefer a shallow sophisticated Layout to a deep nest of simpler ones.

You can usually replace a set of nested LinearLayouts with a RelativeLayout or a ConstraintLayout.

For such a capable Layout, RelativeLayout has only a few Layout properties. They fall into two groups:

- Properties concerned with positioning the control relative to the parent container
- Properties concerned with positioning relative to another control.

At least one of the controls in the Layout has to be positioned relative to the parent container to give the rest of the Layout a position. However, any number of controls can be positioned relative to the parent container if this fits in with what you are trying to achieve.

The RelativeLayout attributes are presented and organized by the Attributes window slightly differently to the way they are represented as attributes in the XML or in code. This description applies to the way Android Studio presents them. Refer to the documentation for the XML or programmatic constants.

## Edge Alignment

The principle is that you can specify the alignment of any pair of edges, one in the parent and one in the child. This will move the child control so that its edge lines up with the parent edge, for example, top edge to top edge. If you specify two pairs of edges then you can change the size of the control as well as positioning it. For example, top to top and bottom to bottom makes the child control the same height as the parent.

## Layout Relative to Parent

The fundamental parent layout attributes are:

- ◆ `layout_alignParentTop`
- ◆ `layout_alignParentLeft`
- ◆ `layout_alignParentBottom`
- ◆ `layout_alignParentRight`

which align the corresponding edge of the control with that of the parent container.

For example: setting layout_alignParentLeft moves the left side of the control to the left side of the parent:

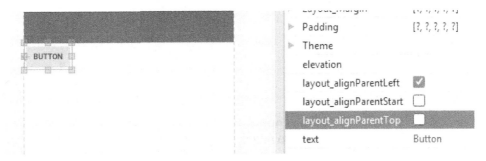

This works without any resizing of the control. If you select two opposing alignments, top and bottom or left and right, then both the edges are moved and the control is resized.

For example, setting layout_alignParentLeft and layout_alignParentRight produces:

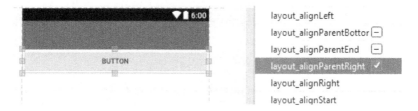

You can also align to the center of the parent with:

- layout_centerInParent
- layout_centerVertical
- layout_centerHorizontal

## Layout Relative to Another Component

The Layout Editor used to map a confusing set of XML properties that positioned a component relative to another component. The latest version no longer performs this simplification. Instead you can either allow the Layout Editor to work out how to set position relative to another component or you can work with the raw attributes in the Attributes window.

The basic idea behind all of the positioning attributes relative to another component is that you simply supply the name of the other component to the relevant attributes:

- `layout_alignTop`
- `layout_alignLeft`
- `layout_alignBottom`
- `layout_alignRight`

For example:

`layout_alignRight= button1`

sets the right-hand edge of the control to align with the right-hand edge of button1. As always, aligning two edges top/bottom and left/right changes the size of the control.

The attributes:

- `layout_above`
- `layout_below`

align the bottom of the control with the top of the referenced control and the bottom with the top respectively.

Similarly the attributes:

- `layout_toLeftOf`
- `layout_toRightOf`

align the left/right of the control with the right/left of the referenced control.

Finally the attribute:

- `baseline`

aligns the text baseline in the parent and child controls.

In API 17 a new feature was added to take account of the direction that text should flow within a layout, this caters for languages such as Arabic that start at the right-hand side and go towards the left. By default Layout_Direction is left-to-right and the start edge is the same as the left edge and the end edge is the same as the right edge. If Layout_Direction is set right-to-left then start is the same as right and end is the same as left. You can set startpadding to control the padding on the left or right depending on the layout direction set. All of the left/right attributes have a start/end version.

## Margin Offsets

So far all we can do is align pairs of edges.

How do you specify exact positions relative to another control or the parent?

The answer is to use the common pattern of setting the margins of the control. If you align top edges but set a top margin of 10dp on the child then the top of the child control will be 10dp lower than the parent control:

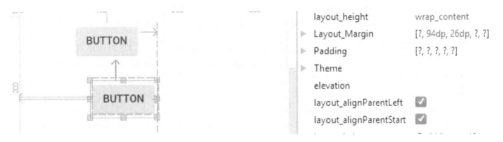

So the edge alignment is used to specify the relative direction of one control to another and the margins set give the exact offset.

## RelativeLayout and the Layout Editor

With all of this understood you can now see how the Layout Editor lets you generate a RelativeLayout. As you move a control around the design surface, the nearest other control or the parent Layout is selected as the parent to use for positioning, the closest edges are used for alignment and that margin is set to the distance between the parent and child.

This works well but it can sometimes be difficult to get the Layout Editor to pick the control or the Layout as you move a control around. You can always use the Attributes window to manually set this if it proves too difficult to set interactively.

Also notice that if you drag an edge of one control close to alignment with the edge of another control then this will result in just that edge being aligned and the control changes its size. For example, if you drag the right side of a control to the right size of the Layout then the width of the control changes. This behavior can confuse beginners using the Layout Editor as it appears to be possible to resize controls by dragging an edge, but most of the time the control snaps back to its original size when released. Of course, it only resizes when the edge you are dragging lines up with a corresponding edge on another control.

It has to be said again that the Layout Editor is not as easy to use with the RelativeLayout as in previous versions of Android Studio. For example, it no longer supplies interactive positioning feedback in terms of pixel offsets and it no longer uses a simplified system of layout properties which map onto the real XML properties. These things might change in future versions, but with the emphasis on ConstraintLayout it seems unlikely.

Once you understand the way that the RelativeLayout works then using the Layout Editor becomes much easier and so does using RelativeLayout to create a complex UI.

# Summary

- You can use different Layout containers to create UIs. Each Layout has its own facilities for how child controls are positioned and sized.

- The default in Android Studio 3 is ConstraintLayout.

- The most important alternatives are FrameLayout, LinearLayout and RelativeLayout.

- Each Layout has its own set of layout properties to control positioning and sizing of a control. Child controls have an instance of the layout properties class to tell the Layout how to position and size them. All Layouts support layout_width and layout_height.

- You can specify position using a number of different units, but in most cases use dp (density-independent pixels) as this works the same way on screens of the same size but different resolutions.

- As far as the Layout is concerned, a control is just a rectangle, width by height, positioned using top and left.

- All controls have padding properties which specify extra space around the control's content.

- Some Layouts provide layout_margin properties that set extra space around the outside of the control.

- Gravity simply sets the simple positioning of an object - top, bottom, right, left. Every control has a gravity property which sets the position of its content, e.g. the text in a Button. Some Layouts have a layout_gravity property that sets how a control will be positioned.

- The FrameLayout is the simplest of all Layouts and just has layout_gravity for positioning. In most cases it holds a single control and it is most often used as a placeholder.

- The LinearLayout can be used to organize controls as a row or a column. As well as gravity, the LinearLayout also supports the specification of a control's weight. After the measured size of each control is determined by the Layout, the remaining unused space is allocated to the controls in the same proportions as their assigned weights.

- Complex layouts can be created by nesting LinearLayouts inside each other to produce a column of rows or a row of columns. This has resulted in the LinearLayout being the most used.

- The general principle is to try to select a Layout that results in the smallest nesting of Layout containers. It is therefore better to use a single RelativeLayout or ConstraintLayout rather than deeply nested LinearLayouts.

# Chapter 7

# The ConstraintLayout

The ConstraintLayout was new in Android Studio 2.2 and it makes use of an additional library. The support library is compatible with all versions of Android back to Gingerbread (2.3, API level 9) and so you can use the ConstraintLayout unless you plan targeting devices running earlier than Gingerbread.

ConstraintLayout was introduced in an effort to make layout more responsive to screen size changes, and to improve the efficiency of layout by making it possible to avoid nesting layouts. It is, essentially, an improved RelativeLayout and if you have read the section on the RelativeLayout much of what follows will seem familiar. The Layout Editor has been changed to work well with the ConstraintLayout at the cost of making the other Layouts harder to work with. This might change as Android Studio continues to develop but with the emphasis on ConstraintLayout being the solution to everything this seems increasingly unlikely.

In the past the ConstraintLayout was underdeveloped and didn't work well in all situations. In Android Studio 3 the support library has improved along with the Layout Editor. It now seems reasonable to base all of your future apps on the ConstraintLayout.

*At the time of writing the default version of ConstraintLayout is 1.0.2. This supports all features including chains and guidelines but not barriers and groups. The current documentation suggests that the Layout Editor supports barriers and groups but if you use the default version of ConstraintLayout they aren't and they do not appear in the context menu.*

*If you want to make use of these features you have to ensure that your project is using 1.1.0 or later. This is currently in beta but could well reach a final version before the next version of Android Studio. To make use of it you need to edit the build.gradle file to read:*

```
dependencies {
implementation fileTree(dir: 'libs', include: ['*.jar'])
implementation 'com.android.support:appcompat-v7:26.1.0'
implementation 'com.android.support.constraint:
                      constraint-layout:1.1.0-beta3'
```

*Only the last line needs changing i.e. from 1.0.2 to 1.1.0-beta3. You will need to resync the project and then you will see group and barriers in the right click context menu.*

If you have an existing Layout then you can ask Android Studio to convert it to ConstraintLayout. All you have to do is right-click on the Layout in the Component Tree and select Convert to ConstraintLayout. This can be used to reduce a nested layout to a single "flat" ConstraintLayout, but be warned that in practice it often gets things very wrong. Often the best you can say of a converted layout is that it provides a starting point for re-implementation.

Let's take a look at how the ConstraintLayout works in the Layout Editor in more detail than in previous chapters.

Using the ConstraintLayout means the only thing that affects where a component displays are the constraints you apply. So how do you apply a constraint? There are two approaches and we have seem them both briefly earlier chapters. You can have the Layout Editor suggest them for you automatically, or you can apply them manually.

## Automatic Constraints

Automatic constraints, which we met in Chapter 3, are supposed to make things easy. There are two ways to get the editor to apply constraints dynamically:

- Autoconnect mode – for a single component
- Infer Constraints – for the entire layout

They do slightly different things and you need to learn to make them work together.

To turn Autoconnect on simply click its icon at the top of the Layout Editor:

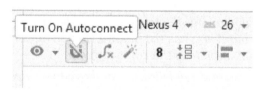

As already explained in Chapter 3, Autoconnect applies constraints to a single component that you are either placing on the design surface for the first time, or to a component that doesn't already have constraints applied that you drag to a new location. When a constraint is added, Autoconnect doesn't attempt to change it if you move the component to a new location where a different constraint might be more appropriate. The other problem already mentioned is that Autoconnect doesn't add constraints that seem obvious. It adds constraints for centering and placing close to an edge, but it doesn't add any constraint relative to another component or to generally position the component.

At the moment Autoconnect is a fairly weak feature and hardly worth turning on in most cases.

The Infer Constraints option is, in many ways, easier to use and more powerful than Autoconnect. All you have to do is position the components where you want them and then click the Infer Constraints icon:

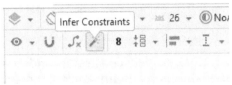

Only constraints that are necessary to fix the position of a component are added – existing constraints are not modified. This means you can use Infer Constraints to make sure that your layout has enough constraints to make it work. If none are added it was OK. It also means that if you click Infer Constraints a second time nothing changes even if you have moved components. To get a new set of constraints you have to delete the constraints you want recomputed and then click Infer Constraints.

You can delete all of the constraints in a layout using the Clear All Constraints button:

You can clear all of the constraints on a particular component by selecting it and clicking on the red cross icon that appears below it:

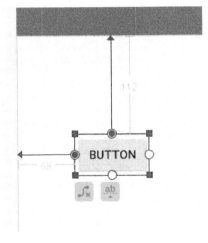

To clear a single constraint simply hover the mouse over the circle that marks the location of the constraint until it turns red and then click it:

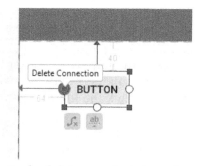

In this way you can selectively delete constraints and re-apply the Infer Constraints operation, or simply manually apply a more appropriate constraint.

Infer Constraints operates in a very simple way. It applies constraints to components according to what they are closest to. This approach results in a layout that works but it might not be the most logical for future modification.

A good strategy is to switch off Autoconnect and use the Infer Constraints option every time you place a new component on the design surface. This allows you to build up a layout one component at a time and check each new set of constraints. You can then modify the newly added constraints and move on to the next component.

Where things get difficult is when you have a multi-component layout and need to make radical changes. Often it is easier in this case to delete all of the constraints and start again.

As long as suitable constraints are in place, the ConstraintLayout works much like the RelativeLayout. For a component that has been placed on its own close to the top and left-hand edge of the screen, constraints will be added that fix its distance from the left and top:

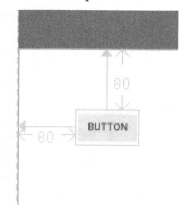

From now on when the button is displayed it will position itself at 80dp from the left and 80dp from the top. These constraints are applied no matter what the size of the physical screen is.

It is worth knowing that the actual positioning is achieved, as in the case of the RelativeLayout, by setting the button's margin properties to 80dp. However, unlike what happens in the RelativeLayout. if you move the Button closer to the right-hand edge, then the constraint will not change to one relative to that edge. Once a constraint is set it stays set unless you delete it and apply a new one. All that happens when you drag a component is that the value of the constraint changes, not its type.

It is also worth knowing that the Attributes window has a diagram that shows you the currently applied constraints and lets you modify them and set distances exactly:

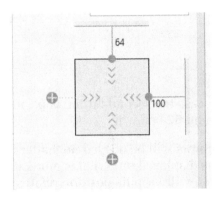

If you click on one of the constraint lines, you can enter a value for the distance. You can also click on the X that appears and delete the constraint completely.

You can also set the default margin that is used for new constraints using the default margin icon in the menu bar:

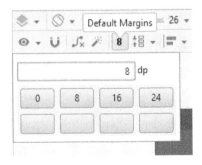

Just like a RelativeLayout, you can set constraints relative to the parent or relative to other controls in the layout. Try placing a second button on the surface and moving it close to the first. Now if you click the Infer Constraints button, the constraints that are applied are taken relative to the first button:

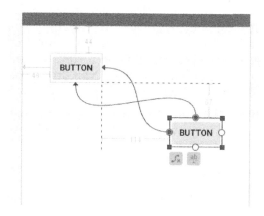

You can see that in this case the second button is positioned 114 from the left edge of the first button and 57 below it.

Once again these constraints will be obeyed no matter how large or small the physical screen the UI is displayed on. What is more, if you move the first button, the second button will keep its position relative to the first. This is exactly like the RelativeLayout and, as long as you set the correct constraints, anything you can do with RelativeLayout can be done with ConstraintLayout.

If you play with the positioning in the Layout Editor you will quickly get the idea.

The big problem with the Layout Editor automatically applying constraints is that it often gets it wrong. Working out how one control should be fixed relative to another really requires some intelligence and, at the moment, the Layout Editor doesn't have it.

# Manual Constraints

You can place constraints on positioning manually. All you have to do is drag a line from the constraint circles on the component to the edge you want to use as a reference point. For example, to position the button relative to the right side of the screen simply drag the circle on the right of the button to the right side of the screen and then move the button where you want it:

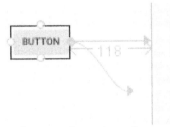

You can mix the automatic and manual setting of constraints and this is often the best way to work. In general, you are specifying the constraint as the distance from some point on the component to a point on some other component.

For example, if you want to place a component relative to another then simply drag the constraint point on the first to an edge of the second. In the case shown below manual constraints have been applied because constraint inference would have placed constraints on the left-hand edge of the screen:

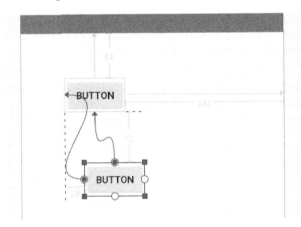

At this point it is worth making a small, but important, point very clear. While you can manually set negative margins in the RelativeLayout, you cannot make use of them in ConstraintLayout. You cannot drag a component so that it needs a negative offset – the Layout Editor stops your drag at zero. If you set a negative margin in the margin properties it will show as negative but be treated as zero.

What this means in practice is that if you align the left side of a component to the left side of another, then the only type of constraint you can apply shifts the second button to the right. If you try to move it to the left then the negative margin that would result is ignored. To understand this try it in the Layout Editor and you will find that you cannot drag the lower button in the previous screen dump beyond the left side of the top button. In the same way, you cannot drag the lower button above the bottom of the upper button. This has a certain logic, but it is also restrictive because it means you cannot set a constraint that connects the top of a component to the top of a component that is below it.

You can use left-side to left-side constraints to left-align components and right-side to right-side constraints to right-align components and so on. To help you do this there is an alignment tool palette:

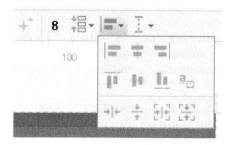

To use it select all the components that you want to align and then click the desired alignment tool. It is important to realize that using these alignment tools simply applies the appropriate constraints. You could achieve the same results by applying the constraints yourself manually.

In addition to being able to align different sides of a control, you can also set a baseline constraint so that text lines up. This was explained in detail in Chapter 3, but put simply – if you click on the second icon that appears when you select a component, an elliptical box appears:

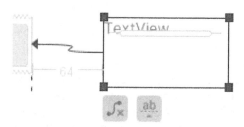

Hover the cursor over the elliptical box until is highlighted and drag from the elliptical box to the baseline of the text in the component that you want to align with:

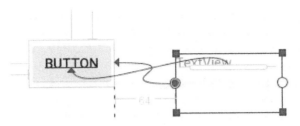

## Bias Constraints

So far the ConstraintLayout hasn't really provided anything new, but it does have a more sophisticated constraint that doesn't have a counterpart in the RelativeLayout. Referred to as "bias" this type of constraint works in terms of ratios, expressed as percentages and displayed as zig-zag lines:

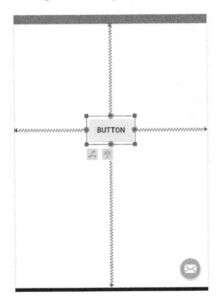

To use it you have to create two constraints that "fight" each other. For example, if you drag one constraint to the left and its counterpart to the right, the result is a horizontal bias used to position the control at the desired proportion of the layout size. You can achieve a vertical bias by dragging constraints from the top and the bottom.

As you drag the control around the screen, the fractions or percentages are updated in the Attributes window. You can use the sliders that appear to set the percentages:

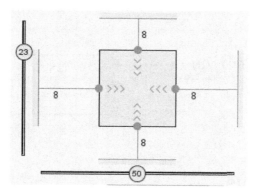

Things are just a little more complicated in that you can also specify a margin which provides a relative component to the bias constraint. If you inspect the display in the Attributes windows shown above, you can see that the constraints have a value of 8 displayed alongside them. This is the default margin assigned when you created the constraint. As you drag the component around the screen you cannot position it closer to the sides than the margin set in that direction.

For example, if you edit the left margin to be 100, then the constraint display acquires a straight portion 100 units long. If you now try to move the button to the left, you will find you cannot get closer than 100 units. Notice that it is the distance between the specified margins that is divided up in the ratio set by the bias. If you want the entire screen to be used, then set the margins to zero:

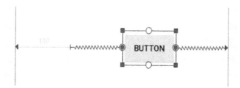

## Chains

A recently introduced feature is the ability to set bias constraints between components as well as to the parent container. That is, you can set pairs of constraints between components that work in the same way as a bias constraint. In doing so you create what is now called a "chain" of components. The reason for introducing chains is to make it easier for ConstraintLayout to create the sort of thing that you would have used

LinearLayout for, namely lines or columns of components with proportional spacing.

Creating a chain is a slightly mysterious process. If you want to create a horizontal chain of say three Buttons the first task is to arrange them roughly into a line:

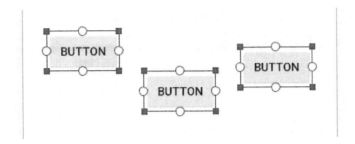

If they aren't in a reasonable line the constraints will be applied separately to each component. Select all three by dragging a marquee around the three and then right click while all three are selected and use the Chain, Create Horizontal Chain:

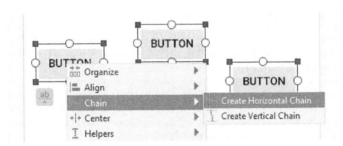

To create a vertical chain you arrange the components in a vertical column, select them all and right click and use the Chain,Create Vertical Chain command. Everything works in the same way but rotated by 90 degrees.

If everything goes to plan and the components are identified as a potential chain, the special constraints will be applied and you will see a chain icon between the inner components:

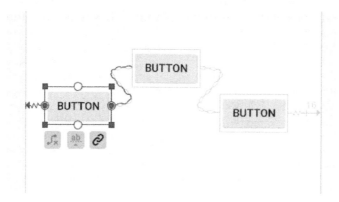

Notice that the default layout for the chain is Spread which distributes the views evenly, taking account of margins. There are three alternative layout modes which are selected by clicking on the chain icon that appears when you select a component that is part of a chain.

If you click this once the layout changes to Spread Inside, which places the first and last component hard against the container and distributes the others evenly in the space available:

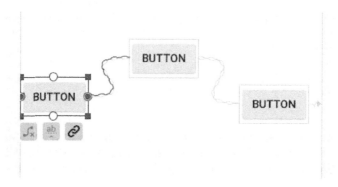

If you click a second time the layout changes to Packed which places each component as close together as possible, allowing for margins, and then places them as a group centered in the container.

You can position the group using the bias setting of the first component in the chain. Notice that the bias setting has no effect in the other chain layout modes:

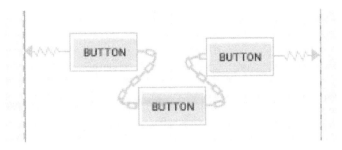

You can set a layout weight using layout_constraintHorizontal_weight and layout_constraintVertical_weight. In spread or spread inside mode this distributes the space in proportion to the weights and mimics the way weights work in a LinearLayout.

## A Chained Keypad

To show how useful chains are, let's implement a keypad of the sort that we used in the calculator project at the end of Chapter 3.

First place nine buttons on the design surface in a rough 3 by 3 grid:

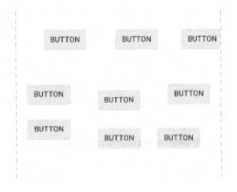

Select each row in turn and use the Chain, Create Horizontal Chain command to convert each one into a chain of three buttons:

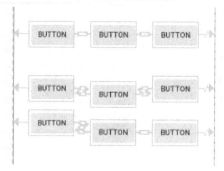

Then select the three chains, i.e. all nine buttons, and use the Chain, Create Vertical Chain command to create the grid:

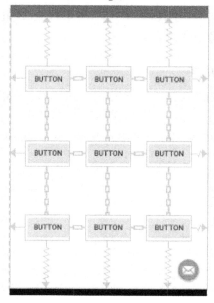

If you want to change the layout to Packed simply select the first button in each row and click the chain icon until you get a packed row:

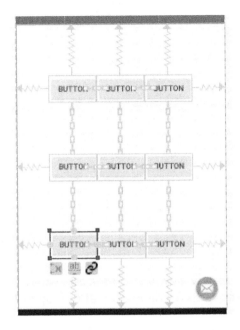

To get a packed column is more difficult because the chain icon only controls the first chain that a component is in. At the time of writing the only way to set packed on the columns is to edit the XML file.

The chain style is controlled by the first component in the chain. If you look at the XML for the first button in the first row you will see:

`app:layout_constraintHorizontal_chainStyle="packed"`

This is responsible for setting the first row to packed layout. To set the first column to packed you have to change the XML to read:

```
app:layout_constraintHorizontal_chainStyle="packed"
app:layout_constraintVertical_chainStyle="packed"/>
```

If you do this you will see the first column in packed format:

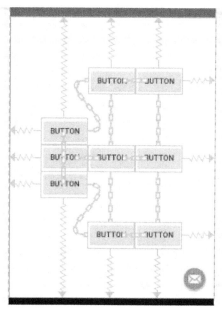

You have to change the XML for the button at the top of the second row and at the top third row to read:

```
app:layout_constraintVertical_chainStyle="packed"/>
```

If you change the top row button's XML correctly you should see a packed array of buttons:

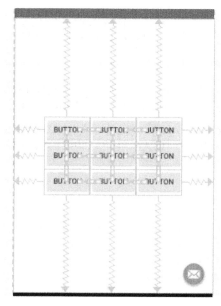

The big problem now is that to position the grid of Buttons you have to adjust the bias settings of the first button in each row, which sets the horizontal bias for that row, and the settings of the first button in each column, which sets the vertical bias. There is no single setting that will position the entire grid, and this doesn't make positioning easy.

What about adding the tenth Button?

It could have been added to the first column but it is just as easy to add it now and set a constraint from the bottom of the last Button in the first column and from the right and left side of the button:

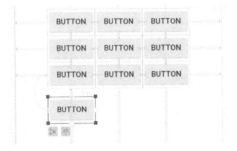

## Guidelines

The final positioning tool you have at your disposal is the guideline. You can now drag-and-drop a horizontal or vertical guideline on the design surface and use it to position other components. The most important thing about guidelines is that they don't exist as a View object, or anything else in the final layout. A guideline is an object in the Layout Editor and any constraints that you set using it are converted to positioning that makes no reference to the guideline when the app is run.

To add a guideline all you have to do is use the Guidelines tool:

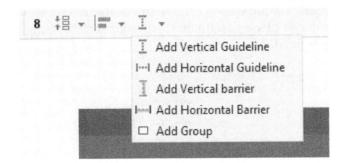

Once the guideline has been added, you can drag it to the desired location and then position components relative to it just as if it was a component in its own right. You can set any constraint that you can use with a component, including bias. Notice that if you move a guideline any components of the UI that are constrained to is will also move – this can be very useful.

You can delete a guideline by selecting it and pressing delete. At the moment the big problem with guidelines is that, while the Layout Editor displays the location as you drag, there isn't an easy way to enter a value to position it exactly:

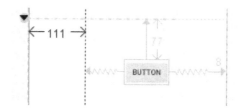

You can enter an exact position if you expand the Attributes you can enter an exact value in the guide_begin attribute which you will find under the Constraints set.

While guidelines are another positioning tool, and you can never have too many, there is nothing you can do with a guideline that you can't do without one. Also, given that guidelines are positioned absolutely on the screen, they don't provide any facilities for adjusting the layout as the screen size changes.

## Groups

*Notice that this is only available in ConstraintLayout 1.1.0 or later – see the start of the chapter for more information.*

A Group gives you the ability to create groups of components. At the moment this only provides a simple way to change the visibility of a set of components. You can place a group on the design surface using the Add Group menu command.

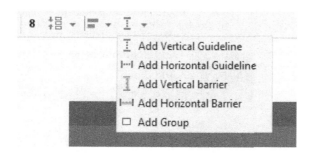

The Group is easiest to use in the Component Tree. You can drag any number of components and drop them on the Group. Notice that there is no sense in which the components are children of the Group, it is not a container. The Group simply maintains a list of the components that it controls the visibility of:

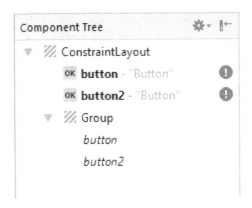

In the example shown above, the Group controls the visibility of button and button2. If the Group's visibility property is set to invisible then button and button2 no longer show in the UI but they still take up layout space. If you set visibility to gone then they are invisible and don't take up space in the UI.

The Group facility is a minor convenience as you could achieve the same result by writing code that sets the visibility of each of the components. However, it might be useful as a way of organizing a complex UI with different sets of components that can be made gone or visible with a single command.

## Sizing

In comparison to positioning, sizing a component is almost trivial but with some interesting twists.

You can see how the component is sized in the Attributes window. The type of lines shown inside the component indicate the size of the component and its relation to its content. Straight lines indicate a fixed size:

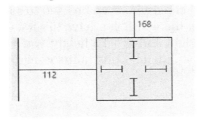

This auto-sizing behavior is set by the layout_width and layout_height properties. You can modify this by typing in an exact size, e.g. 100dp, into the value box next to the property.

An alternative to fixed size components is to allow them to automatically resize to fit or wrap their contents. To set this all you have to do is click on the inner straight lines which change to $<<<$ and allow the component to change its size:

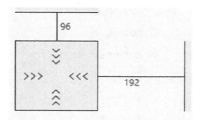

This behavior is controlled by layout_width and layout_height properties set to wrap_content and it is the most common sizing behavior used in Android. That is, most components adjust their size to suit their contents.

There is a third possibility – the size of the component can be set by constraints. If you click one more time on the internal lines they change from $<<<$ to a spring-like graphic:

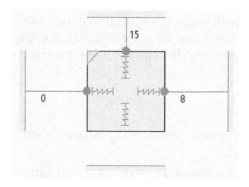

Using Match Constraints you can set sizing independently in the horizontal or vertical. meaning that constraints can be used to set the width or the height of the component. To set the width you have to set a constraint on the left and a constraint on the right and to set a height you set a constraint on the top and one on the bottom. Match Constraints is set by setting a fixed size of 0dp.

For example, if you have a Button and manually apply a constraint from the right and one from the left to the parent and have wrap_content set as the horizontal sizing then the Button stays at its original size, and bias constraints are added to divide up the available space in the Button's position:

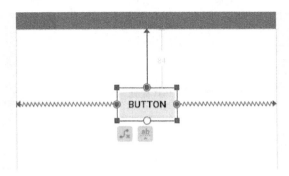

If you leave the constraints in place and change the horizontal sizing to Match Constraints then the button resizes to use the horizontal space available to it:

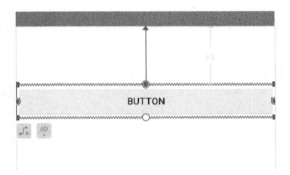

The idea is very simple – the constraints control the position of the component, or the size of the component.

You can apply Match Constraints to components that are constrained relative to other components as well as just the parent container.

For example, if you have two Buttons and you connect the left side of one to the left side of the other and the same for the right side then the constrained Button will position itself to line up with the middle of the other Button:

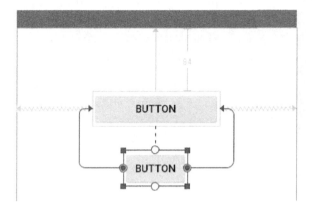

You can also set the alignment point using the bias control to make the Button have a percentage offset.

If you leave the constraints in place and change the horizontal sizing to Match Constraints, then the constrained button resizes to be the same size as the other button:

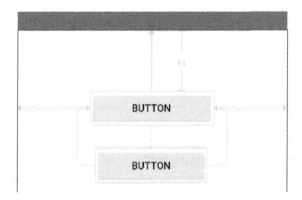

Again, the constraints can be used to set either the position or the size.

The same principle works for chains of components. If you have a chain set to Spread or Spread Inside, but not Packed, you can set MatchConstraints and the components will resize to fill the space. You can set some of the components in the chain to Match Constraints, and only those components will resize to fill the space allocated to them.

For example, in this chain of three Buttons only the second two Buttons are set to Match Constraints and the first is set to Wrap Content:

The final sizing option can be used to set the size of one dimension as a ratio of the other. To make this work, one of the dimensions must have its size set in some other way – either by a Wrap Content, a fixed size or a constraint. The dimension that is going to be set as a ratio has to be set to Match Constraints and then you click the small triangle in the corner of the Attributes window to toggle Aspect Ratio Constraint.

For example, if you place a Button on the design surface and set its width to Wrap Content, and its height to Match Constraint, then a small triangle will appear in the top left:

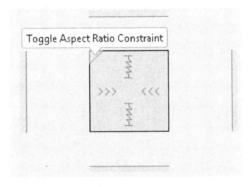

If you click on the triangle, you will set a default ratio for width:height of 1:1.

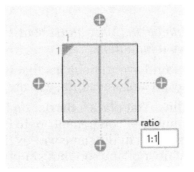

If you type in a value of say 1:2 then the height will be set to twice the width, which in turn is set by the contents:

You can set one of the dimensions using constraints. For example if you manually set right and left constraints on the Button and then set its horizontal size to Match Constraints, the Button will be as wide as the screen. If you now set Match Constants on the height and set the Aspect ratio to 2:1 you will obtain a Button that is as wide as the screen and half as high.

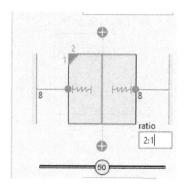

## Barriers

*Notice that this is only available in ConstraintLayout 1.1.0 or later – see the start of the chapter for more information.*

Barriers solve many ConstraintLayout problems that would otherwise be difficult to tackle, but they are not something you are likely to use every day.

A Barrier is a smart guideline. You place a Barrier on the design surface and then drag-and-drop any number of components onto it – most easily within the Component Tree. This works in the same way as the Group component in that the Barrier isn't a container of any sort, but simply keeps a list of components that it is going to work with. The Barrier also has a direction and positions itself to align with the component in its list that is the most extreme in that direction. That is, if the Barrier is set to right it positions itself on the right edge of the component in its list that is furthest to the right. If you think of the group of components that the Barrier has in its list as being surrounded by a box that just contains them, a bounding box, then another way of thinking of this is that the Barrier will position itself on one of the edges of the bounding box – the right-hand edge in our example.

Like a Guideline you can position other components relative to it by setting constraints to it. You can see that this allows you to position components so that they are to the far right, left, top or bottom of a group.

For example, use the Add Vertical barrier menu option to place a Vertical Barrier on the design surface. At this stage you wont be able to see it because its default direction is left and it takes up position as far to the left as possible.

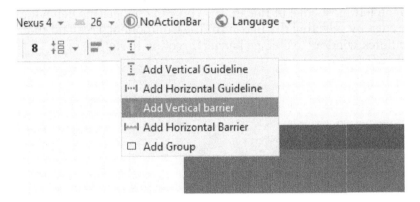

Next place two Buttons on the design surface and, using the Component Tree drag-and-drop them onto the barrier:

The default Barrier direction is left and so it will now position itself to be on the left hand edge of the Button that is furthest to the left.

You can see the Barrier as a gray shaded strip in the diagram below:

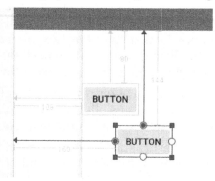

If you move the two Buttons you will notice that the Barrier always anchors itself to the left most edge in the group. You can change this behavior to another edge by selecting the Barrier in the Component Tree and then using the Attributes window to change barrierDirection to right say:

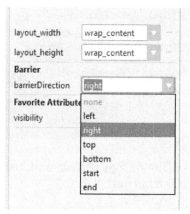

With this change the Barrier positions itself on the right most edge of the group. Now if you place a third Button on the design surface and constrain it to be to the right of the Barrier, then it will always stay to the right of the rightmost edge of the components in the Barrier's list:

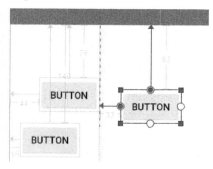

If you move the two Button's around you will soon get the idea that this Barrier is a way of placing components to the right of the rightmost component of the group whichever one this is. Without a Barrier object you would have to put the Button's into a Frame and then position the other components relative to the Frame. This would work but it creates a nested layout. The Barrier approach keeps the ConstraintLayout flat.

The Barrier is useful when ever you have a group of components that change their size due to user input or data or locale or whatever. You can use a Barrier to divide up the screen area into something large enough to accommodate the group and then the rest of the components can position themselves in what is left over.

### Constraint Attributes

As you might guess, there are attributes very similar to those used by the RelativeLayout which set the constraints for a ConstraintLayout. To see all of the attributes you have to click on the View all attributes icon at the top right of the Attributes window – the double arrow.

For example, if you look in the Attributes window you will see:

```
Constraints
    Left_toLeftOf
```

This prompts you to supply the id of the other control being used in the alignment – left-hand side to left-hand side in this case. There are similar constraints for the other possibilities. For example:

```
    Bottom_toBottomOf
```

and so on.

It is also worth understanding that, in allowing you to set the position of a component by simply dragging it to the location you want, the Layout Editor is working out how to set multiple properties correctly. You could do this manually to get the same effect, but the Layout Editor does it simply from where you have positioned a component. This is why it is easier to let the Layout Editor set the properties for you.

## Troubleshooting

The ConstraintLayout provides a way of creating reactive layouts that adjust to the size of the screen. However, doing this effectively is difficult. The amount of intelligence required goes well beyond what the Infer Constraints tool has. It may even be beyond a human. A simpler, but more work-intensive way, is to provide a separate layout for radically different screen sizes and use constraints to make small adjustments.

The ConstraintLayout library uses a linear constraint solver to work out the positions of all of the components. This then produces a layout that is used in your app that is intended to be fast and efficient. Currently the system and the Layout Editor are undergoing rapid change and development. There are many features that don't quite work as advertised, and many features don't have the facilities needed to make them easy to use.

However, ConstraintLayout is the way of the future according to the Android development team.

Given the advantage of producing a single layout that caters for a variety of screen sizes and orientations it is worth persevering with. However, it is very easy to get into a complete mess in the Layout Editor.

One very common problem is for components to apparently go missing. This is usually because they are on top of each other or positioned off the screen. The easiest way to sort this problem out is to go to the Attributes window and manually reset one of the positioning properties.

You will also find the following tips useful:

♦ Use positioning relative to another component if it makes logical sense. That is, if you have a text entry component then it make sense to position its accept button relative to its right-hand side.

♦ If you position everything relative to the parent container then you effectively have an absolute layout that specifies the exact and immutable position of everything.

♦ If the screen size changes then it is possible that components will overlap one another if there isn't enough space. Always make your layouts have plenty of spare space.

♦ A good strategy when working with a group of components is to pick one that you position relative to the container, then position all other components relative to it to ensure that you can move the group and keep alignments.

♦ Remember that some components can change their size as well as location and this can modify the position of components positioned relative to them.

♦ Automatically generated constraints sometimes work, but they are rarely as logical as a set of manually created constraints. If you plan to make use of the layout in the future, then it is worth creating a set of manually applied constraints.

♦ Use Infer Constraints incrementally as you add components and then manually modify what it creates to be more logical.

♦ It is more realistic to produce a separate layout resource for small to medium-sized screens and one for large screens.

# Summary

- The ConstraintLayout is the layout of the future and the new Layout Editor was created to work best with it.

- There are two automatic constraint tools – Autoconnect which works out constraints for a single component, and Infer Constraints which works out any missing constraints for the entire layout. Neither tool is currently particularly useful.

- You can clear all of the constraints in a layout, or just those on a single component or a constraint at a time.

- Constraints can be applied from a component to the parent container and these act like absolute positioning.

- You can set default margins to make positioning components more regular.

- Components can be positioned relative to another component.

- You cannot set negative margins.

- You can align text baselines.

- Bias constraints allow you to set positions that divide the space available in a specified proportion.

- Chains provide some of the features of a LinearLayout. For example, you can use a chain to distribute components across the available space.

- Guidelines can be added to a layout and components can be positioned relative to them, even though they don't appear in the final layout.

- Groups can be created which allow you to set the visibility of all of the components in one go.

- You can set the size of a component absolutely or to be determined by the content. In addition, you can allow a pair of constraints to determine the size.

- An Aspect Ratio Constraint can set one dimension as the ratio of another.

- A Barrier is a smart guideline that tracks a specified group of components and is positioned at the most extreme edge of the group in a specified direction. You can position other components relative to the Barrier.

If you want to be a really good Android programmer, not only do you need to know how to create a UI, but also how the UI is created. To be really confident in what you are doing, you need to understand some of the inner workings of the Android graphics system. This is also essential if you want to modify the UI in code and work with menus.

## A UI Library

There are lots of different UI construction kits for Java and other languages, AWT, Swing, Qt, MFC, WPF and on, and you might think that mastering them all would be a difficult, if not impossible, task. In fact it is a lot easier than you might think because most UI libraries use the same general approach and the Android UI library, which doesn't seem to have a given name, is no different. Let's take a careful look at how it works.

An Activity has a window associated with it and this is usually the entire graphics screen of the device it is running on. In other words, an Activity can allow other objects to draw on the device's screen. However, rather than simply providing direct access to the graphics hardware, there is an extensive set of classes that make building a UI and performing graphics operations easier.

Before we look at general graphics we need to first find out how the UI is constructed.

## The View

The basis of all UI components and general 2D graphics is the View class. This is a general-purpose class that has lots and lots of methods and properties that determine how it will display the component or other graphics entity it represents. It also takes part in the event handling system, which means Views can respond to events. There are View classes that implement all of the standard components that you make use of in the Android Studio Layout Editor, i.e. Button, TextView and so on.

Every View object has an onDraw method that can draw the graphic representation of what it represents onto a Canvas object which is essentially a bitmap with drawing methods. What happens is that the Activity calls the View's onDraw method when it needs to update the UI and passes it a Canvas object that it then renders to the screen – you don't have to worry about how the Canvas is rendered to the screen at this level. You can think of this as, *"every View object knows how to draw itself"*.

To summarize:

- An Activity can be associated with a View object.
- When the Activity needs to draw its UI it calls the View object's onDraw method e.g. view.onDraw(Canvas).
- The View object then draws on the Canvas whatever it needs to, whether a button, text or something else.
- The Activity then displays the Canvas object on the screen.

An Activity can only be associated with a single View object, which determines what is drawn on the screen. This might seem a bit limited but, as you will see, it is far from limited because View objects can be nested within one another.

## Using setContentView

How do you set a View object to show in the Activities window?

The answer is that you use the Activities **setContentView** method, which is what we have been doing all along.

To see this in action, start a new Basic Activity project and change onCreate to read:

```
override fun onCreate(savedInstanceState: Bundle?) {
    super.onCreate(savedInstanceState)
    val b =  Button(this)
    setContentView(b)
}
```

Don't forget to use Alt+Enter to add the import statements needed to allow you to use the Button class, and don't leave any code in onCreate that would use other View objects such as the menu.

The first instruction creates a Button object, which is a subclass of View, and the second sets this as the Activities View. If you run this program what you will see is a gray area that fills the entire screen:

Yes, this is the button! You can even click it although, with no event handler, nothing happens.

To make this button a tiny bit more interesting we can customize it by setting properties. For example:

```
val b =  Button(this)
b.text="Hello Button"
setContentView(b)
```

If you run this you will see a button that fills the screen with the caption "Hello Button".

Don't bother setting any layout properties in code because at the moment there is no layout in force so they will be ignored. How to activate a layout is our next topic.

# The ViewGroup

If an Activity can only show a single View object, how can we ever create a complex UI with multiple buttons, textViews and other components? The answer, and you probably already guessed it, is that there are Layout, or ViewGroup, objects which can be used to host other View objects.

You already know about using Layouts in the Layout Editor or in an XML file, but they, like all UI elements, correspond to particular classes that do the actual work.

A ViewGroup can display multiple View objects. So in nearly all cases the View object that is associated with an Activity is a Layout View. When the Activity asks the Layout View to render itself, by calling its onDraw method, the Layout calls the onDraw method of each of the View objects it contains and puts them together to make a single result. Of course, it also performs a layout operation positioning and sizing the View objects it contains.

So a Layout does two things:

- it hosts other View objects
- it performs the layout function after which it is named.

To see this in action try:

```
override fun onCreate(savedInstanceState: Bundle?) {
super.onCreate(savedInstanceState)
      val linLayout= LinearLayout(this)
      val b =  Button(this)
      b.text="Hello Button"
      linLayout.addView(b)
      setContentView(linLayout)
}
```

If you run this program you will see a button at the very top left of the screen.

The first instruction creates a LinearLayout object. This is a subclass of View that can contain other View objects and it organizes them in a left to right or top to bottom way depending on the setting of its orientation property. Next we create a button object and then use the standard addView method of the LinearLayout to add it to the layout.

All Layouts have an addView method, which can be used to add multiple View objects.

You can add more buttons to see how the default LinearLayout works:

```kotlin
override fun onCreate(savedInstanceState: Bundle?) {
    super.onCreate(savedInstanceState)

    val linLayout= LinearLayout(this)

    val b1 = Button(this)
    b1.text="Hello Button 1"
    linLayout.addView(b1)

    val b2 =  Button(this)
    b2.text="Hello Button 2"
    linLayout.addView(b2)

    val b3 =  Button(this)
    b3.text ="Hello Button 3"
    linLayout.addView(b3)
    setContentView(linLayout)
}
```

## Programming Layout Properties

At the moment we are relying on default settings for the properties, and the layout properties in particular, of the View objects we are creating. However, in practice you could spend the time and lines of code to set all of the properties needed to create any user interface and layout you wanted to.

You now know how to create a UI completely in code. All you have to do is create all of the objects you need, set their properties and add them to suitable layout objects. This is a little more complicated than you might think because each layout type has a different set of layout properties. Exactly how this is done is easy enough, but if you don't want to know about it at this stage you can skip ahead as it doesn't change any of the general principles.

As explained in the previous chapter, each type of Layout has an associated class derived from LayoutParams called *layout*.LayoutParams where *layout* is the name of the Layout class. For example, LinearLayout has the LinearLayout.LayoutParams class, which is used to define all of the layout properties that a View object can use when added to a LinearLayout object.

169

You can probably guess how to make use of the LayoutParams class. All you do is create a correctly initialized instance of the appropriate LayoutParams class and use setLayoutParams on any View object you want to customize.

For example, to set the height and width in a LayoutParams object we could use:

```
val LP= LinearLayout.LayoutParams(100,100)
```

There is a constructor for all of the LayoutParams classes that accepts just the width and the height properties. Once you have a LayoutParams object you can assign it to any View object by setting the View object's LayoutParams property:

```
b3.layoutParams =LP
linLayout.addView(b3)
```

With this change the third button in our previous layout will be exactly 100 by 100 pixels.

Notice that the constructor works in pixels, i.e. px, instead of device-independent pixels, dp. You can also use constants for MATCH_PARENT and WRAP_CONTENT. For example:

```
val LP=LinearLayout.LayoutParams(WRAP_CONTENT,WRAP_CONTENT)
```

There is also a constructor that allows you to set the weight. Other layout properties have to be set using properties after the constructor has done its job. Some properties might have to set using set property methods. For example:

```
LP.setMargins(20,20,20,20)
```

which sets the left, top, right and bottom margins accordingly:

More complex Layout objects have correspondingly more complex LayoutParams that you have to spend time setting up.

So to be clear – there are properties such as text that you set directly on the View object, but there are also Layout properties that you have to set on an appropriate LayoutParams object, which is then set as the View object's LayoutParam property.

## The View Hierarchy

Notice also that a Layout can contain other Layouts and so the set of View objects that make up a UI is structured like a tree, the View hierarchy. When the screen is redrawn each View object is asked to draw itself and this is done for all View objects in the hierarchy from top to bottom.

Normally the View hierarchy is drawn just once when the Activity loads. If an area of the screen is obscured by another graphic for any reason, the redraw is clever enough not to draw the entire View hierarchy. It only redraws View objects that intersect with the invalidated area of the screen. The View hierarchy is also involved in passing events between objects and in determining which component has the current focus.

## XML Layout

So far the principles of the graphic system are simple enough. Every control or component corresponds to a View object and you can build a UI by creating View objects in code and adding them to Layouts. You control the way the View objects are arranged using the LayoutParams object or by directly setting properties. An Activity will draw its View hierarchy to the screen when it needs to. OK, this is how to create a UI in code, but so far we have been building a UI using the Layout Editor.

How does this relate to the View hierarchy?

The Layout Editor creates an XML file which describes the View hierarchy that you want to create. The way that this works is fairly obvious. Each tag in the XML file corresponds to a View object for which you want to create an instance. For example:

```
<LinearLayout>
</LinearLayout>
```

creates an instance of a LinearLayout object.

Nesting tags within a layout indicates that the objects created need to be added to the layout as child Views. For example:

```
<LinearLayout>
 <Button />
</LinearLayout>
```

creates a LinearLayout object and a Button object and then adds the Button object to the LinearLayout using its addView method. You can see that the XML captures the idea of the View hierarchy perfectly.

To set object properties all you have to do is is use the corresponding attributes in the XML. For example to set the button's text:

```
<Button
  android:text="New Button"
/>
```

Layout parameters are set using properties prefixed with layout_property. For example:

```
<Button
 android:layout_width="wrap_content"
 android:layout_height="wrap_content"
/>
```

That is really all there is to it. The XML defines a hierarchy of objects and their properties and the system reads the file and creates the objects. This use of XML as an object instantiation system is not an uncommon one. Of course, the XML created by the Layout Editor looks a lot more complicated than the examples above, but this is mainly because of the number of attributes it defines. The basic idea is still the same.

## Inflation Theory

The final big question to be answered is how does the XML get converted into a real object hierarchy? The answer to this is to use an "inflater".

To inflate a layout is Android jargon for instantiating the objects defined by an XML file. You normally don't have to call an inflater because the system does it for you behind the scenes, but you can if you want to. For example, to inflate a layout you would use an instance of the LayoutInflater. Normally you wouldn't create a fresh instance. Instead you can simply use an existing one supplied by the system using the **LayoutInflater** property of the Activity. Once you have the LayoutInflater you can use one of its many inflate methods to create a View object hierarchy as specified by the XML. Which method you use depends on where the XML is stored. You can simply supply a resource id for an XML file included in the res directory. For example, to inflate the usual activity_main.xml layout you can use:

```
val inf = layoutInflater
val myView = inf.inflate(R.layout.activity_main,null)
setContentView(myView)
```

The second parameter of inflate can be used to provide a View object to act as the root container for the inflated View hierarchy. The container is just used as a reference "parent" for the purposes of calculating the layout. That is, it simply provides the container that everything has to fit into according to the layout rules. Of course this is entirely equivalent to the usual:

```
setContentView(R.layout.activity_main)
```

which calls the LayoutInflater and sets the view in a single instruction.

The only reason that you would manually inflate an XML layout is if you wanted to do something clever, such as put one layout together with another or in some way manipulate the View hierarchy.

Notice that there are other types of inflater objects, e.g. the Menu inflater, which do the same job of converting XML to instantiated objects with the given properties. We will come back to these more specialized inflaters when we look at menus in the next chapter.

There is also a version of the inflate method:

```
inflate(R.layout.activity_main,root, true/false)
```

which will inflate the XML resource using root as its container for the purposes of layout if the last parameter is false, and it will add the inflated View to the root if the last parameter is true.

## Finding View objects

One problem we have to solve if you want to work with the View hierarchy created by an inflater is finding View objects in the hierarchy. In the example where we built the View hierarchy in code it was easy to keep track of a button or a textView by simply keeping a reference to when it was created.

An inflater simply returns the View hierarchy without an easy way to get at a particular object, a button say. One way of solving the problem would be to "walk" the View tree. A ViewGroup object, e.g. a Layout, not only has an addView method but also a range of methods that allow you to access the objects it contains. Each child object is assigned an integer index – think of it like an array. The method:

```
getChildAt(i)
```

will return the child object at index i. You can also use:

```
getChildCount()
```

to find out how many child objects are stored in the container.

Using these methods you can search the hierarchy for the View object you want but how do you know which one it is? The answer is that all View objects have an id property which should identify them uniquely. The id property is set as part of the XML file.

To avoid you having to work out an id value, the standard way of setting an id is to define a resource within the XML file:

```
<Button
    android:id="@+id/my_button"
```

When the XML file is inflated the @+ symbol is interpreted as "create a resource". An integer id is generated using the generateViewId method and this is used to both create the id property and to add a my_button property to the id property of the R object, R.id.

If you are using Kotlin to work with the XML file it automatically converts all of the string labels on the ids to Activity properties and then makes them reference the objects that the inflater creates. To allow this to happen you have to enable the kotin-android-extensions plugin – which is enabled by default in a Kotlin project. You can then specify which layout files you want to create properties for using:

```
import kotlinx.android.synthetic.main.layout.*
```

So to import properties for all of the View created by the two standard XML files main.activity_main.xml and main.content_main.xml you would use:

```
import kotlinx.android.synthetic.main.activity_main.*
import kotlinx.android.synthetic.main.content_main.*
```

These are automatically added to your project file when it is created. Any other layout resource files that you create will also be added automatically so that their ids are properties also.

The only minor complication is that when you set an id using the Layout Editor it will auto generate the @+id/ for you. So in the Attributes window you will see my_button not @+id/my_button which is what is entered into the XML file. This is helpful, but it can be confusing.

There is a lot more to say about resources, but for the moment this is enough to understand what is going on. Resources deserve a chapter all to themselves and you'll come to it after we've looked at menus.

What all this means is that not only do you get an autogenerated id value, but also a way to get this value into running code. You could use the getChildAt methods to step through all of the View objects in the hierarchy, but it is much easier to use:

```
findViewById<Button>(R.id.my_button)
```

which returns the object in one instruction. If you are not using Kotlin's conversion of ids to properties then this is the only sensible way to work and Java programmers make use of the findViewById before they can work with any View object in code.

The general method, in Kotlin, is to inflate the XML, set it as the content of the View, and use the generated Activity properties to work with any View object you want to.

## How to Build a UI?

You now have two distinct approaches to building a UI. You can do the whole job in code or you can create an XML layout. In practice it is usually easier to use the Layout Editor to generate the XML file for you. You can, however, mix the two approaches and change a UI "on the fly". For example you can load a UI by implicitly or explicitly inflating an XML file and then writing code to create and add other components or even remove View objects from the layout. To remove View objects you simply use the removeView or removeViewAt methods of the ViewGroup object.

There are other UI components such as menus that the Layout Editor doesn't support. In this case you have to work with the XML or create the UI in code. This means you do need to know the inner workings of the View hierarchy even though the Layout Editor is the easiest way to create a UI.

# Summary

- All of the UI components are derived from the View class.

- An Activity can host and display a single instance of the View class set by one of its setContentView methods.

- You can create instances of View objects in code and set them to be displayed by the Activity.

- A Layout or ViewGroup object is a View object that can contain many View objects, so creating a sophisticated layout that the Activity can display.

- Each Layout has its associated LayoutParams class, which is used by each View object it contains to control how it treats it within the layout.

- You generally have to create an instance of the LayoutParams class, set the parameters you want to determine, and then set the instance as the LayoutParams of each View object that needs to use it via the LayoutParams property.

- The use of Layout containers results in a View hierarchy, i.e. a hierarchy of View objects which are displayed by the Activity.

- You can also code the View hierarchy using XML. Each XML tag corresponds to a View object and they are nested to define the hierarchy. The properties of the objects are set within the XML as attributes. Layout properties are treated in the same way but with layout_ as a prefix.

- When the time comes for the View hierarchy to be assigned to the Activity, the XML file is converted into a nested set of View objects by the use of an inflater method. This simply reads the XML and converts each tag to an object and sets the object's properties.

- To find particular View objects in an inflated hierarchy the usual approach in Kotlin is to generate properties corresponding to the ids. If you don't want to do this then you have to use use the findViewById method.

# Chapter 9

# Menus – Toolbar

A UI isn't just made up of buttons and other widgets or components; the menu is still a useful way of letting the user select what happens next. Android's menu system is easy to master. We also need to find out about the Toolbar implementation of the action bar.

There is a menu Layout Editor in Android Studio 3.0 and it works quite well, but it is still worth knowing how to create the XML yourself.

The basic principles of menu creation are the same as for building a UI in that a menu is a collection of View objects. You can create the View objects in code or you can use an XML file and a special inflater, a MenuInflater, to convert it into the objects. Defining a menu is more or less the same process every time, although the way in which you use the menu varies according to where and when the menu is shown, but even this follows roughly the same steps. Let's look a the general idea first.

## Creating a Menu Resource

Menus are generally defined by a menu resource file, which is an XML file which is rendered to create the menu. All menu resources are stored in the app\res\menu directory. If you right click on this directory you can select the New, Menu resource option and type in a name – all lowercase as usual:

You can ignore the Available qualifiers for the moment. The idea is that each resource you create will be used in a given situation according to the qualifiers you select. In this way you can create custom menus for particular languages for example. More about this idea in Chapter 11.

When you click the OK button the resource file is created and it will be opened in the layout editor. This in principle should allow you to edit the menu using drag-and-drop just like a general layout, but at the moment it is very limited and tends to create XML that doesn't work. You can place a menu item onto the menu and customize some of its properties, but this is about as far as it goes:

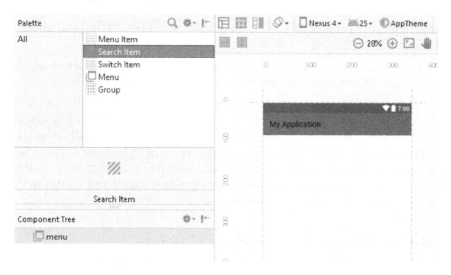

You can work either with the menu editor or the XML directly. You will discover that the XML Editor suggests auto-completions so you aren't entirely without help even if you have to abandon the menu editor.

Before we can create a menu we need to know something about the XML tag.and the corresponding menu items./

## The Menu Tree

A menu is a hierarchy of options. The top-level menu presents a set of items. If any of the items is itself a menu, i.e. a submenu, then it can contain more items.

Android menus make use of three objects, and hence three XML tags:

- ◆ <menu>
- ◆ <item>
- ◆ <group>

At the top level the <menu> tag inflates to a Menu object which is a container for menu items and group elements. The <item> tag inflates to a MenuItem object which is a single option in the menu. It can also contain a <menu> tag which can in turn contain more <item> tags to create a submenu. The <group> tag doesn't inflate to an object. Instead it sets the group id of all of the items it contains. You can set various properties of a group of items in one operation i.e. they act as a group.

There are a range of attributes that can be used with <item> and <group> and not all can be used in every situation. The three that you need to know about are:

- ♦ id - an integer that you use to identify the menu item
- ♦ title - a string that determines what the menu item displays
- ♦ icon - a drawable image used when the menu item can be displayed as an icon.

With all this explained let's define a menu with a single File item and a submenu consisting of two items, New and Open:

```
<?xml version="1.0" encoding="utf-8"?>
<menu xmlns:android=
        "http://schemas.android.com/apk/res/android">
  <item
        android:id="@+id/file"
        android:title="File">

    <!-- "file" submenu -->
    <menu>
     <item
        android:id="@+id/create_new"
        android:title="New" />
     <item
        android:id="@+id/open"
        android:title="Open" />
    </menu>
  </item>
</menu>
```

You can see in the example that we have a top-level menu item that we don't bother giving an id which contains a single <item> tag. This displays the text File when the menu is displayed. In case you have forgotten the notation "@+id/*name*" automatically creates the id resource *name* and sets it to a newly generated integer value. You can then use *name* in code to find and work with the menu item.

The <item> tag contains another <menu> tag which in turn contains two more items that correspond to New and Open file menu options. You can see the structure in the Component Tree:

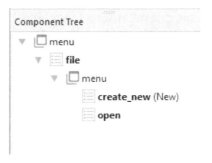

The Component Tree can also be used to do some limited editing of the menu by dragging-and-dropping to modify how items are nested.

Exactly how this simple menu looks depends on how it is displayed, but it defines a menu with a single top-level File option which when selected displays a submenu of two other options, New and Open.

## Displaying a Menu

There are four different ways you can display a menu:

1. Action bar such as the App Bar

2. Context menu

3. Contextual action Bar (CAB)

4. Popup

The action bar or App bar was introduced in Android 3 as a replacement for the original options menu and has become the standard primary menu for apps. With Android 5 a new way of implementing it was introduced, namely the Toolbar, which is a standard widget that can be edited using the Layout Editor. This makes it easier to integrate and work with. If you want to use the ActionBar in earlier versions of Android you need to make use of the Support Library – this is automatically included when Android Studio creates a project for you.

The context menu is a popup menu that appears in response to a long click on a component of the UI.

The Contextual Action Bar appears at the top of the screen when the user long-clicks on a UI element and it is supposed to be used to provide actions that are appropriate for the item that has been selected. It too needs the Support Library to work with older versions of Android.

The popup menu can be displayed in response to almost any user action you care to use. It appears next to the View object that causes it to be displayed. For example you could have a button that displays a popup when clicked or a popup could appear when a user types something into a text field. It is difficult to know exactly when to use a popup menu.

Logically the next step would be to use the XML file we just created to display either a CAB or a popup, but it is better to start with the default project type as it generates the code and menu resource file needed to implement an action bar, the Toolbar, and it is used in most applications.

The remaining menu types are the topic of the next chapter.

## Using the Toolbar

If you start a new Basic Activity project called MenuSample then you will discover that it automatically creates a main_menu resource file and the code needed to display it as a Toolbar.

The Basic Activity template uses the support library to make it possible in earlier versions of Android. This is why the MainActivity class in your project has to derive from the AppCompatActivity class and not the more basic Activity class:

```
class MainActivity : AppCompatActivity() {
```

and why we need the imports:

```
import android.support.design.widget.Snackbar
import android.support.v7.app.AppCompatActivity
```

The Toolbar is defined in activity_main.xml as a custom widget:

```
<android.support.design.widget.AppBarLayout
 android:layout_width="match_parent"
 android:layout_height="wrap_content"
 android:theme="@style/AppTheme.AppBarOverlay">

 <android.support.v7.widget.Toolbar
  android:id="@+id/toolbar"
  android:layout_width="match_parent"
  android:layout_height="?attr/actionBarSize"
  android:background="?attr/colorPrimary"
  app:popupTheme="@style/AppTheme.PopupOverlay"
  style="@style/AppTheme" />

</android.support.design.widget.AppBarLayout>

<include layout="@layout/content_main" />
...
```

Notice that the Toolbar's style is set to AppTheme. This is important as the style selected changes the way the Toolbar is displayed and can stop it from displaying altogether.

Also notice the tag:

```
<include layout="@layout/content_main" />
```

This loads the layout that you design in content_main.xml. As explained in earlier chapters, the layout files are split into two parts – activity_main.xml which defines the layout that should be common to all Android apps, and content_main.xml which is used for the layout specific to your app. The two files are automatically merged together when activity_main.xml is loaded.

When the Activity loads, onCreate runs and inflates the layout in activity_main.xml and the included content_main.xml. This is enough for the Toolbar to display, but for it to be used as an action bar menu by the system we need to add:

```
setSupportActionBar(toolbar)
```

This is generated for you automatically and you will find it in the MainActivity.java file in onCreate:

```
override fun onCreate(savedInstanceState: Bundle?) {
        super.onCreate(savedInstanceState)
        setContentView(R.layout.activity_main)
        setSupportActionBar(toolbar)
```

Now if you run the app you will see the familiar Hello world message and the default App bar:

In fact, this toolbar is so familiar you may not even have realized that it is a menu. It has the name of the app to the left and a three dot icon to the right.

If you select the three dot icon the Settings menu item appears:

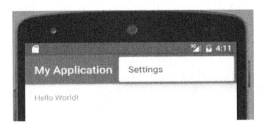

If you take a look at the menu_main.xml file you can see the definition of this menu:

```
<menu xmlns:android="http://schemas.android.com/apk/res/android"
 xmlns:app="http://schemas.android.com/apk/res-auto"
 xmlns:tools="http://schemas.android.com/tools"
 tools:context="com.example.mikejames.myapplication.MainActivity">
<item
  android:id="@+id/action_settings"
  android:orderInCategory="100"
  android:title="Settings"
  app:showAsAction="never" />
</menu>
```

You can see that this defines a single menu with a single item with the title "Settings".

There are some new attributes being used in the item tag. The **showAsAction** attribute is important for the way the Toolbar, or action bar, works. By default the system places menu items into the overflow area that is only revealed when the user selects the three dot icon or more generally the action overflow icon. However, for items that you would like to give the user more direct access, you can set the showAsAction attribute.

This can be set to any of the following:

- **ifRoom** - show if there is room
- **never** - never show in the visible area
- **withText** - show with text
- **always** - always show even if it means overlapping other items
- **collapseActionView** - show a collapsed view of the item.

As you can see, the Settings item in the default Toolbar is set to never show.

The showAsAction attribute works with the orderInCategory attribute to determine the order in which items are shown.

To see this in action let's add another item, one to perform a Send, to the end of the menu_main.xml file before the final </menu> tag:

```
<item android:id="@+id/action_send"
 android:title="Send"
 app:showAsAction="ifRoom" />
```

You can do the same job using the Menu editor. Simply drag-and-drop a Menu Item from the Palette to the Component Tree and use the Attributes window to customize it:

No matter how you do the job the result is the same:

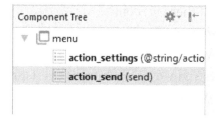

Now if you run the app you will see:

The new Send item will be displayed as long as there is room. If there isn't it will appear when the user selects the three dots icon.

It is usual to show toolbar items as icons so change the item tag to read:

```
<item android:id="@+id/action_send"
  android:title="Send"
  app:showAsAction="ifRoom"
  android:icon="@android:drawable/ic_menu_send"/>
```

which specifies one of the many supplied icons. You can also use the property window to select ic_menu_send in the Resources window:

You can carry on adding menu items to the Toolbar and customizing how they display given different screen widths. The general idea is the same for all menus.

## Creating the App Bar

So far we have just looked at the menu_main.xml file and the XML specification of the action bar menu. There is also some code generated to actually create the menu displayed in the App bar. The Activity will fire a CreateOptionsMenu event when it is ready to display the App bar - recall that before Android 3 there was an options menu rather than an action bar.

All the onCreateOptionsMenu event handler has to do is inflate the XML file that defines the menu:

```
override fun onCreateOptionsMenu(menu: Menu): Boolean {

    menuInflater.inflate(R.menu.menu_main, menu)
    return true
}
```

The onCreateOptionsMenu is called once when the Activity starts. Before Android 3 it was called each time the menu was displayed on the screen, but now the App bar is always on display. How to change a toolbar is discussed later.

All the event handler has to do is use the appropriate inflater object to create the menu from the resource file. The new View hierarchy of menu and item objects is added to the menu object passed to the event handler. This is important because it means that your new menu items are added to any that are already there. This allows other Activities and Fragments to add items to a common toolbar.

## Where's My Toolbar?

If you try any of this out then there is a chance that you will do everything correctly and yet your Toolbar will not show.

There are only two common reasons for this:

1.  You are targeting and using an early version of Android which doesn't support the action bar. This is unlikely, especially if you are using the Support Library.

2.  Much more common is that you are using a theme that doesn't support the type of action bar you are using.

The solution is easy. For Android 5 or later, or when using the Support Library, select one of the AppCompat themes if you want to make use of the new features introduced with Android 5. As always, Android Studio generates the correct XML for the styles that work with the Toolbar.

## Responding to Menu Events

You can attach click event handlers to the various items in a menu in the usual way. This is something that is often overlooked because there is a simpler and standard way of doing the job. However, it is worth seeing the direct method if only to convince yourself that a menu is just another part of the View hierarchy that your application displays. If you aren't fully familiar with how to attach a click event handler to a View object, refer back to Chapters 4 and 5.

When you inflate a menu resource in onCreateOptionsMenu what happens is that the View hierarchy that is created when you inflate the XML is added to the current menu. This is passed into the onCreateOptionsMenu event handler in the menu parameter:

```
override fun onCreateOptionsMenu(menu: Menu): Boolean {
```

Next you use the inflater and inflate the resource:

```
menuInflater.inflate(R.menu.menu_main, menu)
```

After this, menu contains the View hierarchy, that is the entire menu as created so far.

At this point you might be thinking that you can access the menu items using Activity properties that Kotlin adds. You can't and you can't import the menu XML file as you can with a layout. Instead you have to use findViewById however you can't do this because the menu hasn't yet been added to the complete View hierarchy. The menu is only added to the View hierarchy after the onCreateOptionsMenu event handler finishes.

That is, the menu's View hierarchy is built up in menu and this is added to the app's full View hierarchy only when the onCreateOptionsMenu event handler finishes.

To allow you to find the menu item while in onCreateOptionsMenu, the menu object has its own findItem method. So to find the MenuItem that corresponds to the item with id action_send you would use:

```
val mItem = menu.findItem(R.id.action_send)
```

Now that you have the MenuItem object corresponding to the Send item you can add a click event handler:

```
mItem.setOnMenuItemClickListener {item->
                    process event
                false
            }
```

Now the event handler will be called when the Send menu item is selected by the user. The event handler should return true if it has consumed the event and false if it wants to pass it on to other handlers.

The entire onCreateOptions Menu method is:

```kotlin
override fun onCreateOptionsMenu(menu: Menu): Boolean {
        menuInflater.inflate(R.menu.menu_main, menu)
        val mItem = menu.findItem(R.id.action_send)
        mItem.setOnMenuItemClickListener {item->
                                            process event
                                            false
                                        }
        return true
}
```

You can also add an event handler for the menu in the XML resource using the android:onClick attribute. The event handler has to have the same signature as the one demonstrated above, i.e. it has to return a boolean and have a single MenuItem parameter.

For example:

```kotlin
fun myOnClick( item:MenuItem): Boolean {
        return true
}
```

and:

```xml
<item android:id="@+id/action_send"
    android:title="Send"
    app:showAsAction="ifRoom"
    android:icon="@android:drawable/ic_menu_send"
    android:onClick="myOnClick"
/>
```

You can use this method to connect as many individual event handlers as you require for each of the menu items.

This is not the way it is usually done. It tends not to be a good idea to attach event handlers to the click events of each menu item.

Instead the Activity has an onOptionsItemSelected event handler method which is called when any of the items in the menu is selected. Obviously this saves a great deal of effort because you just have to implement a single event handler – and you don't even have to hook it up to the menu.

Android Studio automatically generates an event handler ready for you to use:

```kotlin
override fun onOptionsItemSelected(item: MenuItem): Boolean {
        return when (item.itemId) {
            R.id.action_settings -> true
            else -> super.onOptionsItemSelected(item)
        }
}
```

This just handles the single autogenerated Settings menu option, but you can see the general principle. The event handler is passed the menu item that has been selected - the actual object not just its id. You can then use the menu item's ItemId property to retrieve the id and you can then test it against the ids that you assigned in the resource file.

So in our simple example with a Settings and a Send item we might rewrite the generated event handler as:

```
override fun onOptionsItemSelected(item: MenuItem): Boolean {
        return when (item.itemId) {
            R.id.action_settings -> true
            R.id.action_send -> {
                perform send action
                true
            }
            else -> super.onOptionsItemSelected(item)
        }
}
```

You can see the general idea – test for each of the item's id in each of the clauses and return true if you have processed the item event. This is the standard way of processing item events in menus, that is with a single event handler and a, possibly large, when statement.

## Changing Menus in Code

A menu is just a View hierarchy and so you can make changes to it just like any View hierarchy by adding and customizing View objects. However, menus have some extra considerations because they are displayed in a slightly different way to the rest of the UI. The problem is that the menu items are not always part of the View hierarchy. They are created when the menu is displayed. This means that you might try to modify them before they are present and so cause an application crash.

The key to modifying a menu on the fly is the **onPrepareOptionsMenu** event handler. This is called just before the menu is displayed and the menu View objects are included in the View hierarchy. The onCreateOptionsMenu event only fires once when the menu is created, but the onPrepareOptionsMenu is called every time the menu is redisplayed. Hence you can use it to make modifications to the menu.

Finding a simple example of its use is difficult as we will discover, so let's just add a new item via the onPrepareOptionsMenu. Select a suitable location in the class and right click, select Generate and then Override method. You can select onPrepareOptionsMenu from the list and Android Studio will create a stub for you:

```
override fun onPrepareOptionsMenu(menu: Menu?): Boolean {
        return super.onPrepareOptionsMenu(menu)
}
```

Now all we have to do is use the add method to add a new item. There are a number of overloaded versions of add that allow you to specify the item in detail. The simplest is just add(CharSequence) which adds an item with the specified title:

```
override fun onPrepareOptionsMenu(menu: Menu?): Boolean {
        menu?.add("New Item")
        return super.onPrepareOptionsMenu(menu)
}
```

Now if you run the program you will discover that each time you select the Settings menu a couple of New Items are added to the menu:

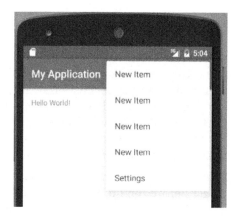

What is going on? The answer is that each time the menu is drawn the onPrepareOptionsMenu is called. For example, if you cause the Settings menu to be displayed, this overwrites the menu display and hence it has to be redrawn and onPrepareOptionsMenu is called.

If you want to modify the menu in this way you need to check if it has already been made. In other words, you need to check the status of the menu to see if the item you want to add is already there.

A slightly more realistic example is to add and remove a menu item depending on the setting of a checkbox. Add a checkbox and change the method to read:

```kotlin
override fun onPrepareOptionsMenu(menu: Menu?): Boolean {
        if (checkBox.isChecked()) {
            menu?.add(Menu.NONE, 10, Menu.NONE, "New Item")
        } else {
            menu?.removeItem(10)
        }
        return super.onPrepareOptionsMenu(menu)
}
```

Notice that all of the items added are given id 10 – there can be more than one menu item with the same id. If the checkbox isn't checked then the menu item with id 10 is removed. If there is no menu item with id 10 nothing happens and if there are more than one just the first is removed. Using this you can add multiple New Items and remove them by simply viewing the Settings menu which invalidates the menu display.

In a more realistic application you wouldn't wait for the menu to be invalidated by a user action. You would call invalidateOptionsMenu() when you wanted the onPrepareOptionsMenu to be called. So perhaps a better example is to add a button that calls invalidateOptionsMenu to update the action bar:

```kotlin
button.setOnClickListener { view-> invalidateOptionsMenu() }
```

and have the onPrepareOptionsMenu only add the item if it isn't already in the menu:

```kotlin
override fun onPrepareOptionsMenu(menu: Menu?): Boolean {
        if (checkBox.isChecked()) {
            if (menu?.findItem(10) == null) {
                menu?.add(Menu.NONE, 10, Menu.NONE, "New Item")
            }
        } else {
            menu?.removeItem(10)
        }
        return super.onPrepareOptionsMenu(menu)
}
```

Finally, how do you set other properties of the MenuItem you have added? The answer is that add returns the MenuItem created. So to set the new item to show in the action bar you would use something like:

```
val menuItem=  menu?.add(Menu.NONE, 10, Menu.NONE, "New Item")
menuItem.setShowAsAction(MenuItem.SHOW_AS_ACTION_ALWAYS)
```

Dynamically modifying the menu is a matter of keeping track of its current state and only then modifying it.

## Controlling the Toolbar

There are a couple of questions that still remain. You can see how to add items, submenus and generally control what the Toolbar displays, but what about controlling when it is displayed or how it looks? The answer to these question is based on working with the ActionBar object and as you might expect this is not something general to all menus.  ActionBar has lots of features for showing menus in different ways and to cover it completely would take too much space. However, it is worth knowing some of the basic customizations that you can apply.

You can get the ActionBar object in an Activity using supportActionBar or actionBar properties. Once you have the ActionBar object you can use its show() and hide() methods to show/hide it as required:

```
supportActionBar?.hide()
```

Similarly you can change the title and subtitle displayed in the action bar:

```
supportActionBar?.title = "My Action Bar"
supportActionBar?.subtitle = "My Subtitle"
```

There are many other properties and methods that you can use to modify the way the action bar looks and behaves.

Things that are worth looking up are: using a split Toolbar; Up Navigation; Action Views; Collapsible Action Views; Action providers; and Navigation tabs.

## Summary

- A menu is a hierarchy of View objects just like any UI element.

- You can create a menu in code, but using a menu XML resource file is the most common way of doing the job.

- There are Menu objects and tags which act as containers for Item objects and tags.

- Submenus can be created by nesting Menu objects within other Menu objects.

- Menu items can have a title, icon, and many other attributes which govern how they are displayed.

- There are four different ways you can display a menu: App bar/Toolbar; context menu; contextual action mode; popup.

- To make use of the App bar/Toolbar and the contextual action mode in earlier versions of Android you need to use the AppCompatActivity and the other support classes.

- To display a Toolbar all you have to do is use the onOptionsCreate event handler to create a menu, usually by inflating a menu resource.

- In general you can handle click events on each menu item or, more usually, you can make use of an item's click event handler that the system provides that responds to a click on any of the items.

- For the Toolbar the item's click event handler is defined in the Activity as

```
override fun onOptionsItemSelected(item: MenuItem): Boolean
```

# Chapter 10

# Menus – Context & Popup

As well as the all-purpose Toolbar which serves as an app's main menu, there are three other commonly encountered menus – the context menu, the contextual action menu, and the popup menu. They share the basic Android approach to menus while having some distinct characteristics.

The context menu is a floating menu that displays commands that take the item clicked as their subject. For example, selecting a line in a table might bring up a context menu that allows you to delete or move the item. The context menu is easy to understand and fairly easy to implement, but there is a slight confusion caused by the introduction of the Contextual Action mode, a context menu in the form of an action bar which is supported in Android 3 and above. A popup menu displays a list of items and is anchored to the View that invoked it. It can be used, for example, to provide additional choices to customize an action.

## The Context Menu

Now that we have the principles of menu construction well understood it is easy to extend what you know about the action bar to other types of menu. To create a context menu is very easy once you know the basic mechanism.

You can register any View object in the UI to respond to a long click. When any registered View object receives a long click, the Activity's **onCreateContextMenu** event handler is called. This is where you create the menu that will be shown as the context menu.

Notice that you can register as many View objects as you like and each one will respond to a long click by onCreateContextMenu being called. This means that if you want to show a different menu for each View object you need to test to see which one has caused the event.

So the recipe is:

1. Create an XML menu resource
2. Register all of the View objects that you want to trigger the context menu using registerForContextMenu
3. Override the onCreateContextMenu event handler and use a menu inflater to create the menu

For a simple example create a new menu resource, right click in the res/menu directory and select the new resource menu file option. Call it mycontext.xml and enter the following:

```xml
<?xml version="1.0" encoding="utf-8"?>
<menu xmlns:android="http://schemas.android.com/apk/res/android">
 <item
      android:title="MyItem1"
      android:id="@+id/myitem1" />
 <item
      android:title="MyItem2"
      android:id="@+id/myitem2"/>
</menu>
```

Next place a button and a checkbox on the UI and in the OnCreate method add the lines as shown below:

```kotlin
override fun onCreate(savedInstanceState: Bundle?) {
    super.onCreate(savedInstanceState)
    setContentView(R.layout.activity_main)
    setSupportActionBar(toolbar)

    registerForContextMenu(button)
    registerForContextMenu(checkBox)
}
```

You can see what is happening here, We find the Button and CheckBox objects and register them using registerForContextMenu. After this a long click on either UI component will trigger the onCreateContextMenu event.

We need to add a handler for this event and we might as well let Android Studio generate the code for us. If you right-click at a suitable place in the Java code for the Activity and select the **Generate** and then the **Override Methods** options in the menu that appears you will see a list of methods you can override:

196

Select onCreateContextMenu and Android Studio will generate a stub for you. You can find the method you are looking for by typing in its name character by character and allowing Android Studio to show you matches in the list. Select the one you want as soon as you can see it.

All you have to do in this stub is inflate the menu resource file or otherwise create a menu object in code:

```
override fun onCreateOptionsMenu(menu: Menu): Boolean {
        menuInflater.inflate(R.menu.menu_main, menu)
        return true
}
```

If you now run the program you will find that the same context menu appears when you long click on either the Button or the CheckBox:

Of course if you really want this to be a context menu then you need to test the View object passed into the onCreateContextMenu event handler and load the menu resource that corresponds to the appropriate menu for the View object.

How do you handle the context menu item selection? n more or less the same way as for the Toolbar.

When any of the items in the context menu is selected the Activity's **onContextItemSelected** event handler is called. So all you have to do is override this and use the item's id to control what should happen. For example:

```
override fun onContextItemSelected(item: MenuItem): Boolean {
    return when (item.itemId) {
        R.id.myitem1 → {
            myitem1 action
            true
        }
        R.id.myitem2 → {
            myitem2 action
            true
        }
        else ->
            super.onContextItemSelected(item)
    }
}
```

The only extra detail is the availability of the **ContextMenuInfo** object which is passed to the onCreateContextMenu handler and can be retrieved from the item in the event handler using **item.getMenuInfo()**. This contains extra information such as which line in a list view has been long clicked. Exactly what information is included depends on the View object that generated the event.

If you want to see a context menu in action add a TextView to the UI and try:

```
override fun onContextItemSelected(item: MenuItem): Boolean {
    return when (item.itemId) {
        R.id.myitem1 -> {
            textView.text = "item1"
            true
        }
        R.id.myitem2 -> {
            textView.text = "item2"
            true
        }
        else ->
            super.onContextItemSelected(item)
    }
}
```

## Contextual Action Bar

The context menu is easy to use but after Android 3 the Contextual Action Bar menu is preferred as it extends the behavior of the action bar, taking over the App bar position at the top of the screen. However, it operates, and is implemented, independently of the App bar.

When a user long clicks a View object a contextual action bar (CAB) appears at the top of the screen, rather than alongside the associated View object as the context menu does, and it gives the user to opportunity to perform multiple actions. This may be the way to do things, but it is more complicated because it requires you to implement more code.

Contextual action mode can be used in earlier versions of Android via the Support Library which Android Studio automatically includes for you.

Unlike the context menu you don't just register UI components that trigger the menu. You have to call the startActionMode method to display the contextual action mode menu, and this means you have to write a long click event handler. Notice that it is up to you what user action triggers the contextual action mode, but it is nearly always a long click.

The steps to creating a contextual action bar are:

1. First create an instance of ActionMode.Callback which contains methods for different stages in the menu's lifecycle.

2. You have to at least override the onCreateActionMode and this usually calls a menu inflater to generate the menu.

3. To handle events on the menu you also have to override onActionItemClicked.

4. To make the menu appear you have to call startSupportActionMode and pass it the instance of ActionMode.Callback you created earlier.

Notice that ActionMode.Callback is the first example of an event object that we cannot implement using a lambda for the simple reason it defines four event handlers. In other words it is not a SAM and we have to implement an object to pass to the setListener method.

For example, if you have a button and you want a long click event to trigger the menu you need to write in the Activity's OnCreate something like:

```
button.setOnLongClickListener { view-> false }
```

So far all we have implemented is an empty long click event handler for the button. To make the long click event display a menu we first need an instance of the ActionMode.Callback interface.

You only have to enter object:ActionMode.callback and then you can use the generate code option to implement the interface:

```kotlin
val mycallback=object : ActionMode.Callback {
    override fun onActionItemClicked(
            mode: ActionMode?, item: MenuItem?): Boolean {
        TODO("not implemented")
    }

    override fun onCreateActionMode(
            mode: ActionMode?, menu: Menu?): Boolean {
        TODO("not implemented")
    }

    override fun onPrepareActionMode(
            mode: ActionMode?, menu: Menu?): Boolean {
        TODO("not implemented")
    }
    override fun onDestroyActionMode(
            mode: ActionMode?) {
        TODO("not implemented")
    }

}
```

The Callback object has four methods each of which is called as part of the menu's life cycle. It is important that you replace the TODOs with code that returns the correct type for each method.

You have to make sure that when you import the class you import the version from the support library:

```kotlin
import android.support.v7.view.ActionMode
```

As you might well guess, to make the menu appear you have to fill in the details for the onCreateActionMode method:

```kotlin
override fun onCreateActionMode(
            mode: ActionMode?, menu: Menu?): Boolean {
    mode?.menuInflater?.inflate(R.menu.mycontext, menu)
    return true
}
```

All we do is inflate the menu resource and the system adds it to the menu. You can also fill out the details of the other methods – you most likely will want to add something to onActionItemClicked, but this involves nothing new.

Finally we need to activate the contextual action menu in the button's onLongClick event handler:

```kotlin
button.setOnLongClickListener { view ->
    startSupportActionMode(mycallback)
    true
}
```

Now when you long click the button a new context action bar menu appears above the usual App bar:

Notice that this behaves a little differently in that the menu stays on the screen until the user clicks the left arrow button in the corner. You can allow the user to make multiple selections or dismiss the menu as soon as the user selects one option. In this sense the contextual action bar is more sophisticated and flexible than the simple context menu.

The complete code to make the contextual action bar appear, with the object changed to an anonymous object withing the setOnLongClickListener is:

```
override fun onCreate(savedInstanceState: Bundle?) {
    super.onCreate(savedInstanceState)
    setContentView(R.layout.activity_main)
    setSupportActionBar(toolbar)

    button.setOnLongClickListener {
        view -> startSupportActionMode(object : ActionMode.Callback {
            override fun onActionItemClicked(
                mode: ActionMode?,
                item: MenuItem?): Boolean {
                    return false
            }
            override fun onCreateActionMode(
                mode: ActionMode?,
                menu: Menu?): Boolean {
                    mode?.menuInflater?.inflate(R.menu.mycontext, menu)
                    return true
            }

            override fun onPrepareActionMode(
                mode: ActionMode?,
                menu: Menu?): Boolean {
                    return false
            }

            override fun onDestroyActionMode(mode: ActionMode?) {
            }
        })
        true
    }
```

This introduction has just scratched the surface of how contextual menus can be used but the general principles follow the ideas of the general Android menu and many of the specifics of the action bar.

## The Popup Menu

The final menu is so simple by comparison with the rest it is hardly necessary to explain how to implement it! What is more difficult is to say when it should be used. It certainly shouldn't be used as a substitute for a context menu where the operations affect the content that it is "attached" to. In the case of a popup it seems that its common use is to refine an action selection by providing parameters that modify it.

To show a popup menu, all you have to do is instantiate a PopupMenu object, set its onMenuItemClick event handler, create the menu by inflating a resource file and finally use its show method. Where on the screen the PopupMenu shows depends on the View object you pass when creating the instance.

The steps are:

1. Create an instance of PopupMenu and pass the View object you want to use to position the menu.

2. If you want to handle item selection, override the onMenuItemClick method.

3. Use the instance's inflate method to create the menu.

4. Use the instance's show method to display the menu.

A popup menu is usually shown in response to some user action and so we need an event handler to create the popup in. If you place a button into the UI you can define its click event handler as:

```
button.setOnClickListener { view ->
    val popup = PopupMenu(view.context, view)
    popup.inflate(R.menu.mycontext)
    popup.show()
}
```

The PopupMenu constructor accepts the context and the View object it will be displayed next to. Usually this is the View object that the user clicked or interacted with i.e. the button in this case. Next we inflate the menu as usual by using the Popups own inflater which adds the menu to the Popup. Finally we call Show which displays the Popup:

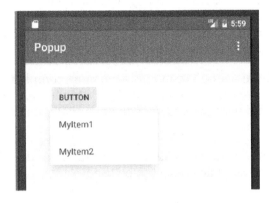

The menu is immediately dismissed if the user clicks on an item or on any other part of the display.

Of course if you were really using the popup menu you would also handle the item click event:

```
popup.setOnMenuItemClickListener { item->
            textView.text = item.title
            false
        }
```

As before you would use a when to discover which item the user had selected and act on that selection.

The complete code is:

```
override fun onCreate(savedInstanceState: Bundle?) {
      super.onCreate(savedInstanceState)
      setContentView(R.layout.activity_main)
      setSupportActionBar(toolbar)

      button.setOnClickListener { view ->
            val popup = PopupMenu(view.context, view)
            popup.inflate(R.menu.mycontext)
            popup.setOnMenuItemClickListener { item->
                textView.text = item.title
                false
            }
            popup.show()
      }
}
```

# Summary

- The context menu is invoked for all View objects in the UI that are registered using registerForContextMenu(View).

- When the user long clicks on any registered object onCreateContextMenu is called and you can use this to display the menu. When the user selects any of the items in the menu, the system onContextItemSelected event handler is called.

- The contextual action bar menu is the most complicated to implement. You have to create an ActionMode.Callback object complete with methods to create the menu and handle events from its items.

- To display the menu you call the startSupportActionMode(Callback) specifying the Callback object to be used.

- If you want to use the contextual action mode menu on earlier versions of Android you have to use the Support Library classes.

- The popup menu is the easiest to implement. Simply create a Popup object, inflate the menu resource, and use its show method to display the menu.

So far we have overlooked resources, but the subject can be ignored no longer. Resources serve too important a purpose in Android. They not only make localization easier, they are key to creating apps that adapt to the device they are being run on.

## Why Use Resources?

Any small scale data that your app uses – strings, constants, graphics, layout files – should all be included as resources rather than hard coded into your app. For example, until now we have entered any text that the UI needed directly as a string property value. For a button this approach has meant setting the Text property by typing in a string such as "Hello World". Android Studio does it best to save you this effort. If you run the Warnings and Errors "linter" by clicking on the red icon in the Layout Editor, then for any string you have entered as a literal into the Attributes window you will see a warning:

While you shouldn't panic about every warning that the linter shows you, this one is a good idea because a resource can be reused in other parts of the program and it is easy to change without having to dive into the code.
A much bigger advantage is that you can provide alternative resources, which are automatically selected by your app according to the conditions. For example, in this case you can provide strings in another language and they will be used automatically according to the locale in which the app runs. This is a very powerful way to create custom apps that work anywhere in the world and on any device.

So how do we create a resource? It does depend on the type of the resource but in Android Studio there are two ways of creating a string resource.

The first is to click the "..." at the right of the property entry box which makes the Resources dialog pop up:

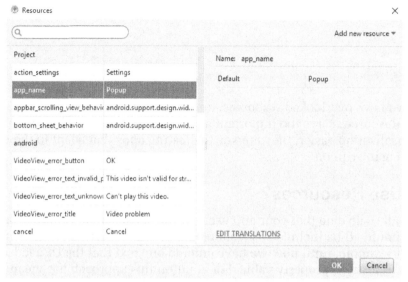

This lists existing resources defined by the system, the project and the theme in use. You can also use the Add New Resource dropdown to create additional resources. In this case a string resource:

All you have to do is enter a resource name and its value – the rest of the entries can be left at their defaults, their meaning will become clear as we proceed.

When you click OK you will see the Attributes window with the entry:

`@string/Greeting`

This is a reference to your newly created resource. You will also see the string that you have specified appear as the button's caption. You can now reuse the string resource by entering @string/Greeting anywhere the "Hello World" string is required – of course it has to be used with a property that accepts a string. If you change the definition of a resource then obviously all of its uses are updated.

The second way of creating a string resource is to edit the resource XML file. If you look at the file strings.xml in the res/values directory you will find it contains:

```
<resources>
 <string name="app_name">Resources1</string>
 <string name="hello_world">Hello world</string>
 <string name="action_settings">Settings</string>
 <string name="Greeting">Hello World</string>
</resources>
```

You can see the hello world string that we have just added and some other strings that Android Studio creates automatically for you, including another hello world string which is used in the initially generated UI. You can edit the resource file directly or you can use the Resources dialog to create and edit existing string resources.

## What are Resources?

● Resources are any data that your program wants to use.

Resources are compiled into your program's executable ready to be distributed to your end users as part of your app. For a string this doesn't seem particularly useful, after all you could just as easily use a string constant in code, but for other types of resource it can be the only way to get the data included in the app's executable.

For example, drawables, a range of different types of graphics objects, can be included as resources. If you include a .gif file as a resource then that .gif file is incorporated into your app by the compiler. This means you don't have to provide the gif as a separate file and you don't have to worry about where it is stored. Notice, however, that adding a .gif file to your app increases its size.

All resources are stored in folders within the res directory. The folder name gives the type of the resource and, as we shall see, can specify when the resource is to be used.

You can see a list of resource types in the documentation but the commonly used ones are:

- drawable/

  Any graphic – typically .png, .gif or .jpg but there are a range of other less frequently used types. The rule is – if it's in any sense a graphic it belongs in drawable.

- layout/

  We have been using layouts since we started programming Android and XML layout is a resource compiled into your app ready to be used.

- menu/

  The XML files that specify a menu are also resources and compiled into your app.

- values/

  XML files that define simple values such as strings, integers and so on. You can think of these as defining constants for your program to use. Although you can put any mixture of value-defining XML into a single file in the values/ directory, it is usual to group values by data type and or use.

  Typically:

  - arrays.xml for typed arrays
  - color.xml for color values
  - dimens.xml for dimensions
  - strings.xml for strings
  - styles.xml for styles.

You can also include arbitrary files and arbitrary XML files in raw/ and xml/. There are two directories dealing with animation, animator/ and anim/. There is also a directory where you can store icons suitable for different screen resolutions, but more of this when we look at conditional resources.

# Drawables

Drawables are slightly different from other resources in that there is no XML file that defines them. To create and use a drawable all you have to do is copy the graphic file that you want to use into the drawable/ directory. You don't need XML to define the resource because the resource's id is just the file name.

The best way to explain how drawable resources work is via a simple example. If you want to create a jpg bitmap resource all you have to do is copy the jpg file into the correct resource directory. Android Studio automatically creates the drawable/ directory for you and all you have to do is copy the bitmap file into it – but how?

The first thing to say is that the file name for a drawable resource can only contain lower case letters and digits. If the original file name doesn't conform to this pattern you can rename it after you have copied it into the directory.

There are two fairly easy ways:

1. You can find the file in the usual file directory structure and use copy and paste to paste it into the directory displayed in Android Studio.

2. Alternatively you can right click on the drawable folder in Android Studio and select Show in Explorer which opens the folder as a standard file system folder to which you can copy the bitmap file in any way that you like, drag-and-drop for instance:

Once you have the file, dsc0208.jpg in this case, in the drawable/ directory you can make use of it. Place an ImageView control on the UI using the Layout Editor. The Resources window opens automatically for you select the drawable you want to use.

If you want to change the drawable at a later time, find its src property in the Attributes window and click on the ... button at the far right and the Resources window will open.

Select the Project tab and scroll down until you can see the name of the file you have just copied into the drawable folder and select it:

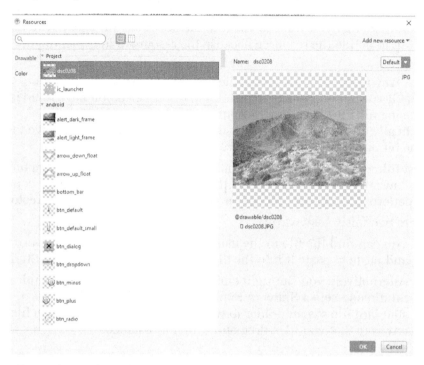

You will see that @drawable/dsc0208.jpg has been entered as the value of the src property – you could have entered this string directly without the help of the Resources window. You will also see the image displayed in the ImageView control:

That's almost all there is to drawable/ resources, but there is a bit more to learn about the different types of drawables that you can store there. This is best discussed when we cover graphics in general in the next chapter.

## Values

The easiest of the resource folders to use is probably values/, but it also tends to be the least often used. The strings.xml file tends to be employed, but the others are underutilized. The reason for is is that the system tends to prompt you to enter strings as resources and there is an obvious advantage to string resources in that they allow easy localization. However, putting constants of all types in resources is a good idea.

Although the documentation only mentions string, arrays, colors, dimensions and styles, you can include a wider range of data types in the XML file:

- Bool

  ```
  <bool name="resourcename">true</bool>
  ```

- Integer

  ```
  <integer name="resourcename">1234</integer>
  ```

- String

  ```
  <string name="resourcename">A String</string>
  ```

  There is also a string editor which you can use to manage a collection of strings including translations to other languages. Its use is fairly self evident:

There are also two array types:

- Integer Array

  ```
  <integer-array name="resourcename">
   <item>123</item>
   <item>456</item>
  </integer-array>
  ```

- Typed Array

  ```
  <array name="resourcename">
  <item>resource</item>
  <item>resource</item>
  </array>
  ```

Dimension is also two easy-to-understand value resources:

- Dimension is simply an integer value complete with a units designator. For example:

```
<dimen name="resourcename">10px</dimen>
```

Obviously you can use any of the standard Android measurement scales – pt, mm, in, and so on. You use dimensions anywhere that you need to specify a size or location in a particular set of units.

Finally Color lets you organize the colors you are using in your app:

- Color provides easy to use names for hex color codes.

For example;

```
<color name="resourcename"> #f00 </color>
```

defines a red color. You can specify a color using any of:

```
#RGB, #ARGB, #RRGGBB or #AARRGGBB
```

where each of the letters represents a single hex character with R= Red, G=Green, B=Blue and A=Alpha (transparency).

## IDs

Ids are value resources and can be set up just like any other value resource. For example, if you want to set up an id for a button you might use:

```
<item type="id" name="resourcename" />
```

Notice that this is slightly different from other value resources in that you don't have to provide a value. The reason is that the system provides a unique integer value for each id. You don't often need to define an id in an XML file all of its own because ids can be created on the fly within other XML files. Putting a + in front of a resource id creates the resource without having to explicitly do the job. For example:

```
<Button
 android:text="@string/Greeting"
 android:id="+@id/button2"
```

creates the button2 resource.

On the other hand:

```
<Button
 android:text="@string/Greeting"
 android:id="@id/button2"
```

will only work if you have defined button2 in a resource file in the values/ folder.

Of course in Android Studio you can simply type in an id in the property window say and the system will automatically provide the +@id to make it auto-create. Also keep in mind that the Kotlin plugin converts ids into properties that reference the View objects. So in the example above there will be a button2 property that references the Button object.

## Accessing Resources in Code – The R Object

For much of the time you really don't need to bother with accessing resources in code because the job is done for you automatically. For example, if you assign a string resource to a button's text:

```
<Button
  android:text="@string/Greeting"
```

then the system retrieves the string resource and sets the button's text property to it when the layout is inflated. You don't have to do anything to make it all work. However, sometimes resources are needed within the code of an app and you have to explicitly retrieve them.

When your app is compiled by Android Studio it automatically creates a resource id, a unique integer, for every resource in your res/ directory. These are stored in a generated class called R - for Resources. The directory structure starting with res/ is used to generate properties for the R object that allows you to find the id that corresponds to any resource. This means that a resource id is always named something like R.*type.name*. For example:

```
R.string.Greeting
```

retrieves the resource id for the string resource with resource name "Greeting" that is:

```
<string name="Greeting">Hello World</string>
```

Notice that the resource id is an integer and not the string it identifies.

So how do you convert a resource id to the resource value?

The first thing to say is that you don't always have to. There are many methods that accept a resource id as a parameter and will access the resource on your behalf. It is usually important to distinguish when a method is happy with a resource id and when you have to pass it the actual resource value.

If you do have to pass the resource, or you want to work with the resource, then you have to make use of the Resources object. This has a range of **gettype(resource_id)** methods that you can use to access any resource. For example, to get the string with the resource name "Greeting" you would write:

```
var myString=resources.getString(R.string.Greeting)
```

and myString would contain "Hello World". If you are not in the context of the activity you might have to use applicationContext.resources.

The only problem with using the Resources object is trying to work out which get methods you actually need.

There are also utility methods that will return any part or all of its resource name given the id:

- `getResourceEntryName(int resid)`

  Returns the entry name for a given resource identifier

- `getResourceName(int resid)`

  Returns the full name for a given resource identifier

- `getResourcePackageName(int resid)`

  Returns the package name for a given resource identifier

- `getResourceTypeName(int resid)`

  Returns the type name for a given resource identifier.

There are also some methods that will process the resource as well as simply retrieve it. For example, if you have a raw XML resource, getXml(int id) returns an XmlResourceParser that lets you work through the XML retrieving tags, attributes, etc.

## Conditional Resources

So far resources have just been a way to get data into your app. You might have thought that if there was another way to do the job then it might be just as good. However, Android Resources are central to customizing your app so that it works with the wide range of device types and user that an Android app has to cope with. The clever part is that you can make use of conditional resources to provide a set of resources customized for the current device at runtime.

The idea is simple. First you provide a default resource file. This is the one that is located in the appropriate directory, /res/values say, but now you use qualifiers as part of the directory name.

For example, you can create a directory called /res/values-es which is intended to provide resource values for the app when running on a device set to a Spanish language locale. What happens is that first any values that you have defined are taken from the XML files in the values directory, these are considered the default. Next, if the app is running on a Spanish language device the XML files in values-es are processed and any resources with the same name replace the ones provided by the defaults.

214

You can see that this provides a fairly easy way to make sure that your app presents a UI in the local language, but there are more qualifiers than just locale, and these allow you to customize the app for other features of the device. You can even stack up qualifiers as part of folder names to get more precise targeting. For example, the directory values-es-small would only be used if the language was Spanish and the screen was similar to a low density QVGA screen. The only thing to be careful of is that the qualifiers are used in the order in which they are listed in the documentation.

There are qualifiers for locale, screen density, size and orientation, device type, night v day, touch screen type, keyboard availability and platform version (API level). You can find them all listed in the documentation, but in most cases this is unnecessary because Android Studio helps you to create qualified resources.

If you select a resource directory, values say, and right click you will see a New,Values resource file in the context menu. If you select this option then the New Resource File dialog opens. You can use this to create a resource file – just enter its name - and you can apply any qualifiers you want to by simply selecting from the list of available quantifiers to the left:

If you select Locale then you will be allowed to enter any details of the qualifier. In the case of Locale you can select the languages and regions you want to apply from a list:

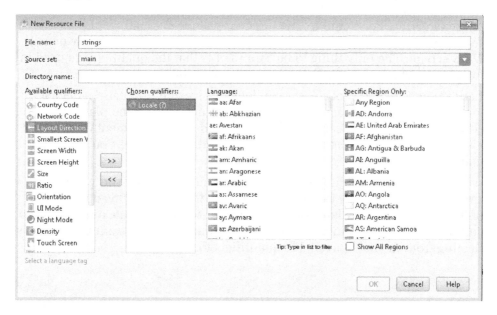

Using the New Resource File dialog saves you a lot of time looking up qualifiers and language/region codes. It is much simpler than hand coding the directories and XML files. However, you need to be aware of how Android Studio presents qualified resources to you in the project browser. For example, if you create a new strings file in the values directory and select Locale and es for the Spanish language in Any Region then this creates a directory res/value-es and a strings.xml file within it. So now you have:

`values/strings.xml`

and:

`values-es/strings.xml`

This is not what the project browser shows by default which is the Android view. It shows the new file as being in the values directory within another folder called strings.xml.

The project browser is trying to show you the resource files with all of the similar files, i.e. strings, all grouped together in a single directory, but with qualifiers displayed to the right. In the case of locale it even shows the country flag as an icon:

This is a conceptual way of organizing things and it arguably makes working with multiple resource files easier. In this case you can see that the two strings.xml files are displayed as variations on strings.xml.

You can see the actual file structure by selecting Project Files from the drop-down menu in the upper left-hand corner.

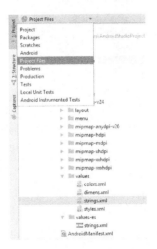

Select the Android view to return to the familiar view of your project.

Working with Android Studio you can, for the most part, ignore the actual file and directory structure and simply add additional resource files using the New Resource File dialog, or for adding locales the Translation Editor described in the next section. Occasionally, however, you will need to find a file and manually edit the directory structure. In particular, there are no commands that allow you to modify the qualifiers associated with a resource file. The simplest solution is to delete the file and re-create it with new qualifiers if necessary. It is also worth mentioning that you can create custom layout files in the same way and that the Layout Editor also has facilities to allow you to clone an existing portrait layout as a landscape layout, for example.

## A Simple Localization

As we have already created a Spanish strings.xml file it is trivial to provide a Spanish version of the greetings string. All you have to do is edit the Spanish strings.xml to read:

```
<?xml version="1.0" encoding="utf-8"?>
<resources>
 <string name="Greeting">Hola Mundo</string>
</resources>
```

Now all you have to do is run the app and change the locale of the emulator or the real Android device. The simplest way to change the locale is to use the Custom Locale app:

When you run this you can see the current locale and select a new one:

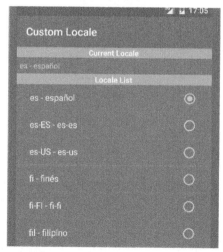

When you run the app in the emulator you will see the string resource retrieved from the Spanish strings.xml file:

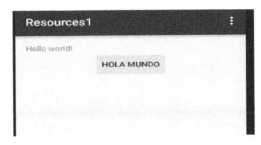

Notice that while the button's text has changed the default strings.xml has been used for the other strings in the app.

It is very important to make sure that all of the resources you use have a default value. If you miss a resource out of a locale file that doesn't have a default, your app will not run.

## Android Studio Translation Tools

Android Studio also has some additional tools to allow you to preview conditional resources. The World icon displayed in the Layout Editor allows you to select a locale. It is worth using this to check that your app looks good in other locales:

However, new locales only show in the drop-down list if they have been added using the Translation Editor. If you have manually added the Spanish locale using the instructions earlier add it in the Translation Editor any translations that you have already added will be retained.

If you are trying to maintain an app that supports a number of languages then the easiest way to maintain it is to use the Edit Translations option. This display an editor for string resources that shows each locale version on the same line:

You can use this to enter translations of default strings and you can create new string resources across all of the locales with a single operation – enter the key, default and translations. You can also use the world icon at the top left to create new locales and this is by far the best way to do the job. There is even a link to order a translation from Google Translate.

# Summary

- Use resources for as much data as you can. It makes it easier to change things.

- You can use the Property window to create and use resources or you can edit the XML directly.

- There is a wide range of resource types. In addition to layouts and menus, you are certain to use values and drawables.

- Drawables are an example of a resource that doesn't use an XML file. You simply copy the graphics resource files into the drawables directory.

- You can store simple data types in the values resource directory and this is often a better way to do things than using constants in the code.

- The R object is automatically generated and its structure mimics the resource directory structure. For each resource the R object has an integer resource id.

- Many methods take a resource's id and retrieve the resource for you. If you want to explicitly access a resource in code then use the methods that the Resources object provides.

- Conditional resources allow you to provide resources that suit the current device – locale, screen resolution and so on.

- Conditional resources work by applying qualifiers to the names of the directories that hold the resource files.

- Android Studio provides a simplified view of conditional resources that groups all variations on a resource file in the same organizational folder. This does not correspond to the file structure, but it is simpler.

- You can use the New, Resource File command to create conditional resources.

- The Layout Editor lets you select which locale resource is used so that you can work directly with the localized layout.

- If you want to localize your app then make use of the Android Studio Translation Editor.

# Chapter 12

# Bitmap Graphics

Android graphics is a huge subject, but you have to start somewhere. In this chapter we look a simple 2D bitmap graphics, which is often all you need, and discover the basic principles of Android graphics.

## Android Graphics

Graphics support in Android is extensive – from the simple display of images and 2D graphics through animation and on to full 3D rendering. To cover it all needs a separate book, and even then there would be topics left untouched. This chapter is an introduction to the minimum you need to know about 2D bitmap graphics in Android. It isn't all you need to know to get the job done, but it is enough to get you started on many common simple graphics tasks. With this grounding you'll also be in a position to seek out some of the additional information you need to do the less common things.

The key difference between this account of Android graphics and the typical approach you find in other documents is that it concentrates on the principles as well as the how-to. By the end of this chapter you should have a clear idea of what the different Android graphics classes are all about.

## The Bitmap

You could say that the bitmap is the foundation of any use of Android graphics. The reason is that no matter how a graphic is specified or created, it is a bitmap that is eventually created and displayed on the screen.

There are many ways of creating or obtaining a bitmap. We have already seen how a bitmap file, .jpg, gif or .png can be included in the drawable/ resource directory and displayed in an ImageView control. In many cases a bitmap can be acquired by loading a file, reading in a collection of bytes, or even taking a photo with the Android camera.

In this instance we will simply create a Bitmap directly:

```
val b = Bitmap.createBitmap(500, 500, Bitmap.Config.ARGB_8888)
```

A bitmap is simply a rectangle of pixels. Each pixel can be set to a given color but exactly what color depends on the type of the pixel. The first two parameters give the width and the height in pixels. The third parameter specifies the type of pixel you want to use. This is where things can get complicated. The specification ARGB_8888 means create a pixel with four channels ARGB - Alpha, Red, Green, Blue, and allocate eight bits of storage to each channel. As four eights are 32 this is 32-bit graphics. The alpha channel lets you set an opacity.

There are many different pixel formats you can select, and there is always a trade off between the resolution and the amount of space a bitmap occupies. However, ARGB_8888 is a very common choice.

Now you have a bitmap what can you do with it? The answer is quite a lot!

Most of the methods of the Bitmap object are concerned with things that change the entire image. For example:

```
b.eraseColor(Color.RED)
```

sets all of the pixels to the specified color, red in this case. Using the setPixel and getPixel methods you can access any pixel you want to and perform almost any graphics operation you care to. You can also work with the pixel data at the bit level.

## The ImageView Control

How can you see a Bitmap that you have just created? The simple answer is to use an ImageView control. This isn't a popular approach, however, because it isn't as flexible as alternatives such as overriding the onDraw event handler. This said, the ImageView control is very easy to use and sufficient for many tasks.

Start a new project and place an ImageView into the UI, accepting the defaults. The Layout Editor wont let you place an empty ImageView on the design surface so select any drawable as a temporary filler.

As a demonstration of how you can use the ImageView to display a Bitmap, change the onCreate event handler to read:

```
override fun onCreate(savedInstanceState: Bundle?) {
    super.onCreate(savedInstanceState)
    setContentView(R.layout.activity_main)
    setSupportActionBar(toolbar)

    val b = Bitmap.createBitmap(500, 500, Bitmap.Config.ARGB_8888)
    b.eraseColor(Color.RED)
    imageView.setImageBitmap(b)
}
```

If you run the program you will see a fairly large red square appear where the ImageView control has been placed:

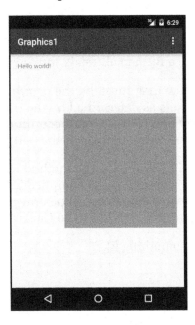

Notice the ImageView control has been automatically resized to show the Bitmap.

The ImageView control has a range of methods similar to setImageBitmap that makes it useful for displaying a range of different types of graphic.

## Canvas

You can just use a Bitmap and work with individual pixels, but this isn't a very "high level" way to create graphics. What we need are some larger scale methods that draw useful things like lines, rectangles, circles and so on.

The Bitmap object doesn't have this sort of method, but the Canvas object does and you can use it to draw on any Bitmap. That is you create a Canvas object, associate it with a Bitmap, and you can use the Canvas object's methods to draw on the Bitmap. There are lots of different Canvas drawing methods, and even a facility to transform the basic coordinate system to anything you care to use, but we have to start somewhere so a simple example first.

You can create a Canvas and attach it to a bitmap in one operation:

```
val c = Canvas(b)
```

Now when you use the drawing methods of the Canvas they draw on the Bitmap b. There are many occasions when a control or object provides a Canvas object attached to a Bitmap all ready for you to draw on.

It is also important to know that, initially, the coordinate system of the Canvas object is set to pixels as determined by the Bitmap. That is, if the Bitmap is *width* by *height* pixels, the default coordinate system runs from 0,0 at the top left-hand corner to *width,height* at the bottom right.

Using Canvas can be as simple as calling a method like drawLine to draw a line between two points. The only slight complication is that you have to use the Paint object to specify how the line will be drawn. In general Paint controls how any line or area is drawn by the Canvas methods.

A typical Paint object is something like:

```
val paint = Paint()
paint.setAntiAlias(true)
paint.strokeWidth=6f
paint.color=Color.BLUE
paint.style=Paint.Style.STROKE
```

After creating the Paint object we set AntiAlias to true, i.e turn it on. This creates a higher quality but slightly slower rendering. Next we set the width of the line to 6 pixels, color to blue, and sets it as a stroke, i.e. a line rather than an area fill. If you are puzzled by the 6F in the setStrokeWidth it is worth saying that this is how you specify a float constant.

Once created you can use a Paint object as often as it is needed and you can modify it and reuse it. You can also use an existing Paint object to create a new Paint object which you then modify.

# A First Graphic

Now we have a Paint object we can draw a line:

```
c.drawLine(0f, 0f, 500f, 500f, paint)
```

This draws a line from 0,0 to 500,500 and as the Bitmap is 500 by 500 pixels this draws a diagonal line across the entire bitmap. Again the numeric values all end in f because the method needs float values, for reasons that will become clear later:

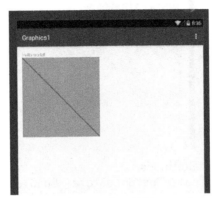

All you have to do now is get to know the different drawing methods provided. Here we use a few of the most common.

First we need to set the Paint object we created earlier to a FILL style so that we draw solid blocks of color and not just outlines:

```
paint.style=Paint.Style.FILL
```

To draw a yellow circle all we need is:

```
paint.color=Color.YELLOW
c.drawCircle(400f, 200f, 50f, paint)
```

The first two parameters give the position of the center and the third is the circle's radius.

To draw a green rectangle:

```
paint.color=Color.GREEN
c.drawRect(20f, 300f, 180f, 400f, paint)
```

The first two parameters give the top left-hand corner and the next two the bottom right-hand corner.

Finally let's add some text:

```
paint.color=Color.BLACK
paint.textSize=50f
c.drawText("Hello Graphics",0,14,90f,80f,paint)
```

The Paint object has a number of properties that let you set the font and style. In this example we simply set the text size. The drawText method takes a string, the start and end positions of characters in the string that will be displayed, and the coordinates of the starting location.

If you put this all together and run it you get this very tasteful graphic:

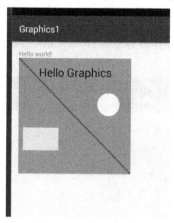

The complete code to create this is:

```
override fun onCreate(savedInstanceState: Bundle?) {
    super.onCreate(savedInstanceState)
    setContentView(R.layout.activity_main)
    setSupportActionBar(toolbar)
    val b = Bitmap.createBitmap(500, 500, Bitmap.Config.ARGB_8888)
    b.eraseColor(Color.RED)
    val c = Canvas(b)

    val paint = Paint()
    paint.setAntiAlias(true)
    paint.strokeWidth=6f
    paint.color=Color.BLUE
    paint.style=Paint.Style.STROKE
    c.drawLine(0f, 0f, 500f, 500f, paint)
    paint.style=Paint.Style.FILL
    paint.color=Color.YELLOW
    c.drawCircle(400f, 200f, 50f, paint)

    paint.color=Color.GREEN
    c.drawRect(20f, 300f, 180f, 400f, paint)

    paint.color=Color.BLACK
    paint.textSize=50f
    c.drawText("Hello Graphics",0,14,90f,80f,paint)

    imageView.setImageBitmap(b)
}
```

You can use this to try out other Canvas graphics methods.

It is worth pointing out that there is a set of drawBitmap methods that you can use to draw an existing Bitmap onto the Bitmap associated with the Canvas. This might seem like a strange thing to do, but it is one of the most useful drawing operations because you can use it to implement simple sprite animation.

## Transformations

Now we come to one of the more sophisticated options that Canvas offers. Before anything is drawn, the coordinates you supply are acted on by a transformation matrix. By default this is set to the identity matrix which leaves the coordinates as they were. However, the following methods modify the transformation matrix:

- rotate(float degrees)
  rotate about the origin through degrees

- rotate(float degrees, float px, float py)
  rotate about the point px,py through degrees

- scale(float sx, float sy)
  scale about the origin by sx and sy

- scale(float sx, float sy, float px, float py)
  scale about the point px,py by sx and sy

- skew(float sx, float sy)
  skew by sx and sy

- translate(float dx, float dy)
  translate by dx and dy

There are also some properties and methods that let you work directly with the transformation matrix:

- matrix
  set or get the transform matrix

- concat(Matrix matrix)
  multiply the transform matrix by the matrix provided

If you already know how matrices and transformation matrices work then this will be seem quite straightforward. If not, there are a lot of traps waiting to trip you up. The main one, that troubles just about everyone at first, is that the order in which you do things matters. A translation followed by a rotation isn't the same thing as a rotation followed by a translation. Try it if you don't believe me. Another is that these transformations change the coordinate system and don't affect anything you have already drawn. They only change what happens when you draw something after the transformation has been applied.

For example, we can rotate the text in the previous example:

```
paint.color=Color.GREEN
c.drawRect(20f, 300f, 180f, 400f, paint)
c.rotate(15f)
paint.color=Color.BLACK
paint.textSize=50f
c.drawText("Hello Graphics",0,14,90f,80f,paint)
```

In this case there is a 15 degree rotation after the rectangle has been drawn and before the text is drawn. The result is that the rectangle stays where it was but the text is rotated:

After the rotation everything you draw will be at 15 degrees.

Notice that the rotation is about the origin, i.e. 0,0 the top left-hand corner. If you want to rotate about a different point, usually the center of some object, you need to use rotate(d,x,y).

For example to rotate the rectangle about its center you would use:

```
c.rotate(45f,100f,350f)
paint.color=Color.GREEN
c.drawRect(20f, 300f, 180f, 400f, paint)
```

where 100,350 is the center of the rectangle:

You can also see that the text is now in a different position and not simply rotated about the origin. This is because the 15 degree rotation is added to the 45 degree rotation around the center of the rectangle. To keep your transformations separate and non-interacting you have to remember to return the transformation matrix to the identity after you have changed it to something else.

How do you set the matrix back to the identity?

You could use:

```
c.matrix= Matrix()
```

as Matrix() creates an identity matrix by default, or you could just use:

```
c.matrix= null
```

because setting it to null causes the matrix to be reset. However, needing to make a change to the transformation matrix and then restore the original is such a common operation that Canvas supports:

```
c.save()
```

which saves the current matrix and:

```
c.restore()
```

which restores the current matrix.

For example:

```
c.save()
c.rotate(45f,100f,350f)
paint.color=Color.GREEN
c.drawRect(20f, 300f, 180f, 400f, paint)

c.restore()
c.rotate(15f)
paint.color=Color.BLACK
paint.textSize=50f
c.drawText("Hello Graphics",0,14,90f,80f,paint)
```

With the save before the first rotate, the restore before the second decouples the two transformations.

# A Logical Approach to Transforms

One approach to keeping track of transformations is to draw everything centered on the origin, and then translate, scale and rotate it to its final position. For example, to draw the rectangle:

```
c.drawRect(20f, 300f, 180f, 400f, paint)
```

rotated through 45 degrees you would first draw a unit square centered on the origin:

```
c.drawRect(-0.5f, -0.5f, 0.5f, 0.5f, paint)
```

then you would then scale it to its desired size:

```
c.scale(160f,100f)
```

and rotate it:

```
c.rotate(45f)
```

Finally you would move it to its correct location:

```
c.translate(100f, 350f)
```

If you try out these steps, you will discover that you don't get what you expect. The reason is that we have been transforming the object: draw a square, scale the square, rotate it and move it to the desired location. However, the Canvas transformations don't transform graphical objects but the coordinate system. You can immediately see that this means you should draw the square last after you have performed all of the transformations. Indeed this is the rule:

- do everything you would have done to the geometric shape in the reverse order when changing the coordinate system.

So the correct transformation sequence is:

```
c.save()
c.translate(100f, 350f)
c.rotate(45f)
c.scale(160f,100f)
c.drawRect(-0.5f, -0.5f, 0.5f, 0.5f, paint)
c.restore()
```

Notice that when you do a scale this applies to any strokeWidth you may set i.e. double the scale and a strokeWidth of 1 becomes an effective strokeWidth of 2.

You can always work out the transformation sequence you need by considering the graphical object, working out the transforms needed to change it to what you want and applying them in the reverse order.

Some programmers take to this idea and think it is the best and only way to do logical systematic graphics. Some adopt it a little bit, and others draw things where they are needed in the size and orientation needed.

## Setting Your Own Coordinates

When you first attach a Canvas to a Bitmap the coordinate system is in terms of the number of pixels in the Bitmap. Often, however, you want to work with a different coordinate system. For example, you might want to work with the origin in the middle and the x and y coordinate ranging from -1 to +1.

You can set any coordinate system you care to work with using suitable transformations.

If your coordinate system runs from xmin to xmax and from ymin to ymax you can apply it to the canvas using:

```
c.scale(width/(xmax-xmin),height/(ymax-ymin))
c.translate(-xmin,-ymin)
```

where *width* and *height* are the size in pixels of the bitmap.

Using this formulation the y coordinate increases down the screen, as did the original pixel coordinates.

If you want the y coordinate to increase up the screen then use the transformation:

```
c.scale(width/(xmax-xmin),-height/(ymax-ymin))
c.translate(-xmin,-ymax)
```

and notice the change to ymax in the second line.

So, for example, if you wanted to draw a graph using coordinates between 0,0 in the bottom left corner and 10,10 in the top right, i.e. y increasing up the screen, you would use:

```
c.save()

val xmax=10f
val xmin=0f
val ymax=10f
val ymin=0f
val width=500f
val height=500f

c.scale(width/ (xmax-xmin), -height / (ymax-ymin))
c.translate(-xmin, -ymax)

paint.setStrokeWidth(.4f)

c.drawLine(0F, 0F, 10F, 0F, paint)
c.drawLine(0F, 0F, 0F, 10F, paint)
c.drawLine(0F, 0F, 10F, 10F, paint)

c.restore()
```

This draws axes and a 45 degree line:

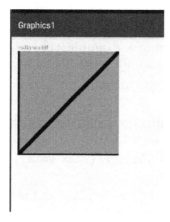

Notice that when you change the coordinate system all other measurements change as well. Hence the stroke width has to be set to 0.4 as it is no longer in terms of pixels.

## Simple Animation

To bring this chapter to a close we will animate a ball bouncing around a Canvas, or a Bitmap depending how you look at it. This might seem like a strange topic to end on, especially since we are not going to do the job in the way that most Android programmers would go about it. Indeed Android has a range of different animation facilities – View animation, Value animation and so on. However, none of them demonstrates the fundamental way that dynamic graphics work and before you move on to learn more sophisticated ways of creating animation it is a good idea to find out how things work at the lowest level.

This example not only teaches you something about animation, but also about the problems of creating dynamic graphics of any kind in the Android UI. One warning – do not assume this is all there is to know about Android animation or that this is the best way to do things.

To animate something in the simplest and most direct way all you have to do is draw the shape, change the shape, erase the old graphic, and draw it again.

In most systems this is usually achieved at the lowest possible level by using a timer to call an update function which erases the shape, does the update to the shape and then draws it at its new location. You can take this approach in Android, but for various reasons it isn't the way things are usually done. It has to be admitted that there are some slight difficulties, but overcoming them isn't hard and is very instructive.

To see how it all works let's just bounce a "ball" around the screen. This is more or less the "hello world" of simple 2D sprite-based graphics.

So start a new Android Studio project and place an ImageView on the design surface. This is the only UI element we need.

We need a set of objects and values that are accessible from a number of methods and that have a lifetime the same as the app. The simplest way of achieving this is to set up private properties:

```
private val b = Bitmap.createBitmap(width, height,
                                    Bitmap.Config.ARGB_8888)
private val c: Canvas=Canvas(b)
private val paint: Paint = Paint()
```

First we create a bitmap and associate it with a Canvas. The Paint object is created to avoid having to create an instance every time we update the graphics.

Notice that other parts of the program are going to need to access width, height of the play area:

```
private val width = 800
private val height = 800
```

We are also going to need properties to record the ball's position, its radius and velocity. For simplicity we might as well just use the default pixel coordinates of the Bitmap:

```
private var x = 463f
private var y = 743f
private var vx = 1f
private var vy = 1f
private var r = 30f
```

Now we have all of these variables defined we can move on with the OnCreate function and set up the color of the play area and the Paint object used to draw the ball:

```
c.drawColor(Color.WHITE)

paint.setAntiAlias(false)
paint.style = Paint.Style.FILL
```

You might be wondering why AntiAlias is set to false, i.e. turned off. The reason is that its dithering algorithm makes it hard to remove a graphic by redrawing it in the background color. Try changing false to true in the final program to see what the problem is.

We also need to set the bitmap we are drawing on to the display:

```
imageView.setImageBitmap(b)
```

Now we are all ready to start drawing the animation.

## Timer and Threads

Now we come to the inner workings of the animation.

We need a Timer object that runs a function every so many milliseconds:

```
val timer = Timer()
```

The timer object has a range of schedule functions which run a function, actually a method in a TimerTask object, at different times. The one we need is:

```
timer.schedule(TimerTask,delay,repeat)
```

which runs the TimerTask after *delay* milliseconds and every *repeat* milliseconds after that. The timings aren't accurate and it could take longer than specified for the TimerTask to be run.

The simplest way to create the TimerTask is to use an object expression. You can't use a lambda because the TimerTask is an object with a constructor and some additional methods i.e. it isn't a SAM:

```
timer.schedule(object : TimerTask() {
                    override fun run() {
                        update()
                    }
                }
        , 0, 10)
```

This creates a new TimerTask and overrides its run method. The run method is called when the Timer is triggered. All it does is to call the new function update, which we have yet to write, that does the update to the ball's position etc. The final two parameters specify a 0 millisecond delay in triggering the first call and then 10 milliseconds as the repeat period. That is, update will be called every 10 milliseconds or so. If the processor is busy doing something else it could be more than 10 milliseconds between repeats.

The update function is fairly easy:

```
fun update() {
    paint.color=Color.WHITE
    c.drawCircle(x, y, r, paint)
    x = x + vx
    y = y + vy
    if (x + r >= width) vx = -vx
    if (x - r <= 0) vx = -vx
    if (y + r >= height) vy = -vy
    if (y - r <= 0) vy = -vy
    paint.color=Color.RED
    c.drawCircle(x, y, r, paint)
    imageView.invalidate()
}
```

First it sets the color to white and draws the ball, a circle. This erases the ball at its old position, remember the background is white. Next it updates the position by adding the velocities in each direction. To make sure that the ball bounces we test to see if it has reached a boundary and if it has its velocity is reversed. Finally, the color is set to red and the ball is drawn at the new position.

If the function was to stop at this point then everything compiles and runs, but you won't see the ball move. The reason is simply that the UI is drawn once at when the program is initially run and then only when it is necessary because the user has interacted with it or the orientation has changed, etc. As a result the bitmap displayed by the ImageView object would be changed every 10 milliseconds, but it would not be redisplayed.

To make the UI update we need to call the ImageView's invalidate method which basically tells the UI to redraw it. However, if you put this in at the end of the update function you get an error message something like:

> *android.view.ViewRootImpl$CalledFromWrongThreadException: Only the original thread that created a view hierarchy can touch its views.*

The reason for this is that the Timer object uses a new thread to run the TimerTask. This is often what you want to happen, but in this case it is a problem. It is a problem that often occurs in creating a sophisticated Android app and something you are going to have to learn to cope with.

If you are new to the idea of threading, this explanation might help.

*When you run an Activity it is assigned a single thread or execution. A thread is a unit of execution and it is what obeys your instructions. In a complete system there are many threads of execution – some running and some suspended. The operating system picks which threads get to run in a way that attempts to make them all seem to be making progress.*

*The single thread that the Activity gets is generally called the UI thread because its job is just to take care of the UI. It responds to events from the Activity like OnCreate and from the user like a Button click. When the UI thread responds to an event it obeys the event handler and then goes back to waiting for the next event. This is the sense in which every Android app is simply a collection of event handlers that the UI thread executes when the corresponding event occurs.*

*The big problem is that the UI event is really only happy when it has nothing to do. Then it just waits for an event and processes it at once. This makes the user think your app is very responsive because clicks and other input are acted on at once. If you give the UI thread a long task to do, for example you write a lot of processing into an event handler, then it isn't just waiting for the user to do something, and the user starts to think that your app is slow and sluggish. At the extreme the UI thread can be kept 100% busy doing something and then the entire UI seems to freeze up.*

*In short the UI thread should not be used for intensive computation or anything that takes more than a few milliseconds. The way to achieve this is to use other threads. This is a main topic of **Android Programming: Structuring Complex Apps**.*

The UI thread creates the UI and to avoid problems of synchronization only the UI thread can interact with the UI. That is, only the UI thread can access the UI. This is a fairly common approach to implementing a UI and not at all unique to Android.

So what happens is that the Timer tries to run its TimerTask and this in turn runs the update function, but using the thread the Timer runs on rather than the UI thread. Everything is fine until the last instruction of update, which attempts to use a method that belongs to an ImageView object and this it cannot do because it is not the UI thread. Hence the error message.

At this point many Android programmers give up and try a completely different approach. Some of these approaches do have advantages, see the Handler class for example for a good alternative. However, the Android framework provides a method for just such a situation:

```
runOnUiThread(Runnable)
```

This is a method of the Activity object and you can use it from any thread that has access to the Activity object's methods to run a function on the UI thread. If the thread using it happens to be the UI thread then no harm done, the function is just called. If it isn't the UI thread then the call will be deferred until the UI thread is available and then the function will be run. As always the function shouldn't keep the UI thread busy for too long or the UI will become sluggish or even freeze completely.

The Runnable is an Interface that has a single run method that is the function that is executed on the UI thread – this means it is a SAM (Single Abstract Method) and we can use a lambda to simplify the code:

```
   runOnUiThread { update() }
```

This ensures that update is run on the UI thread.

Putting this all together gives:

```
 timer.schedule(object : TimerTask() {
                          override fun run() {
                               runOnUiThread { update() }
                          }
                  }
, 0, 10)
```

This looks like a mess of nesting and curly braces, but you should be able to follow the logic.

Now when you run the program you will see the red ball bounce slowly and smoothly around the screen. How good the animation is depends what you run it on. On the emulator is can be slow and irregular; on a real device it should be fine:

*Animation complete with a trail to show how the ball moves*

Now you know at least one way to allow a non-UI thread interact with the UI. There are so many ways to implement animation that this is just one of many starting points, but with an understanding of this one the others will seem easier. If you wanted to use this approach, the structure of this demonstration program could be improved. For example, the ball really should be a Ball class complete with its position and velocity properties and its update method. This way you gain the benefits of object-orientation and you can animate lots of balls around the screen with very little extra effort.

## Listing

The complete listing of the animation program is:

```
import android.os.Bundle
import android.support.design.widget.Snackbar
import android.support.v7.app.AppCompatActivity
import android.view.Menu
import android.view.MenuItem
import kotlinx.android.synthetic.main.activity_main.*
import android.graphics.Bitmap
import android.graphics.Canvas
import android.graphics.Color
import android.graphics.Paint
import kotlinx.android.synthetic.main.content_main.*
import java.util.*
```

```kotlin
class MainActivity : AppCompatActivity() {

        private val width = 800
        private val height = 800

        private var x = 463f
        private var y = 743f
        private var vx = 1f
        private var vy = 1f
        private var r = 30f

        private val paint: Paint = Paint()
        private val b = Bitmap.createBitmap(width, height,
                                        Bitmap.Config.ARGB_8888)
        private val c: Canvas = Canvas(b)

        override fun onCreate(savedInstanceState: Bundle?) {
                super.onCreate(savedInstanceState)
                setContentView(R.layout.activity_main)
                setSupportActionBar(toolbar)

                c.drawColor(Color.WHITE)
                paint.setAntiAlias(false)
                paint.style = Paint.Style.FILL
                imageView.setImageBitmap(b)

                val timer = Timer()
                timer.schedule(object : TimerTask() {
                                override fun run() {
                                        runOnUiThread { update() }
                                }
                        }
                    , 0, 10)

        }

        fun update() {
                paint.color = Color.WHITE
                c.drawCircle(x, y, r, paint)
                x = x + vx
                y = y + vy
                if (x + r >= width) vx = -vx
                if (x - r <= 0) vx = -vx
                if (y + r >= height) vy = -vy
                if (y - r <= 0) vy = -vy
                paint.color = Color.RED
                c.drawCircle(x, y, r, paint)
                imageView.invalidate()
        }
```

There is so much to learn about graphics it is difficult to pick out things you need to know. If you want to find out more about how the standard UI works you need to look into the OnDraw event and how to create your own View object that render graphics. You need to find out about Android's vector graphics using shapes and path. You need to know about the different types of animation that are available and eventually you need to learn about OpenGL and its support for hardware accelerated 2D and 3D graphics.

# Summary

- The subject of Android graphics is huge and there is always more than one way to approach any task. This chapter is a first look at what you might call UI-based graphics.

- The Bitmap is the basic graphics object. It consists of a rectangle of pixels that can be set to any color.

- The ImageView is a general purpose UI component that can be used to display a range of graphics objects including a Bitmap.

- You can draw on a Bitmap using a Canvas object which has a large number of different drawing methods.

- The color and drawing style used by many of the Canvas methods is determined by the properties of a Paint object.

- The Canvas object also supports transformations which can be used to modify where a graphic is drawn, its size, rotation, etc.

- Transformations can be used to standardize the drawing of graphics objects at the origin.

- Transformations can also be used to change the default pixel coordinate system to anything you want to use.

- Simple animation is possible using nothing but a Bitmap, Canvas and an ImageView.

- Only the UI thread can modify the UI.

- The Android Timer can be used to animate 2D graphics, but you have ensure that it runs the code on the UI thread using the runOnUIThread method.

# Chapter 13

# Life Cycle Of An Activity

One of the things that you have to get used to when programming for a mobile platform is that your app can be shut down and restarted without much warning. This is something that often causes beginners and programmers from other platforms to make mistakes. You have to learn how to cope with this start-stop existence and that, for an Android app, it is a tough life just trying to stay alive.

I recently encountered an Android app, created by a large well known company, that asked me to fill in a form. I was just about to press the Submit button when I accidentally tilted the phone and the screen auto-rotated. When I looked again there was a blank form! I had to start over and, being a programmer, I couldn't resist testing to see if the data vanished from the form when I rotated the phone a second time – it did! The programmers from this high-profile company had no idea about creating an Android app beyond the basics.

Don't fall into the same trap. Find out about app lifetime, state and persisting data. It may sound like a boring topic but it is vital to the working of a UI.

## Lifetime and State

Most programmers are used to the idea that their application will be started by the user, used and then terminated by the user. If the application is restarted then it is usually up to the user to load whatever context they need by way of documents, etc. Sometimes an application has to automatically retain state information from run to run. For example, a game might keep track of which level a player had reached and the cumulative score, but this is about as complicated as things get.

For an application running on a mobile device things are very different. The very nature of the device means that any application could be interrupted at any moment by an incoming phone call or the user making a phone call. To a certain extent this need to make apps "interruptible" has been taken up by mobile phone operating systems as a more general principle. Android, for example, will stop your application running just because it needs the memory or wants to save battery life. It even terminates and restarts your application if a media reconfiguration is required.

For example, as we discovered in a previous chapter, if the user changes the orientation of the device then your app is terminated and restarted. This is not quite a restart from scratch because the system saves and restores some state information automatically, but exactly how all this works is something we have to find out.

The bottom line is that when you program under Android – and most other mobile operating systems – you have to care about the life cycle of your app and you have to take steps to ensure that its state is preserved so it can seem to the user that nothing at all has happened – even though your app has effectively been hit on the head and disposed of before being dragged back to continue from where it was.

Being an Android app is a dangerous existence and not at all like a Windows or a Linux app which can behave as if they have the machine all to themselves.

## The Life Cycle of an App

The different states that an Android app can be in and the transitions between them can seem complicated – that's because they are. If you are still thinking in terms of a desktop app that starts, runs and is terminated by the user, this level of complexity can seem unnecessary – and perhaps it is. However, these are the rules that we have to play by.

The Activity class has a set of overrideable event handlers for each of six states an Activity can be in. These work in pairs, bracketing the phases of the Activity:

- **onCreate and onDestroy** bracket the entire life of the Activity in memory and can be considered to be at the outermost level.
  This pair is called when the app is loaded into memory or unloaded from memory and bracket the entire lifetime of an Activity. When it is first loaded the onCreate is triggered and when the app is disposed of onDestroy is triggered. You clearly have to use these two to set up and destroy any resources which are needed for the entire lifetime of the app. However, if your app is removed by the system it will call onDestroy just before unloading the Activity and onCreate when it reloads it. This means that onCreate may be called when you need to restore the state of the Activity so that the user doesn't notice any interruption.

- **onStart and onStop** bracket any period that the app is visible.
  It could be that the Activity is behind, say, a modal dialog box. The Activity is visible but not interacting with the user. This pair of events can be triggered multiple times during the entire lifetime of the app. Simple apps can mostly ignore the onStart and onStop events because the Activity is still in memory and doesn't lose any resources or state.

The main use of onStart and onStop is to give the app an opportunity to monitor any changes that might affect it while not interacting with the user. To confuse the issue even more there is also an **onRestart** event which occurs before the onStart event but only if this isn't the first time the Activity has fired the onStart - that is this is a true restart.

- **onResume and onPause** bracket the period that the Activity is in the foreground and interacting with the user.
  Again this pair of events can happen multiple times during the entire lifetime. The onResume event occurs when the Activity returns to the foreground and doing its usual job. The onPause event occurs when the user switches away to another app for example.

## The Simple Approach

At this point you have every right to be confused with so many changes of status and having to respond to each one. The main thing to worry about is the complete restart of your app which triggers an onDestroy and an onCreate. This is the only one that destroys the current state of the app, the others are simply opportunities for your app to reduce the load on the system, or to save some user data just in case. As the onDestroy is usually just an opportunity to clean up resources to avoid leaks, most simple apps really only have to handle the onCreate event.

It is tempting to think that this starting and stopping is just like a desktop app being terminated and then the user deciding to use it again, so that it's fine for the app to start off as if it was being run for the first time. In the case of an Android app this isn't what the user expects at all. Your app can be terminated by the system without the user knowing anything about it. When the user tries to regain access to an app they will generally expect it to carry on from where they left it. It may be a complete restart as far as you are concerned, but the user just switched to another app for a few minutes and expects to find yours as they left it.

What this means is that you cannot think about onCreate as if it was the constructor for your app. When onCreate is fired it might be the first time your program has ever run or it might be a restart with some things that you created on a previous start still in existence. For simple applications you can often simply create everything again as if it was the first time your app had run, and in some cases you need to test the savedInstanceState to see if you are actually just restarting.

Notice also that often these events also tend to occur in sequences. For example, an app that has just received the onPause event is likely to go on to receive the onDestroy event because the system will remove it to free up memory. It is a mistake to try to think too much about sequences of events and ask which one should do any particular initialization or clean up. Just think about the state that your app is moving into and place the necessary code into that event handler.

## Lifecycle Explorer

There is no better way to feel comfortable with the lifecycle and its events than to write a short demo program that shows you when they occur.

Start a new Android Basic Activity project, accepting all defaults, call it Lifecycle and then accept all the defaults to get started quickly. In the Layout Editor remove the "Hello World" string and place a TextView on the design surface. Next resize it so that it fills most of the area and remove its default text entry, make sure it is constrained and has a large margin around it:

The code we need is fairly easy, the only trick is to remember to call each of the system-provided event handlers that you have overridden. If you don't do this the app simply terminates when you run it.

The OnCreate event handler still has to construct the UI, but now we get a reference to the Java object representing the TextView into a global variable so that the event handlers can access it:

```
override fun onCreate(savedInstanceState: Bundle?) {
    super.onCreate(savedInstanceState)
    setContentView(R.layout.activity_main)
    setSupportActionBar(toolbar)

    textView.append("Create\n")
```

The rest of the program simply overrides each of the event handlers in turn, calls the original event handler and then adds a text message to textView:

```kotlin
override fun onStart() {
        super.onStart()
        textView.append("Start\n")
}

override fun onPause() {
        super.onPause()
        textView.append("Pause\n")
}

override fun onResume() {
        super.onResume()
        textView.append("Resume\n")
}

override fun onStop() {
        super.onStop()
        textView.append("Stop\n")
}

override fun onRestart() {
        super.onRestart()
        textView.append("Restart\n")
}

override fun onDestroy() {
        super.onDestroy()
        textView.append("Destroy\n")
}
```

A very simple and tedious sort of program.

## Trying It Out

If you now run this program you can use it to find out when the life cycle events happen. You might be surprised to learn that when you first run the program you get:

If you think about it for a moment, this isn't unreasonable as the app is being loaded, becoming visible and in the foreground, and hence the appropriate events are fired in turn.

Beginners often assume that the life cycle events somehow override each other. That is, if an onCreate has been fired then this is the big event in the Activity's life and so the others won't happen. This isn't the case and you need to make sure that you put actions into the event handlers that really are appropriate to the life cycle state. For example, if you put something in the onResume event handler make sure you realize that it is going to be fired when the app first starts up as well as when it just being resumed.

If you try other things, like pressing the Home key and selecting another app, then you will see other event sequences, but of course only when you resume the Lifecycle app.

For example, pressing the Home key, then showing the task manager by long pressing the Home key and reselecting your app results in: Pause, Stop as the app is removed from the foreground and then Restart, Start, Resume as the app is loaded, becomes visible and then resumes the foreground and interacts with the user.

You can try other actions out but there is one thing you must try out – changing the orientation. If you are using the emulator then press Ctrl-F11. When the screen orientation changes you will see that the TextView has been cleared and Create, Start, Resume have been added.

This is because when you change orientation the app is completely stopped and then completely restarted, i.e. it is as if the app was being run from scratch for the first time.

This statement is almost true – but not quite.

## Retaining State – the Bundle

When you change orientation your app is stopped and restarted. When this happens the TextView is reset to its default state when the app loads. This description of what is happening is perhaps what you might expect. However, this isn't the complete story.

The system does try to help you with the problem of having your app stopped in its tracks and restarted. It will automatically retain the state of UI elements that can be modified by the user, and it automatically restores them when the app starts. So in principle you can initially ignore the problem of an app restart because the system restores your UI. This is the reason that some Android programmers assume that everything is "normal" and there is no need to study the lifecycle of an app. This is true at first, but later your app will evolve beyond what the system provides by default.

Automatically saving and restoring the UI's state is what the **savedInstanceState** parameter in the onCreate event handler is all about:

```
override fun onCreate(savedInstanceState: Bundle?) {
```

A Bundle is a set of key/value pairs which is used to save the values stored in UI elements when the app is stopped by the system. It stores id/value pairs and when the app is restarted the Bundle is used to initialize the values in the corresponding UI elements. Notice that if the user stops your app by removing it from the recent apps list then the savedInstanceState is destroyed, the app really does start over afresh, and the onCreate isn't passed a Bundle to restore the UI. In other words, savedInstanceState only restores the UI when the app has been stopped by the system.

It is also worth noticing that the restore will work to an alternative layout loaded because of a configuration change. For example, it will restore state to a landscape version of a layout as well as the original portrait version. All that matters is that the current layout has View objects with the correct ids.

At this point you are probably wondering why the TextView object wasn't restored by the system when the device was rotated? The simple answer is that a TextView object isn't intended for user interaction – it is supposed to just be used to show static text labels and so the system doesn't save and restore it.

You can see the automatic save and restore in action if you add an EditText input field on the design surface of the Lifecycle Explorer. Now if you enter some text into the EditText field it will be retained if you rotate the device. However, if you press and hold the Home key, remove the app and then start it afresh you will see that the EditText field is blank again:

The text in the EditText field at the bottom of the screen is preserved during a screen rotation.

- The general principle is that any UI element that can be modified by the user is automatically saved and restored. Any changes that your code makes or that the user makes in complex UI components are lost unless you take steps to preserve them.

## Saving Additional UI Data

The system will save and restore the state of the UI elements that the user can change, but it will not store any that your code changes. It also doesn't automatically save and restore any other data that the user or your code may have generated that isn't within the UI. In these cases you have to write some code that saves the values and restores them.

There are lots of ways of saving the state of an app as it is started and stopped by the system. One of the simplest is to use the Bundle object that the system uses.

The system fires the **onSaveInstanceState** event when it is about to add data to the Bundle and save it. If you want to save some additional data all you have to do is override the default event handler. For example, suppose you want to save and restore the data in the TextView in the Lifecycle Explorer. First you have to save the data:

```
override fun onSaveInstanceState(outState: Bundle?) {
    super.onSaveInstanceState(outState)
    outState?.putCharSequence("myText",textView.text)
}
```

Notice that we save the text content of the textView object as the value and use the key "myText". In most cases it would be better to create a string constant for the key. The key can be any identifier you care to use, but it has to be unique within the Bundle as it is used to retrieve the data you have stored in the Bundle.

Now to retrieve the data and place it into the TextView we need to change the onCreate event handler:

```
override fun onCreate(savedInstanceState: Bundle?) {
    super.onCreate(savedInstanceState)
    setContentView(R.layout.activity_main)
    setSupportActionBar(toolbar)

    textView.append("Create\n")
    if (savedInstanceState != null){
     textView.text=savedInstanceState.getCharSequence("myText")
    }
```

This starts off in the usual way but now we check to see if savedInstanceState has any data. If it does we retrieve the stored text using the key "myText".

There is no reason not to use the onCreate event handler in this way, but the system also fires an **onResetoreInstanceState** event when it is about to perform its own "automatic" restore of the UI for you. You can override this event handler if you want to keep the code that restores the app's state kept out of the onCreate event handler.

For example, you could have written:

```
override fun onRestoreInstanceState(savedInstanceState: Bundle?) {
    if (savedInstanceState != null) {
      textView.text = savedInstanceState.getCharSequence("myText")
    }
    super.onRestoreInstanceState(savedInstanceState)
}
```

Do remember to call the **super.onRestoreInstanceState** if you want the system to restore the rest of the UI in the usual way. There are put and get methods for a range of standard data types. All simple types, byte, integer and so on, are supported, as are strings, arrays and other simple data structures. You can also create your own classes that can be stored in a Bundle by implementing the Parcelable interface. Notice you can save arbitrary data, and not just data for the layout. You can also create your own Bundle instance and make use of it for data storage, persistence and for transferring data to other parts of a program. There are many standard classes the Bundle doesn't support. In these cases you have to make your own arrangements to save data to storage.

Often all you need to do to make sure that your app maintains its state between system restarts is to use the savedInstanceState Bundle object. This approach also reduces much of the practicality of lifecycle management to implementing the onSaveInstanceState and onRestoreInstanceState event handlers. This is so much simpler than having to worry about all of the different life cycle events.

As an exercise, you can now go back to the iCalc example in Chapter 3 and make its display and current value persist through a screen rotate.

## Complex UI Elements

One of the traps waiting for you is the problem of exactly what is automatically saved and restored. For example, at the start of this chapter we had the story of the app that lost the user's form data when it was rotated. Given what we now know of the auto-saving and restoration of user modifiable UI elements, you might be wondering how this could happen? The answer is that the programmers of the app had probably grown accustomed to the automatic persistence of UI state and didn't bother to check that rotation had no effect. It did have an effect because the form was being downloaded from a website and displayed in a WebView control. A WebView control is persisted by the system, but it reloads the page when it is restored. This means that on a rotation the form was reloaded as empty and the user's data was lost.

- You always have to check that things work as you expect. Always test what happens to your UI on a rotation.

## Advanced State Management

For completeness it is worth noting that there are many more approaches to maintaining state. Later you will need to discover how to store lots of user data locally for longer term persistence, and this is often enough to implement state management though a configuration change.

There are also more advanced state management problems when you come to make use of Fragments, the subject of *Android Programming: Mastering Fragments & Dialogs*. In this case you can use retainedInstance to ask the system not to destroy an entire Fragment. This means that all of the data stored in the Fragment is retained even though the Activity may be removed from memory. This makes it possible to use a Fragment as a repository of state.

The ultimate in making sure that things happen as you want is to handle the configuration change yourself. You can do this by making a change to the manifest. If you do this then it is up to you to make the changes needed when the **onConfigurationChanged** event occurs. You could, for example, opt to animate buttons and other UI objects into new positions or just ignore the need to reconfigure altogether.

This is all advanced and for most applications you can get by using just the onSaveInstanceState and onRestoreInstanceState event handlers.

# Summary

- Android, like many other mobile OSs, will remove your app from memory and restart it as it needs to.

- The user will not be aware that your app has been destroyed and recreated and will expect it to continue from where they left off.

- The system signals changes in state to your Activity via a complicated set of events. You need to understand how these work in order to make your Activity resume correctly after the various levels of suspension.

- onCreate should not be regarded as the "constructor" for your app because it is called when the app is restored as well as when it is run for the first time.

- The system will store the state of any user modifiable UI components and restore it when the Activity resumes.

- The data is stored in a special instance of a Bundle, a set of key/value pairs, called savedInstanceState.

- The system alerts you when it is about to save and restore data from savedInstanceState by firing the onSaveInstanceState and onRestoreInstanceState event handlers.

- You can override both of these event handlers to save and restore extra data in the savedInstanceState Bundle.

- For many simple apps you can mostly ignore the lifecycle events and concentrate on using the onSaveInstanceState and onRestoreInstanceState event handlers to persist data.

- You must always check that UI and other elements are persisted through a suspension of your app. You can test using a rotation configuration change.

- There are other more advanced ways of saving state which you will need to discover later on. You can't use a Bundle for everything.

# Chapter 14

# Spinners

Working with Android Studio makes building the UI easy with an interactive editor, the Layout Editor, but you still need to find out how to handle the things it isn't quite so good at. In the next two chapters of our exploration of Android we look at spinners and pickers, the next step up from buttons and text controls.

Spinners are what are referred to as drop-down lists or something similar in other UIs. They allow the user to pick from a list of possible items. Pickers, which are the subject of Chapter 15, also allow the user to pick an item, but in this case the items are more narrowly defined – a date, a time or a number.

## The Spinner and the Layout Editor

- The spinner presents a set of alternatives to the user and lets them select one.

Putting a Spinner into your project is as easy as using the tool Palette in the Layout Editor, but you can't get away without some code to make it all work. In particular, you need to define the list of items that the Spinner will display when the user activates it.

When you place a Spinner on the design surface all you get is a blank control with a non-functioning dropdown icon:

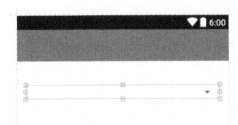

At the moment the Layout Editor only provides minimal support for setting up the Spinner with some data to display. The simplest sort of thing to show the user is a list of text items, and you might well think that the most direct way of doing this is to use a String array. It is, but things are slightly more complicated than this. They are simple, however, if you create a resource to specify the String array because in this case the system will do everything necessary to load the data.

Setting the contents of the Spinner using a String array in code is a good way to see how the Spinner works, and this is what we do next, but it isn't the way it usually happens.

Android provides a comprehensive system of resources – strings, images and lots of XML files. The idea is that you can produce customized versions of you application just by changing the resource files, i.e. without having to modify your code. For detailed information on using resources refer back to Chapter 11.

In the case of a Spinner you could set up a resource that was a String array that provided the list of items to be displayed. If you then wanted to create a version of your app for a foreign market you could get the list translated to create a resource in the new language.

Resources are a great idea and you should use them for all fixed strings and fixed data in general. So far, the examples have tended to avoid resources to make things simpler, but for a Spinner you need to know how to code up a String array resource and use it.

Android Studio does have some good resource support but in some areas it is lacking. For example, in an ideal world the system would help you create a String or String array resource, but at the moment it only provides help for simple string values. It will help you create a String resource, but offers no assistance for a String array, for which we have no choice but work with the XML file.

Find the file strings.xml in the res/values directory and open the file strings.xml. Add to this the String array definition:

```
<string-array name="country">
 <item>Canada</item>
 <item>Mexico</item>
 <item>USA</item>
</string-array>
```

The meaning of the XML is obvious and this is the advantage of a human readable markup language.

If you have explored resources using the Resource window which appears when you select the three dots option in the Attributes window you might worry that this new resource, i.e. SpinnerList, doesn't appear. It also doesn't appear in the Resource editor that you can select while editing the XML file.

The reason is that, currently, Android Studio doesn't support the assignment, editing or creation of String arrays other than manually. However, making use of the new resource is fairly easy. The id of the resource is @array/country and this has to be typed into the entries property in the Attributes window as the Resource picker doesn't support arrays at the moment:

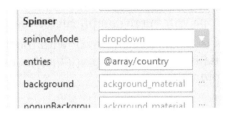

If you enter the id correctly you will see the first item appear in the Spinner within the editor. When you run the app you will see all of the entries when you drop down the list:

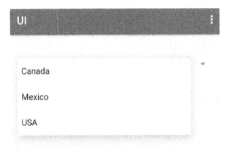

For simple lists of options that can be specified at design time this is all you need to know about how to load a list of items into a Spinner. In practice, however, a Spinner usually has to be loaded with a list at runtime and then you need to know about the ArrayAdapter.

## Introducing the ArrayAdapter

In the case of UI widgets that display lists of things, Android has a much more general mechanism to cope with the different type of things you could display. Widgets that show lists of things generally work with an example of an "adapter". For more on adapters in general see Chapter 15.

An adapter basically takes a list of objects and converts them into something that can be displayed in the widget. In general, you can create custom Adapters to do clever things with lists of objects of your own so that they display appropriately. In most cases, however, you can get by with just using the provided built-in adapters.

In the case of the spinner the most usual choice is the ArrayAdapter. This takes an array of objects of any type and makes them suitable for display by calling their **toString()** method. As long as the toString() method produces what you want to see in the Spinner then everything should work.

In the case of an array of Strings calling the toString() method on each array element might seem like overkill, but it is the price we pay to build mechanisms that can cope with more complicated situations.

So the plan of action is to create a String array with the items we want to display, use this to initialize an ArrayAdapter object, and then attach the ArrayAdapter to the Spinner.

Creating the array is easy:

```
val country = arrayOf("Canada", "Mexico", "USA")
```

The ArrayAdapter constructor can seem to be complicated. It seems even more complicated because ArrayAdapter uses generics to allow you to specify the type of each element in the array.

*If you haven't used generics before, all you need to know is that, in general, generics are a way of creating useful classes, often collections of objects that can be of a type you specify. You know you are working with a generic when you have to specify the type it is to work with using <type>.*

So instead of creating a special array Adapter for each type of array, an IntArrayAdapter, a StringArrayAdapter and so on, you simply have to specify the type as <int> or <String> when you use the generic ArrayAdapter type. For example, to create an ArrayAdapter for an array of Strings you would use:

```
val stringArrayAdapter=ArrayAdapter<String>(constructor parameters)
```

The pattern is the same for all the constructors and for different array types.

There are quite a few ArrayAdapter constructors, but they all need some basic information. They need to know the current context, usually `this,` and the layout to be used to display the list and the array of data items.

The only difficult one is the layout to be used to display the list. This sounds like a lot of hard work until you discover that the system provides some basic standard layouts that you can just use.

In our case the layout is:

```
android.R.layout.simple_spinner_dropdown_item
```

Notice that `this` is actually an integer that determines the layout resource to use and nothing more complicated. Putting it all together gives:

```
val stringArrayAdapter=ArrayAdapter<String>(
                    this,
                    android.R.layout.simple_spinner_dropdown_item,
                    country)
```

If you are wondering what country is, remember that we defined a String array called country earlier.

The final step is to specify the ArrayAdapter to use in the Spinner. We can use its **adapter** property:

```
spinner.adapter=stringArrayAdapter
```

You could have done the job in one line and the onCreate event handler:

```
override fun onCreate(savedInstanceState: Bundle?) {
        super.onCreate(savedInstanceState)
        setContentView(R.layout.activity_main)
        setSupportActionBar(toolbar)

        val country = arrayOf("Canada", "Mexico", "USA")
        spinner.adapter=ArrayAdapter<String>(
            this,
            android.R.layout.simple_spinner_dropdown_item,
            country)
}
```

If you run the program you will see the same drop-down list we produced using just the Layout Editor.

## Handling the Selection

The next question is, how do you discover that the user has made a selection?

The simple answer is that we have to hook up to the Spinner's events and the OnItemSelectedListener is the interface that has the onNothingSelected and onItemSelected event handlers. As the interface defines two event handlers it isn't a SAM and so we have to use an object.

If you enter the following line:

```
val onSpinner=object:AdapterView.OnItemSelectedListener{
```

You can then use the right click Generate, Override Methods option to create a stub:

```
val onSpinner=object:AdapterView.OnItemSelectedListener{
        override fun onNothingSelected(p0: AdapterView<*>?) {
            TODO("not implemented")
        }

        override fun onItemSelected(p0: AdapterView<*>?,
                                    p1: View?, p2: Int, p3: Long) {
            TODO("not implemented")
        }

    }
```

It also adds an import for AdapterView.

You can see at once that you have to implement two event handlers:

- onItemSelected – triggered when the user selects an item
- onNothingSelected – triggered when the Spinner has no items or the user deselects all items

You might be surprised to see two occurrences of <*> in the generated code. Both events are generic and, as already explained, they can work with a range of different types. The <*> is a type projection which essentially allows any type to be used. For example List<*> is a list of any type. Of course, the actual type isn't known until runtime and so every element of the List is treated as an Any type and it's up to you to cast it to something more specific. Kotlin adds checks to make sure your casts are safe.

Let's look at the onItemSelected event handler in more detail:

```
override fun onItemSelected(
  p0: AdapterView<*>?,
  p1: View?,
  p2: Int,
  p3: Long)
```

What is this p0:AdapterView that has suddenly appeared? As explained in earlier chapters, all of the visible components of the UI correspond to View objects of one sort or another. An AdapterView is the View object that corresponds to one of the displayed items in the Spinner. You could, for example, use the AdapterView passed to the event handler to modify the appearance of the displayed item.

The p1:View parameter is just the child of the AdapterView that was actually clicked. Note that an item can be composed of more than one View item.

Finally the p2:int parameter and the p3:long provide the position of the view that was clicked in the adapter and the row id of the item that was selected.

You can populate a Spinner from a database. In this case the row id gives the database row number, which isn't necessarily the same as its position in the Spinner. For a simple ArrayAdapter the position and id are the same. In most cases the only parameter you will be interested in is the int position which gives you the item the user selected. For example, place a TextView on the design surface and change the onItemSelected event handler to read:

```
override fun onItemSelected(p0: AdapterView<*>?,
                            p1: View?,
                            p2: Int,
                            p3: Long) {
    textView.text=p2.toString()
}
```

All that happens is that the position parameter is displayed in the TextView.

Finally to connect the event handling object to the Spinner we need to add it using its `onItemSelectListener` property:

```
spinner.onItemSelectedListener=onSpinner
```

Of course you could define the event handling object and assign it in one instruction. Putting this together gives the new `onCreate`:

```
override fun onCreate(savedInstanceState: Bundle?) {
        super.onCreate(savedInstanceState)
        setContentView(R.layout.activity_main)
        setSupportActionBar(toolbar)

        val country = arrayOf("Canada", "Mexico", "USA")
        spinner.adapter=ArrayAdapter<String>(
            this,
            android.R.layout.simple_spinner_dropdown_item,
            country)

        spinner.onItemSelectedListener =
                object:AdapterView.OnItemSelectedListener {
                    override fun onNothingSelected(
                            p0: AdapterView<*>?) {
                    }

                    override fun onItemSelected(
                            p0: AdapterView<*>?,
                            p1: View?,
                            p2: Int,
                            p3: Long) {
            textView.text = p2.toString()
        }
    }
}
```

If you now run the program you will see something like:

The position displayed corresponds to the element in the array that has been selected, counting from zero of course.

Most of the time is it enough just to have the index number of the selected item, but the AdapterView object has a few methods that enable you to get the selected item. If you want to review the selected item you could use the position to index the original ArrayAdapter, or even the original String array, but these aren't generally available to the event handler. So to retrieve the item you would use the getItemAtPosition method. For example, to display the country name you would modify the `setText` call to:

```
textView.text = p0?.getItemAtPosition(p2).toString()
```

Notice that the selected item is returned as an object type and you have to cast it before you can do anything with it.

There are other methods that can be used to retrieve information or manipulate the selected element, but for most simple applications the itemAtPosition property is all you really need.

## Creating an ArrayAdapter from a Resource

To create an ArrayAdapter from a resource you need to make use of a static method of the ArrayAdapter class, createFromResource. This just needs you to specify the context, the resource id, and the Spinner layout. All you have to do is to replace the creation of stringArrayAdapter:

```
spinner.adapter=ArrayAdapter.createFromResource(
                this,
                R.array.country,
                android.R.layout.simple_spinner_dropdown_item)
```

With this change everything works as before, but now to change the items that appear in the Spinner you simply edit the XML file.

You could also use the resources object to retrieve the String array and then proceed as if the String array had been defined in code:

```
val country=resources.getStringArray(R.array.country)
```

## Changing The List

There are lots of more advanced things that you can do with Spinners, but these aren't encountered that often and mainly occur when trying to build a custom user experience.

The one thing that does occur often is the need to dynamically change the list of items. There are many slight variations on this, but essentially what you do is change the String array and then call the adapter's notifyDataSetChange method. For example, if you want to change Mexico, i.e. element one, to Greenland you would use:

```
country[1]="Greenland"
(spinner.adapter as ArrayAdapter<String>).notifyDataSetChanged()
```

You have to explicitly cast the adapter property as it is too complex for the compiler to infer.

The ArrayAdapter also has add, clear, remove and insert methods which can be used to modify the underlying data, but for this to work the object holding the data has to be modifiable.

You can't modify a String array in this way. What you need instead is an ArrayList.

If you change the declaration of country to:

```
val country= mutableListOf("Canada", "Mexico", "USA")
```

you can add "Greenland" to the end of the items using:

```
(spinner.adapter as ArrayAdapter<String>).add("Greenland")
```

Notice that in this case the ArrayAdapter constructor used changes from one that accepts an array to one that accepts a List of objects.

You can always find out how many items there are using the count property.

How do you modify a list of items that are created using a resource? This is a tricky question because the ArrayAdapter creates a String array to hold the data which means you can't use the methods that modify a list. There are a number of ways of fixing this, but the simplest is to construct your own List from the resource directly:

```
val country= mutableListOf(
            *resources.getStringArray(R.array.country))
spinner.adapter=ArrayAdapter<String>(
            this,
            android.R.layout.simple_spinner_dropdown_item,
            country)
```

With this version of the ArrayAdapter you can once again use the add, and other methods, to modify the list of items. Notice the use of the Kotlin spread operator to unpack the String array into individual Strings so that mutableListOf works correctly.

# Summary

- Spinners are a way of presenting a list of options for the user to select from.

- Spinners can be complex in terms of their layout and what they show, but the simplest example is to work with an array of Strings.

- The array of Strings can be created in the code or within a resource file.

- The array of Strings has to be converted into an ArrayAdapter object to be used with the Spinner.

- The ArrayAdapter provides a View object for each item displayed in the Spinner.

- There are two ways (at least) to load a String array resource into an ArrayAdapter – using its createFromResource or by loading the resource as String array and then proceeding as before.

- Loading the String array has the advantage that you can change it into a List, which can be modified in code by adding or deleting elements. You cannot change the length of a String array.

- To find out what the user has selected simply use the onItemSelected event handler.

- To retrieve the item that the user has selected use the getItemAtPosition(position) method.

Android currently supports three Pickers for dates, times and general numbers and they are important ways to get user input. However, they have been through so many revisions that they lack simple documentation or guidelines how to use them. Let's clear up the confusion.

## Working with Pickers

- A picker is a "dial" that you can use to select one of a predetermined set of values.

In this sense it is a lot like the Spinner covered in the previous chapter, but one that has a restricted set of choices.

There are two ways to make use of a Picker, as a widget, or as a dialog box. You will find the TimePicker and the DatePicker, ready to place on the design surface, in the Date&Time section of the Palette. The NumberPicker, however, is much lower down, in the Advanced section:

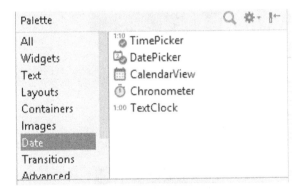

Although in some cases you probably will want to create a Dialog box and will need to use a complex DialogFragment to wrap the Dialog and manage its lifecycle, and there are many situations where using the raw widget will do the job well enough. For more on DialogFragment see: ***Android Programming: Mastering Fragments & Dialogs.***

# TimePicker

The TimePicker is a very easy way to get started. If you create a new Android project, called TimeAndDate and accept all of the defaults you can place a TimePicker, listed top of the Date & Time section of the Palette, on the design surface just like any other widget, and size and locate it as required. In its default configuration it shows in the Layout Editor using the style android:timePickerStyle and has an analog clock face and an input area that can be used to set the time by dragging the hands on the clock face:

Pickers are complex widgets that have multiple components, each of which can change appearance depending on how they are styled and which version of Android you are targeting. While you can select from a range of themes, they don't all work with all SDK/APIs and they may to be removed at some time in the future. For example, before API 14 this theme was used:

API 14 adopted the Holo theme and the picker looked like this:

What follows is what you get if you simply accept the defaults. However, it is important to realize that exactly what the user sees depends on the version of Android they are using. For example your up-to-date app running on the latest Android might look like the clock TimePicker but it you run it on a pre-Lollipop API such as Jelly Bean (API 18) then you will see the Holo-themed version as above. If you want to support older versions then it is important to remember to test using them. If you want to use something that looks like the Holo-themed version on all versions then all you have to do is find timePickerMode in the Attributes window and use the drop-down list to select spinner or clock depending on the type you need.

For easy backward compatibility use compatibility library v7 appcompat, which is included in your projects automatically by Android Studio, and stick with the AppCompat themes.

## TimePicker in Code

To interact with the TimePicker all you have to use is the get/set methods for Hour and Minute. You can also programatically change the 12 hour/24 hour mode. Notice that the time is always returned in 24-hour form no matter what the widget's mode is.

Although the currentMinute and currentHour properties are deprecated, the alternatives which do exactly the same thing, minute and hour, don't work on earlier versions of Android. So for the moment it seems preferable to use the deprecated methods and ignore the warnings. For example to set the TimePicker you would use:

```
timePicker.setIs24HourView(true)
timePicker.currentMinute=10
timePicker.currentHour=13
```

The only task remaining is figuring out how to discover when the user has selected a time.

You could provide a button which the user has to click to confirm the new time. For example, place a Button and a TextView on the design surface and add the following Button click event handler:

```
button.setOnClickListener { view ->
        textView.text=  timePicker.currentHour.toString() + ":" +
                        timePicker.currentMinute.toString()
}
```

This provides a way for the user set the time:

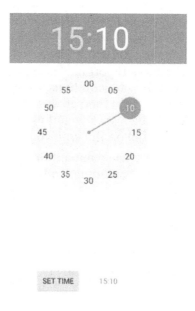

In most cases the difficult part in using a Picker isn't setting it up or getting the data from it, but in processing that data into a form in which your program can use it. In this case we simply convert the time into a slightly formatted string representation.

## Updating the Time

What about getting an update every time the user changes the TimePicker? This requires an event handler for an OnTimeChanged event which can be implemented with an OnTimeChangedListener interface as a lambda.

You can guess that when the time is changed by the user, the onTimeChanged method is called and the TimePicker that triggered the event is passed as view, and its hour and minute setting as hourOfDay and minute, and all that is now needed is to set the event handler using the setOnTimeChangedListener method.

For example, to transfer the new time to the TextView used in the previous example you would use:

```
timePicker.setOnTimeChangedListener { timePicker, h, m ->
    textView.text=h.toString() + ":" + m.toString()

}
```

Now if you run the program you will see the TextView change every time the user alters the TimePicker by whatever method.

The full program, including the code for the button and the event handler is shown below:

```
override fun onCreate(savedInstanceState: Bundle?) {
        super.onCreate(savedInstanceState)
        setContentView(R.layout.activity_main)
        setSupportActionBar(toolbar)

        timePicker.setIs24HourView(true)
        timePicker.currentMinute = 10
        timePicker.currentHour = 13

        button.setOnClickListener { view ->
            textView.text = timePicker.currentHour.toString() + ":"
                            + timePicker.currentMinute.toString(
        }

        timePicker.setOnTimeChangedListener { timePicker, h, m ->
            textView.text = h.toString() + ":" + m.toString()
        }
}
```

## DatePicker

There are two date widgets in the current Android system, DatePicker and Calendar view. The DatePicker has been in use since API 1 but Calendar view was only introduced in API 11. The main difference between the two is the way that they look. As they work in much the same way and the DatePicker is more versatile this is the widget we will use. Also once you have experienced the way TimePicker works there is very little to add to cover its date counterpart.

To see the DatePicker in action simply start a new project called Date and accept all of the defaults. Place a DatePicker on the design surface at the top left-hand corner. The DatePicker underwent the same changes with the introduction of Material Design as did the TimePicker. As long as you use the latest API and the default layout it will show in a calendar format:

As is the case with the TimePicker, if you run your app on an older pre-Lollipop version of Android then you will see the Holo-themed spinner version:

You can opt to display the Holo spinner version in all Android versions by setting the datePickerMode to spinner. As an alternative you can also opt to also show a full Calendar in spinner mode by setting CalendarViewShown to true. The spinnerShown property can also be set to false to remove the spinners:

As well as playing with the way the DatePicker looks, you can also set and get all of the parts of a date using:

- DayOfMonth
- Month
- Year

You can also set and get maximum and minimum dates that the widget will show using properties.

When it comes to interacting with the widget you can set up a button to allow the user to set the date as with the TimePicker or you can use the OnDateChanged event to track the value. Doing this follows the same steps as for the OnTimeChanged event but with a small difference - there was no setOnDateChangedListener method in early versions of Android. Instead there is an init method which can be used to set the date and the event handler. However as the final parameter of init is SAM you can use a lambda and you can place the lambda outside of the function call parentheses i.e.

```
init(y,n,d){event handler}
```

For example, if you add a TextView to the bottom of the design surface and the following code for the event handler then you can see the date change each time the user makes a change:

```
datePicker.init(2018, 4, 6)
        { datePicker, y, m, d ->
            textView.text = m.toString() + "/" +
                            d.toString() + "/" + y.toString()
        }
```

which sets the year, month and day and the event handler.

If you run the app you will see:

This tells you at once, May is selected and the date is 4/6/2018, that the months are numbered starting with Jan at zero not 1. The solution is to add one to the month number.

## Number Picker

You might be worried that the NumberPicker is going to be trouble when you notice that it is in the Advanced section of the toolbox palette! In reality it is very easy to use, all you have to do is select it and place it on the design surface. To try it out start a new project called Number and accept all of the defaults. If you have any problems with the rendering of the NumberPicker simply ignore the errors and build the project. The errors should then go away.

If you run the app then you will see the NumberPicker styled for the latest API which in this case looks very odd because there is nothing loaded into the spinner:

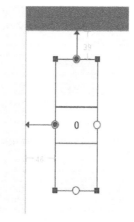

The reason for this is that the NumberPicker is slightly more complicated than the other Pickers in that it allows you to set what the spinner displays.

There are two distinct ways in which you can set the range that is displayed, as a pair of max/min values, or as the values stored in an array.

For example, if you just want the NumberPicker to show 0 to 9 you might use:

```
numberPicker.maxValue = 9
numberPicker.minValue = 0
```

If you don't want the number spinner to wrap around you can use:

```
numberPicker.wrapSelectorWheel=false
```

If you want to give the user the choice of 0, 10, 20 and so on up to 90 you first have to initialize a string array of the correct size for these values. In this case, the difference between MaxValue and MinValue properties plus 1 gives the number of elements in the list.

To create the array we need to use the Array constructor with a lambda that initializes it:

```
val values=Array(10,{i-> (i*10).toString()})
```

Once we have the array of values to display it can be assigned to the Picker using its setDisplayedValues method:

```
numberPicker.maxValue=9
numberPicker.minValue=0
numberPicker.displayedValues=values
```

You may have noticed that the array used to specify the values is a String array. What this means is that the NumberPicker, despite its name, can allow the user to pick from a list of arbitrary strings that you can set.

For example:

```
val values=arrayOf("mike","sue","harry")
numberPicker.maxValue=2
numberPicker.minValue=0
numberPicker.displayedValues=values
```

produces:

When it comes to retrieving the data you can use the getValue method, which always returns an integer. This is either the index in the String array, or the actual value if you are not using a String array, of the item the user picked.

If you want to get a live update of the value the user selects you can use the OnValueChange event. The event handler:

```
public void onValueChange(
 NumberPicker picker,
 int oldVal,
 int newVal)
```

provides you with the NumberPicker object that the event occurred on as picker and the index of the old and new values. The only problem is getting the values from the String array that was used initially. This is probably not accessible from the event handler and may not even exist any longer. The solution is to use the NumberPicker's getDisplayedValues, which returns a String array of values currently loaded in the NumberPicker.

For example to transfer the value to a TextView

```
numberPicker.setOnValueChangedListener { numberPicker, old, new ->
                        val values =numberPicker.displayedValues
                        textView.text=values[new]
        }
```

This uses the picker to get the array of displayed values, which it then transfers to the TextView using the newVal as an index.

In fact given that values is already defined and likely to be accessible to the lambda via closure we could write:

```
numberPicker.setOnValueChangedListener { numberPicker, old, new ->
                        textView.text=values[new]

        }
```

Notice however that this would fail if the list of items in the NumberPicker had changed.

Now when you run the program the TextView is updated as soon as any changes are made:

That's about all there is to basic use of the NumberPicker.

## Multi-Digit Input

If you want to create a multi-digit input – for hundreds, tens, units, say – then simply use three NumberPickers. This is more tricky than it first appears if you want to dynamically track the current value across more than one NumberPicker. For example, to build a three-digit input you first need to place three NumberPickers on the design surface with ids numberPicker1, numberPicker2 and numberPicker3. Place numberPicker1 on the far left, then numberPicker 2 and then numberPicker3. Also add a TextView somewhere convenient:

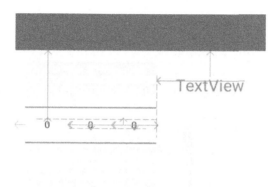

You could initialize each of the NumberPickers in turn, but it is instructive to use an array of NumberPickers to do the job:

```
val nps=arrayOf(numberPicker1,numberPicker2,numberPicker3)
```

Note that you can create an array of object of any type using arrayOf.

Now we have an array of NumberPicker objects we can initialize them all in the same way, but first we need the array of values:

```
val values=Array(10,{i->i.toString()})
```

As we are using 0 to 9 this could be done as an index without using an array, but this makes the example more general. Now we have the array of values we can initialize the NumberPickers:

```
for( i in nps.indices){
     nps[i].maxValue=values.size-1
     nps[i].minValue=0
     nps[i].displayedValues=values
     nps[i].setOnValueChangedListener(onValueChanged)
}
```

Notice that the same event handler is used for all of the NumberPickers. In some cases this is the way to do things, in others it is better to have an event handler for each widget.

The next small problem is how to update the value displayed in a TextView when one of the NumberPickers changes its value. Again the simplest solution for an example is to get the values from each of the NumberPickers using a for loop:

```
val onValueChanged= {picker:NumberPicker,old:Int,new:Int->
        var temp=""
        for(i in nps.indices){
                temp+=values[nps[i].value]
        }
        textView.text=temp
}
```

In this case we don't use any of the event method's parameters we simply use the values array which is available due to closure and lookup the values that each NumberPicker is currently set to.

If you run the program, you should be able to alter what is displayed in the TextView in a sensible three-digit place value way:

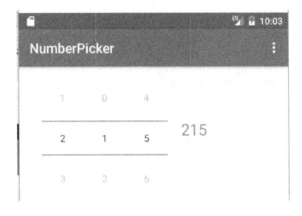

The complete program is:

```kotlin
import android.os.Bundle
import android.support.design.widget.Snackbar
import android.support.v7.app.AppCompatActivity
import android.view.Menu
import android.view.MenuItem
import android.widget.NumberPicker

import kotlinx.android.synthetic.main.activity_main.*
import kotlinx.android.synthetic.main.content_main.*

class MainActivity : AppCompatActivity() {
    override fun onCreate(savedInstanceState: Bundle?) {
        super.onCreate(savedInstanceState)
        setContentView(R.layout.activity_main)
        setSupportActionBar(toolbar)


        val values=Array(10,{i->i.toString()})
        val nps=arrayOf(numberPicker1,numberPicker2,numberPicker3)

        val onValueChanged= {picker:NumberPicker,old:Int,new:Int->
            var temp=""
            for(i in nps.indices){
                temp+=values[nps[i].value]
            }
            textView.text=temp
        }
        for( i in nps.indices){
            nps[i].maxValue=values.size-1
            nps[i].minValue=0
            nps[i].displayedValues=values
            nps[i].setOnValueChangedListener(onValueChanged)
        }
}
```

There is much more to say about the Pickers and how to customize them, but the methods explained here are the most common, and customization generally only involves the use of fairly obvious properties and methods.

The biggest omission here is the use of the Pickers within a DialogFragment. This is a big topic that is covered in **_Android Programming: Mastering Fragments & Dialogs._**

## Summary

- TimePicker, DatePicker and NumberPicker provide easy to use ways of getting user input without having to use an on-screen keyboard.

- Pickers are usually introduced as dialog boxes or dialog fragments. This is a good way to use them, but they are also useful if you don't use a dialog.

- With the introduction of Material Design with Android Lollipop, the look of the Pickers has changed. For easy backward compatibility use compatibility library v7, appcompat, which is included in your projects automatically by Android Studio, and stick with the AppCompat themes.

- If you stick with these defaults your app will use Material Design on Lollipop and later, but the Holo theme for earlier versions of Android. If you stray from AppCompat themes things tend not to work.

- It is possible and very easy to replace the Material Design with the Holo look on all versions of Android. Simply set the timePickerMode and/or datePickerMode properties to spinner. The NumberPicker always shows as a spinner.

- Use the OnXChangedListener event handler to respond to user input.

- The DatePicker in spinner form can also display a calendar using the CalendarViewShown property.

# Chapter 16

## ListView

ListView is probably the most commonly used UI component in an Android app. It isn't difficult to use, but you need to get to grips with the idea of an "adapter", and understanding what is going on pays dividends.

For a range of reasons, one of the most common things you need to do in an Android UI is to display a list of things that the user can select from. We have already looked at the basic Picker, but the ListView is a more general category of "picker".

If you are familiar with desktop development then you probably think of lists that the user can select from as being similar to a drop-down list. Android and portable devices often need something more than just a small list. Because of the limited screen size, it is often the case that the user can only be shown an overview of quite a few different items. When the user selects an item they are then presented with more details of the item, commonly called a details view.

Displaying lists and other collections of data is so common that Android has a mechanism that makes it easier once you understand how it all works.

The key idea is that to display a collection, each item in the collection has somehow to be converted to an appropriate View object. It is the View object that the container displays for each item of data in the collection.

## Understanding the Adapter

Displaying a collection of items has a number of similarities no matter what the collection of items are, or what container is used. The container has various positions that are visible on the screen for displaying items. For example, a ListView has horizontal slots, one per item, and a GridView has a 2D grid of slots. Each container accepts a View object and displays it in a slot. For example, you could provide the ListView with TextView objects and it would simply display text in each of its slots.

You might be wondering why not just supply a set of Strings to the ListView and let it work out how to display the Strings as text? Things could be organized in this way and it would be simpler, but only if you wanted to display Strings. If you wanted to display a list of images, say, then you would need a ListView that understood images and so on.

It is much more flexible to provide the container with a set of prepared View objects because then the container simply has to display the View object without having to perform any conversions.

All containers that derive from the AdapterView class make use of adapters to supply what they display in terms of View objects. As well as the ListView and GridView, they include the Spinner, Gallery and StackView.

We have already looked at the use of the Spinner and its associated adapter, so this time it is the turn of a more advanced UI element – the ListView and its adapter.

This approach also has the advantage that you can provide the container with a View object that is a complete layout, i.e. it could itself be a container with lots of View objects to display. For example, you could supply a ListView with a View object that contains an image, and a TextView to create a multimedia list of pictures and text.

Of course the container isn't doing the conversion from the data object to the View object – you are going to have to do it. This is where the adapter comes in. The ListView and the GridView containers both make use of the ListAdapter class as their basic adapter.

## Extending the ListAdapter Class

In general you have to take the ListAdapter class and extend it to create your own custom Adapter which generates a custom View object for the container to use in each of its slots. The container asks for the View object to be used to display item i or using whatever indexing suits the particular container. The Adapter returns the View object and the container displays it – without worrying what it is or what it corresponds to. This might sound complicated, but it turns out to be very simple in practice.

However, to make things even simpler there is also an ArrayAdapter which lets you display a single text item for each element of an array of arbitrary objects. How can this possibly work if the object in the array can be anything? The first thing to point out is that ArrayAdapter is a generic class and can accept an array of any type as long as you specify it when you create the ArrayAdapter instance. The second point to note is that Array adapter calls each item's toString method to get some text to display in the container, which is very simple but also very restrictive. In fact, it is quite easy to modify what the ArrayAdapter displays, and this makes it more versatile than you might expect and hence well worth getting to know.

Before proceeding a quick summary is helpful:

- Containers like ListView and GridView display View objects in a particular arrangement – as a vertical list or as a 2D grid in these two cases respectively.

- An Adapter converts the data that is to be displayed in each slot into a suitable View object.

- For complex data and displays you need to create a custom Adapter.

- In many cases the ArrayAdapter, a predefined custom Adapter for converting Arrays to TextView objects, can be used.

- The ArrayAdapter, at its most basic, can supply TextView objects to a container from an array of any type simply by calling the object's toString methods.

## Using the ArrayAdapter

Rather then starting with an example that is completely general, it is worth looking at how the ArrayAdapter is used in conjunction with a ListView.

Start a new Android Studio project called ListViewExample based on a Basic Activity and accept all the defaults. For a simple example all we are going to do is display a list of names in a ListView.

First delete the usual "Hello World" textView. In the Layout Editor scroll down the Palette until you can see the Containers and place a ListView on the design surface. At the moment the listView isn't always automatically assigned an id. If this is the case type listView into the id in the Attributes window. If you do this then a dummy content will be generated for you:

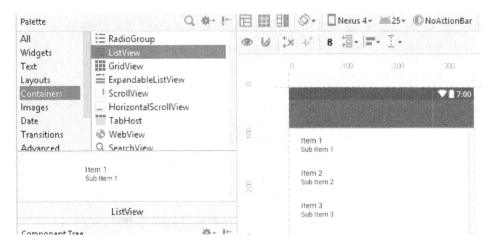

You will see that, for the sake of allowing you to work with the layout, the Layout Editor shows you the ListView filled with some two-item text objects.

Our Adapter is going to be simpler than this dummy display with just a single line of text.

If you run the program at this early stage you won't see anything in the ListView – it will be blank. The text that you see in the Layout Editor is just to help you visualize the UI – there is no Adapter associated with the ListView and hence when you run it there is nothing to display.

Our next task is to create an ArrayAdapter object to supply the ListView with something to display. First, however, we need a String array to hold the text we are going to display. For simplicity we might as well add the code to the onCreate method.

To create a simple String array we can use:

```
val myStringArray = arrayOf("A", "B", "C")
```

Feel free to think up something more creative than A, B, C. In the real world the Strings would probably be read from a file or a database, etc.

Now we can create the ArrayAdapter. To do this the constructor needs the context, usually this, and a layout to use to display each String and the String array:

```
val myAdapter= ArrayAdapter<String>(
                        this,
                        android.R.layout.simple_list_item_1,
                        myStringArray)
```

Notice the way that the type of the array is specified as <String>. If you are not familiar with generics then you need to look up how it all works. Also notice the use of the standard supplied layout simple_list_item1. You can create your own layouts and we will see how this is done in a moment.

Finally we need to associate the adapter with the ListView:

```
listView.setAdapter(myAdapter)
```

The complete onCreate method is:

```
override fun onCreate(savedInstanceState: Bundle?) {
     super.onCreate(savedInstanceState)
     setContentView(R.layout.activity_main)
     setSupportActionBar(toolbar)

     val myStringArray = arrayOf("A", "B", "C")
     val myAdapter = ArrayAdapter<String>(
                        this,
                        android.R.layout.simple_list_item_1,
                        myStringArray)
     listView.setAdapter(myAdapter)
}
```

You will also have to remember to add import statements for each of the classes used – ListView and ArrayAdapter – easily done with Alt+Enter.

If you now run the program you will see a neat list with each array element displayed on a line:

So far this doesn't look impressive but the ListView gives you some basic facilities. For example, if you increase the number of elements in the array:

```
var myStringArray =
    arrayOf("A", "B", "C", "D", "E", "F", "G", "H", "I", "J")
```

you will discover that you can automatically scroll through the list using the usual flick gesture.

## Working with the Data

The whole point of showing the user a list of items is so that they can interact with it. You can manipulate the data on display in various ways and handle events when the user selects an item.

### Get Selection

Perhaps the most important thing is to deal with the user selecting an item. The usual way of doing this is to write a handler for the OnItemClickListener, which passes four parameters:

```
onItemClick(AdapterView parent,View view,int position, long id)
```

The AdapterView is the complete View displayed by the container, the View is the View object the user selected, the position is the position in the collection, and the id is the item's id number in the container. For an ArrayAdapter the id is the same as the array index.

You can use this event to find out what the user has selected and modify it. For example the event handler:

```
listView.setOnItemClickListener({parent, view, position, id ->
            (view as TextView).text="selected"
    })
```

sets each item the user selects to "selected".

It is important to know that changing what the View object displays doesn't change the data stored in the associated data structure. That is, in this case setting a row to "selected" doesn't change the entry in the String array.

You can also set the selection in code using:

```
listView.setSelection(position)
```

where position is the zero-based position of the item in the list, and you can scroll to show any item using:

```
listView.smoothScrollToPosition(position)
```

A subtle point worth mentioning is that you can't make use of the View object that is passed to the event handler to display the selection in another part of the layout. A View object can only be in the layout hierarchy once. In most cases this isn't a problem because you can usually manually clone the View object. For example, in this case the View object is a TextView and so you can create a new TextView and set its Text property to be the same as the one in the list:

```
val w = TextView(applicationContext)
w.text = (view as TextView).text
```

This can be more of a nuisance if the View object is more complex.

## Changing the Data

One of the slightly confusing things about using adapters is the relationship between what is displayed and what is in the underlying data structure. You can change the data, but if you want to see the change in the container you have to use an adapter notify method to tell the adapter that the data has changed.
For example, if you change an element of the array:

```
myStringArray[0]="newdata"
```

then nothing will show until you use:

```
(listView.adapter as ArrayAdapter<String>).notifyDataSetChanged()
```

Notice that you have to cast the ListAdapter in adapter to an ArrayAdapter<String> to call the notify method.

There is a second way to change the data using the ArrayAdapter itself. This provides a number of methods to add, insert, clear, remove and even sort the data in the adapter. The big problem is that if you use any of these then the underlying data structure associated with the adapter has to support them. For example, the add method adds an object onto the end of the data structure but, with the program as currently set up, if you try:

```
myAdapter.add("new data")
```

the result will be a runtime crash. The reason is that in an array has a fixed size and the add method tries to add the item to the end of the array, which isn't possible.

If you want to add items to the end of an array-like data structure, you need to use a List and not just a simple array – we met this idea before in Chapter 14 in connection with Spinners. A List can increase and decrease its size. For example we can create a List from our existing String array:

```
val myList=mutableListOf(*myStringArray)
```

and you can associate this new List with the adapter instead of the String array:

```
val myAdapter = ArrayAdapter<String>(
                        this,
                        android.R.layout.simple_list_item_1,
                        myList)
```

Following this you can use:

```
myAdapter.add("new data")
```

and you will see the new data at the end of the displayed list. You may have to scroll to see it.

As long as you are using a List you are safe to use all of the adapter data modifying methods:

```
add(item)
addAll(item1,item2,item3...)
clear() //remove all data
insert(item,position)
remove(item)
```

You can also make use of:

```
count() // number of elements
getItem(position) // get item
getItemId(position) //get item id
getPosition(item)
```

## A Custom Layout

So far we have just made use of the system provided layout for the row. It is very easy to create your own layout file and set it so that it is used to render each row, but you need to keep in mind that the only data that will be displayed that is different on each row is derived from the item's toString method.

The simplest custom layout has to have just a single TextView widget which is used for each line. In fact this is so simple it has no advantage over the system supplied layout so this is really just to show how things work.

Use Android Studio to create a new layout in the standard layout directory and call it mylayout.xml. Use the Layout Editor or text editor to create a layout with just a single TextView object. Create a new layout and accept any layout type for the initial file. You can then place a TextView on the design surface. You won't be able to delete the layout, however, as the editor will not allow you to do it. Instead you need to switch to Text view and edit the file to remove the layout:

```
<?xml version="1.0" encoding="utf-8"?>
 <TextView
  xmlns:android="http://schemas.android.com/apk/res/android"
  android:text="TextView"
  android:layout_width="match_parent"
  android:layout_height="wrap_content"
  android:id="@+id/textView" />
```

Notice that you need the xmlns attribute to make sure that the android namespace is defined.

To use the layout you simply provide its resource id in the ArrayAdapter constructor:

```
val myAdapter = ArrayAdapter<String>(
                            this,
                            R.layout.mylayout,
                            myStringArray)
```

If you try this you won't see any huge difference between this and when you use the system layout android.R.layout.simple_list_item_1.

The next level up is to use a layout that has more than just a single TextView in it. The only complication in this case is that you have to provide not only the id of the layout but the id of the TextView in the layout that you want to use for the data. For example, create a layout with a horizontal LinearLayout and place a CheckBox, and two TextViews. The simplest way to do this is to place the LinearLayout in the default ConstraintLayout and use the Layout Editor to design the layout. Then start a new layout resource and copy and past the LinearLayout XML tag and all it contains as the base layout in the new file:

```xml
<?xml version="1.0" encoding="utf-8"?>
<LinearLayout
xmlns:android="http://schemas.android.com/apk/res/android"
    xmlns:app="http://schemas.android.com/apk/res-auto"
    xmlns:tools="http://schemas.android.com/tools"
    android:layout_width="368dp"
    android:layout_height="wrap_content"
    android:descendantFocusability="blocksDescendants"
    android:orientation="horizontal"
    tools:layout_editor_absoluteX="0dp"
    tools:layout_editor_absoluteY="25dp">

    <CheckBox
        android:id="@+id/checkBox2"
        android:layout_width="wrap_content"
        android:layout_height="wrap_content"
        android:layout_weight="1"
        android:text="CheckBox" />

    <TextView
        android:id="@+id/textView"
        android:layout_width="wrap_content"
        android:layout_height="wrap_content"
        android:layout_weight="1"
        android:text="TextView" />

    <TextView
        android:id="@+id/textView2"
        android:layout_width="wrap_content"
        android:layout_height="wrap_content"
        android:layout_weight="1"
        android:text="TextView" />
</LinearLayout>
```

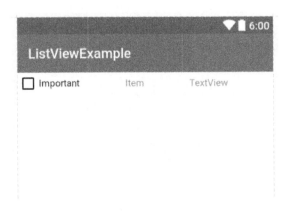

You can use this layout by creating the ArrayAdapter with:

```
val myAdapter = ArrayAdapter<String>(
                              this,
                              R.layout.mylayout,
                              R.id.textView2,
                              myStringArray)
```

assuming that the TextView you want the data to appear in is textView2.

The resulting ListView example is a little more impressive than the previous example

Notice that each of the View objects in the layout gives rise to a distinct instance per line. That is, your layout may only have had one CheckBox but the ListView has one per line. This means that when the user selects the line you can retrieve the setting of the CheckBox, say. It also means that a ListView can generate several View objects very quickly and this can be a drain on the system.

There are a few things that you need to know if you are going to successfully handle onItemClick events. The first is that your layout can't have any focusable or clickable Views. If it does then the event isn't raised and the handler just isn't called. The solution is to stop any View object in the container from being focusable by adding:

```
android:descendantFocusability="blocksDescendants"
```

to the LinearLayout, or use the Property window to set it to blocksDescendants:

With this change the event handler should be called, but now you need to keep in mind that the View object passed as view in:

```
listView.setOnItemClickListener({ parent, view, position, id ->
```

is the complete View object for the row and not just the TextView. That is, in the case of the example above it would be the LinearLayout plus all of its children.

If you are going to work with the View object, you have to access the objects it contains and you can do this is in the usual way.

For example:

```
listView.setOnItemClickListener({ parent, view, position, id->
    view.findViewById<TextView>(R.id.textView).text="Selected"
})
```

Notice that you can use findViewById in the View that is returned.

## A Custom ArrayAdapter

If you only want to display a String in each row you can use the standard ArrayAdapter and the object's toString method. You can even customize the object's toString method to display something different from the default, but it is still just a String.

If you have an array of general objects and want to display multiple items from each object, or items which are not Strings, then you need to create a custom ArrayAdapter. This isn't difficult, although there are one or two more advanced points to take note of.

For this first example, let's keep it as simple as possible. First we need some objects to hold the data we are going to display – a record type, say, with a field for name and one for number in stock. You could also add a photo of the item, but in the spirit of keeping it simple a String and int are enough.

If you know other languages you might be thinking that we need a struct or something similar. In Java or Kotlin there are no structs. If you want to create a record you create an object with the necessary properties. However Kotlin supports data classes which are designed for the task and in many ways are a superior "record" type to what you find in other language.

Start a new project called CustomList and accept all the defaults. Remove the default text and add a ListView.

In Java it is a rule that every new class you create has to be in a separate folder. You can follow this convention in Kotlin but it is often easier to add utility classes to the file you are working in. You can always separate them at a later date.

We are going to create a data class complete with properties that we can use to store data:

```
data class MyData (var myTitle:String, var myNum:Int)
```

The new class has two public fields, myTitle and myNum, and a primary constructor allowing us to initialize these fields.

For example, in the onCreate method you can add:

```
val myDataArray=arrayOf(
        MyData("item1", 10),
        MyData("item2", 20),
        MyData("item3", 30)
)
```

You might need to add more data than this to try out the ListView properly but this at least gets us started.

Now we have some data to display we need to add the custom adapter. Once again we can create a new class called MyAdapter in the same file. MyAdapter has to inherit from ArrayAdapter:

```
class MyAdaptor(    val mycontext: Context?,
                    val resource: Int,
                    val objects: Array<out MyData>?) :
            ArrayAdapter<MyData>(mycontext, resource, objects) {
```

This looks complicated but it is the code you get using Alt+Enter on the partially declared class. The <out MyData> is the compiler protecting you from an unlikely problem but it is still worth playing by its rules. Notice also that we have to change the generated context parameter to mycontext to avoid a name clash.

Notice that we want the generic ArrayAdapter to work with MyData objects. Most of the methods of ArrayAdapter will work perfectly well with arrays of arbitrary objects.

The primary constructor that we have just defined will also automatically create read only properties for each of the parameters that start val. This is another of Kotlin's simplifications and we don't need to define a more elaborate constructor.

Notice that with this constructor our adapter is used in the same way as in the previous example, that is we supply context, resource id, and the array of data. These values are also passed on to the constructor of the super class i.e. ArrayAdaptor.

We now reach the key part of the customization, overriding the adapter's getView method. This is the core of the functionality of the adapter. Each time the ListView needs to display a new row, it calls the adapter's getView method and expects to get back a View object that it can display as the row.

To override the method you can use Android Studio to generate some code. Right-click in the adapter class and select Generate, Override method and then select getView. The generated code isn't particularly helpful, but at least it gets the method signature correct:

```
override fun getView(      position: Int,
                           convertView: View?,
                           parent: ViewGroup?): View {
        return super.getView(position, convertView, parent)
}
```

It really doesn't matter how getView generates the View object it is going to return, but the most common way of doing the job is to inflate a layout file.

To give the inflater something to work with, right-click on the res/layout folder and select New,Layout file. Call the file mylayout, change the LinearLayout to horizontal, and add two TextViews with ids, title and number. Feel free to change the layout to make things look pretty - it won't change the code you need to write:

```
<?xml version="1.0" encoding="utf-8"?>
<LinearLayout
    xmlns:android="http://schemas.android.com/apk/res/android"
    xmlns:app="http://schemas.android.com/apk/res-auto"
    xmlns:tools="http://schemas.android.com/tools"
    android:layout_width="368dp"
    android:layout_height="wrap_content"
    android:descendantFocusability="blocksDescendants"
    android:orientation="horizontal"
    tools:layout_editor_absoluteX="0dp"
    tools:layout_editor_absoluteY="25dp"
    layout_height="wrap_content"
    layout_width="match_parent">

    <TextView
        android:id="@+id/title"
        android:layout_height="wrap_content"
        android:layout_weight="1"
        android:layout_width="wrap_content"
        android:text="TextView" />

    <TextView
        android:id="@+id/number"
        android:layout_height="wrap_content"
        android:layout_weight="1"
        android:layout_width="wrap_content"
        android:text="TextView" />
</LinearLayout>
```

Our first task is to get an inflater and inflate the layout file:

```
val inflater=(mycontext as Activity).layoutInflater
val row=inflater.inflate(resource,parent,false)
```

Notice that we make use of the resource id we stored when the constructor ran and we use the parent View object passed in to the getView method. The only purpose the parent View object serves is to allow the system to lay out the resource in a known container. The final false parameter tells the inflater not to add the resource generated object to the parent – this is a job for the ListView.

Before this happens we have to put the data into the View object. To do this we need to find the two TextView objects that we placed into the layout and this is just a matter of using the familiar findViewById pattern:

```
val title=row.findViewById<TextView>(R.id.title)
val number=row.findViewById<TextView>(R.id.number)
```

Once you have the View objects you need to change, you can use the position parameter to get the data from the array of objects that was set by the constructor:

```
title.text= objects?.get(position)?.myTitle
number.text= objects?.get(position)?.myNum.toString()
```

All we need to do now is return the row View object:

```
        return row
}
```

The complete myAdapter class is:

```
class MyAdaptor(val mycontext: Context?,
                val resource: Int,
    val objects: Array<out MyData>?) :
      ArrayAdapter<MyData>(mycontext, resource, objects) {

      override fun getView(position: Int,
                           convertView: View?,
                           parent: ViewGroup?): View {
      val inflater=(mycontext as Activity).layoutInflater
      val row=inflater.inflate(resource,parent,false)
      val title=row.findViewById<TextView>(R.id.title)
      val number=row.findViewById<TextView>(R.id.number)
      title.text= objects?.get(position)?.myTitle
      number.text= objects?.get(position)?.myNum.toString()
      return row
      }
}
```

Now all we have to do is write some code that makes use of the new class and this is exactly the same as the code that made use of the standard ListView:

```
val myAdapter=MyAdaptor(this,R.layout.mylayout,myDataArray)
listView.adapter=myAdapter
```

Don't forget to put a ListView component on the main layout:

If you run the program you will now see a list consisting of two TextViews, each with something different to display on each line. In a real app you probably wouldn't create a new class for two text items, overriding the toString method would be easier, but the principles are the same no matter what the multiple View objects created by the adapter are.

## Reuse, Caching and General Layouts

We have a working custom adapter class but there are some things we can do to make it better. The first relates to efficiency. If you recall, it was pointed out that a big list of objects could result in the creation of a lot of View objects. In practice, however, we really only need the number of View objects that correspond to rows actually being displayed on the screen.

To avoid having to dispose of and create new View objects all the time, the ListView gives you the opportunity to recycle the View objects you have already created. This is what the convertView parameter in the getView method is all about. If it is null you have to inflate and create a new View object. If it is non-null then it is a View object ready to be used and you don't have to create a new one.

Modifying the previous example to make use of convertView is easy:

```
val row:View
if(convertView==null){
        val inflater=(mycontext as Activity).layoutInflater
        row=inflater.inflate(resource,parent,false)
}else{
        row=convertView
}
```

Notice that this is null safe as the compiler checks that row gets a value one way or another.

This is a speed-up worth making and saves having to create lots of View objects and dispose of them. However, we are still looking up the child View objects every time we want to change the data:

```
val title=row.findViewById<TextView>(R.id.title)
val number=row.findViewById<TextView>(R.id.number)
```

This is also very wasteful and can be avoided with the application of the ViewHolder pattern. All we have to do is save the references to the children in an object, and store this in the parent View's tag property. Then the next time we see the parent View we don't have to find the children we are looking for - they are stored in the parent's tag as a ViewHolder object.

First we need to create a ViewHolder data class:

```
data class ViewHolder(var title:TextView,var number:TextView)
```

Notice that this has fields capable of holding references to our two TextView objects. The logic of the getView method is now to also create and store a ViewHolder object if we are not recycling a View object:

```
val row: View
if (convertView == null) {
      val inflater = (mycontext as Activity).layoutInflater
      row = inflater.inflate(resource, parent, false)
      val viewHolder =ViewHolder  (
            row.findViewById<TextView>(R.id.title),
            row.findViewById<TextView>(R.id.number))
            row.tag=viewHolder
}
```

Notice that we have stored the references to the TextViews in the viewHolder and stored this in the row's Tag field – this is what tag fields are generally used for.

If we do have a recycled View object, we need to get the viewHolder object:

```
} else {
  row = convertView
}
```

Finally, no matter where the viewHolder object came from, we just use it:

```
(row.tag as ViewHolder).title.text =
                        objects?.get(position)?.myTitle
(row.tag as ViewHolder).number.text =
                        objects?.get(position)?.myNum.toString()
return row
}
```

With this change we have avoided creating a View object each time and we have avoided having to look up the child objects each time, a very useful saving in time and resources.

Finally there is one last embellishment to apply. At the moment the layout for the row has to have the ids of the TextView objects set to title and number. It is much better to let the user set these in the constructor:

```
class MyAdaptor(    val mycontext: Context?,
                    val resource: Int,
                    val resTitle:Int,
                    val resNumber:Int,
                    val objects: Array<out MyData>?) :
        ArrayAdapter<MyData>(mycontext, resource, objects) {
```

This constructor has two extra parameters used to specify the id numbers of the two ViewText objects in the layout. These are automatically created properties of the class.

Finally we need to change the getView method to use the two new private variables:

```
val viewHolder =ViewHolder  (
                row.findViewById<TextView>(resTitle),
                row.findViewById<TextView>(resNumber))
```

With these changes the adapter can be used as:

```
val myAdapter = MyAdaptor(this,
                            R.layout.mylayout,
                            R.id.title,
                            R.id.number,
                            myDataArray)
```

and the user is free to use any ids for the layout as long are there are two TextViews.

There are aspects of the ListView that haven't been covered. In particular, what do you do if your data structure isn't an array? The ArrayAdapter can handle Lists by simply overriding the appropriate constructor. Anything more complex and you will have to create a custom Adapter. In most cases, however, this isn't necessary because most data structures can be mapped onto an array.

There are a range of formatting topics not covered, the header and separator for example, but these are relatively easy. More complicated are the multi-selection options and any custom list displays such as a list with multiple columns or pop-out detail windows.

## Custom Adapter

Putting together all the code introduced so far gives:

```kotlin
class MyAdaptor(
        val mycontext: Context?,
        val resource: Int,
        val resTitle: Int,
        val resNumber: Int,
        val objects: Array<out MyData>?):
            ArrayAdapter<MyData>(mycontext, resource, objects){
    override fun getView(
                position: Int,
                convertView: View?,
                parent: ViewGroup?): View {
        val row: View
        if (convertView == null) {
            val inflater = (mycontext as Activity).layoutInflater
            row = inflater.inflate(resource, parent, false)
            val viewHolder = ViewHolder(
                            row.findViewById<TextView>(resTitle),
                            row.findViewById<TextView>(resNumber))
            row.tag = viewHolder

        } else {
            row = convertView
        }

        (row.tag as ViewHolder).title.text =
                            objects?.get(position)?.myTitle
        (row.tag as ViewHolder).number.text =
                            objects?.get(position)?.myNum.toString()
        return row
    }
}

data class ViewHolder(var title: TextView, var number: TextView)
```

# Summary

- Containers like ListView work together with an adapter to display data.

- The adapter accepts a data structure – usually an array or a list – and converts any data item into a View object that represents the data.

- You can handle a selection event to find out what the user has selected.

- The View object can be complex with an outer container and any number of child objects.

- The basic ArrayAdapter uses each object's toString method to provide the data to display in a ViewText object.

- If you want to display something other than the result of calling toString, you need to implement a custom ArrayAdapter. To do this you have to override the inherited getView method.

- The ListView is clever enough to provide you with View objects to recycle – although you don't have to if you don't want to.

- The ViewHolder pattern can make your use of nested View objects more efficient.

# Chapter 17

# Android The Kotlin Way

After seeing Kotlin at work making your Android code shorter and, more importantly, clearer, it is time to gather the ideas together. This chapter is a collection of the ways Kotlin makes Android easier in comparison with Java. If you are not a Java programmer many of these differences will not seem impressive.

This chapter is at the end of the book because it can serve as a reminder to a Java programmer learning Android what a difference Kotlin makes. It could also be read first by a fairly experienced Android programmer wanting to know what their Android Java idioms look like in Kotlin.

If you want a good grounding in Kotlin I can do no better than recommend my own *Programmer's Guide To Kotlin* **ISBN 978-1871962536.** This chapter is more about how Kotlin affects your approach to Android programming than a general Kotlin tutorial.

## What You No Longer Have To Type

- Semicolons, type specifiers and new

The first joy of Kotlin is that you no longer have to type a semicolon to mark the end of each line. You can type a semicolon if you want to and Android Studio doesn't mark it as an error, but it does suggest that you might want to remove it:

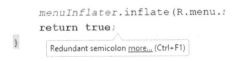

In Kotlin the end of a line is the end of a line and you don't need a special additional symbol to mark it. However, if you include more than one statement on a line, you do need to indicate where each one ends by placing a semicolon between them.

If you are a long time Java programmer you might well find it difficult to stop typing semicolons – eventually you will.

The second obvious simplification is that in most cases you no longer have to specify a type when it is obvious.

For example in place of:

```
String myString=new String();
```

you can now write

```
var myString=String()
```

Java beginners have long been confused by the need to write String... new String and now we don't have to. If you do need to specify a type you do it as a trailing qualifier:

```
var myString:String=String()
```

This example also highlights the third simplification – you no longer write new in front of a constructor. After all new signified that the function call was a constructor, but what is and what is not a constructor is fairly obvious from the class declarations.

## var & val

Of course, one new thing is that you have to use either var or val when you declare a variable.

If you write:

```
var myVariable=1
```

then you will get a true variable that you can read and write.

If you use:

```
val myVariable=1
```

then you get a read-only variable which you cannot use on the left of an assignment.

**In most cases you should use var for simple types and val for objects.**

A more general principle, however, is to always use val unless you are forced to use var by the nature of the algorithm. Notice that all val promises is that you cannot assign to the variable – you can modify the properties of any object that it references. This is read-only rather than immutable.

## No More get & set

Kotlin classes have properties that come complete with get and set mutator functions. Properties declared using var have default getters and setters and those declared using val have only a getter i.e. val properties are read-only.

All properties are accessed via getter and setter functions and, unlike in Java, you don't have to explicitly create them – the compiler will do the job for you.

It will also automatically put get or set in front of the property's name so that you can use Java properties implemented in this way without having to modify property names. In Java you might have a setText and a getText method. You can still use these in Kotlin:

```
var myString=view.getText()
view.setText()=myString
```

But in many cases you can simply write:

```
var myString=view.text()
view.text=myString
```

In other words, the mutator methods have been converted into properties with the same name, but with a lower case first letter.

Kotlin can also deal with Booleans that are named starting with is.

For example, instead of:

```
button.isShown()
```

you can write:

```
button.isShown
```

In most cases, when you see a set or get you can simply use the equivalent property, but not always. There are many odd problems that can crop up to stop the transformation from getters/setters to properties. Consider the well known and used:

```
setOnClickListener
```

If this was converted to onClickListener this would confuse the issue with the OnClickListener interface. In this case you have to use the setOnClickListener method but as it accepts a SAM – an interface that defines a Single Abstract Method it can be written using a lambda:

```
button.setOnClickListener { view -> instructions}
```

At the moment the best advice is to try to use any get/set methods as properties and see what Android Studio supplies as an auto-complete.

The range and quality of auto-complete features is likely to improve as Kotlin support is developed.

## View Objects As Properties

In Java finding a View object uses the findViewById method, and this is still needed in Kotlin in many cases. It is even easier to use in Kotlin because it is implemented as a generic extension function and you can avoid having to cast to the correct type:

```
val button = findViewById<Button>(R.id.my_button)
```

However, if you are using Kotlin to work with the XML file it automatically converts all of the string labels on the ids to Activity properties and then makes them reference the objects that the inflater creates. You can then specify which layout files you want to create properties for using:

```
import kotlinx.android.synthetic.main.layout.*
```

As you enter the id of a View object defined in the XML file Android Studio will ask if you want to import the "synthetic" definition it has created.

So. to import properties for all of the View created by the two standard XML files main.activity_main.xml and main.content_main.xml you would use:

```
import kotlinx.android.synthetic.main.activity_main.*
import kotlinx.android.synthetic.main.content_main.*
```

What this means is that you can simply use variables with the same name as the id string assigned to the View object so, for example, instead of having to use findViewById for the R.id.my_button object you can simply use the button property as if you had executed:

```
val button = findViewById<Button>(R.id.my_button)
```

## Event Handlers

With the whole of Chapter 4 about event handling, only a brief summary is given here.

In Java event handlers are methods that belong to event listener objects often defined using an interface. In many cases there is a single event handler defined in a single interface and this is a SAM – Single Abstract Event.

For example the View.OnClickListener interface is defined as:

```
    public interface OnClickListener {
        void onClick(View var1);
    }
```

and you need to create an object which implements this interface to pass to the setOnClickListener method. The Kotlin compiler accepts a lambda expression, an anonymous local function or a function reference of the correct type and compiles it to an object that implements the interface with the function. Notice that the setOnClickListener is passed an object and not a lambda or a function.

For example:

```
button.setOnClickListener {view -> button.text="Clicked"}
```

Using a lambda is the most common way of creating an instance of the event listener object for a SAM.

There are instances where the event listener object isn't a SAM. It might not even be defined as an interface. Some event listeners are defined as classes with a mix of virtual and implemented methods. The implemented methods are often utility functions that allow you to do things such as cancel event handling or modify it in some way. Even when event listeners are interfaces, they can define multiple related event handlers and so do not qualify as a SAM.

For example, in Chapter 10 we meet the ActionMode.Callback which is an interface with four event handling methods defined. In this case the simplest solution is to use a local object that implements the interface:

```
val mycallback=object : ActionMode.Callback {
        override fun onActionItemClicked(
            mode: ActionMode?, item: MenuItem?): Boolean {
                TODO("not implemented")
        }

        override fun onCreateActionMode(
            mode: ActionMode?, menu: Menu?): Boolean {
                TODO("not implemented")
        }

        override fun onPrepareActionMode(
            mode: ActionMode?, menu: Menu?): Boolean {
                TODO("not implemented")
        }
        override fun onDestroyActionMode(
            mode: ActionMode?) {
                TODO("not implemented")
        }

}
```

The same approach works if the event listener is defined as a class with some implemented methods and some virtual methods. Simply create an object that implements the class and all of the virtual methods.

# Data

Kotlin essentially reuses Java's data types including arrays and strings, but it augments them and has its own approach to them. However, essentially a Kotlin array is a Java array and a Kotlin String is a Java String.

You create an array using:

```
var a=arrayOf(1,2,3)
```

which creates an array of three integers.

For larger arrays you can use:

```
var array=Array(size, initializer)
```

where size gives the number of elements and *initializer* is a lambda expression that used to initialize the array. For example:

```
var a = Array(1000, { i -> i * 2 })
```

If you want the equivalent of an ArrayList in Java use List or MutableList.

Kotlin's Strings are much like Java's but it is worth knowing that they support templating. For example:

```
var s = "Name $name and Address $address"
```

will insert the values of the variables – name and address – into the string.

Although Kotlin doesn't have a record or structure type, it does have data classes. If you create a class with a primary constructor something like:

```
class MyPersonClass{
 var name:String=""
 var age:Int=0
}
```

then you get a class with two properties initialized as specified.

If you also add the modifier "data" in front:

```
data class MyPersonClass{
 var name:String=""
 var age:Int=0
}
```

you also get some auto-generated methods including, equals, copy, hashcode, toString and componentN. The componentN methods are particularly useful as they provide destructuring:

```
var myDataObject=MyDataClass("Mickey",89)
var (myName,myAge) = myDataObject
```

which unpacks the properties in to the separate variables.

A special case of destructuring is the spread operator *. If you have a function that accepts a variable number of arguments you can pass it an array using;

```
val a=arrayOf(1,2,3)
val list =asList(*a)
```

# Null Safety

Perhaps one of the most subtle features of Kotlin you have to get to know and use is its null safety.

References can be either non-nullable or nullable.

If you declare a variable in the usual way you get a non-nullable:

```
var myVariable:sometype= something
```

and you cannot set the variable to null because:

```
myVariable=null
```

throws a compiler error.

The compiler tracks operations that could generate a null, and flags any operation that could possibly set a non-nullable variable to null. For example, if a function could return a null you cannot assign it to a non-nullable. This often occurs if you are trying to use a Java function which, of course, doesn't support non-nullable types.

If you need a nullable reference then you have to explicitly declare it using ? as in:

```
var myVariable:sometype?=something
```

Now myVariable can be set to null:

```
myVariable=null
```

and this works without a compiler error or warning.

Kotlin tracks your use of nullables and makes sure you don't assign a nullable to a non-nullable without checking that it isn't null. If you do use a nullable without checking that it is safe, the compiler will warn you and refuse to compile the program.

There are various operators that make life easier if you are working with nullable types.

The safe call operator ?. will only access a property if the object is non-null.

For example:

```
var myVariable=myObject.myProperty
```

will not compile if myObject is a nullable. Using the safe call operator:

```
var myVariable:Int?=myObject?.myProperty
```

does work and myVariable is set either to the value of the property or to null if myObject is null. Notice that myVariable has to be nullable for this to work. If you only want to perform an operation if something is non-null you can use the let method:

```
a?.let {a=a+1}
```

the block of code in the curly brackets is only executed if a is non-null.

Finally there is the safe cast `as?` which will return null if the cast isn't possible. So:

```
variable as? type
```

will evaluate to null if the cast to type isn't possible.

## Java Types and Null

When working with Kotlin then you can keep nulls under control. All the variables you use can be non-nullable and the only cost of this is that you have to initialize them when they are declared or soon after. In principle, it is very difficult of a null to occur in pure Kotlin, but when you are working with Android you cannot avoid interworking with Java and null is a possible value for any Java variable. Not only this but the type being used by a Java method that you have to call may not be a Kotlin type at all. In this case Android Studio studio shows them as T! meaning they could be referenced by a non-null or nullable variable, i.e. a T or a T?

Similarly, Java collections can be treated as mutable or immutable and can be nullable or non-nullable. The IDE shows these as (Mutable) Collection <T>!. Finally a Java array is shown as Array<(out) T>! meaning that it could be an array of a sub-type of T nullable or non-nullable.

Given that Java types are nullable you have two choices in handling this. You can set the type to a Kotlin non-nullable of the equivalent type, or you can keep the nullable type and check for nulls. For example, the savedInstance Bundle passed into the onCreate method is a Java object and so it is a nullable:

```
override fun onCreate(savedInstanceState: Bundle?)
```

If you try to use one of its methods in the usual way then you will see the following message:

```
var value= savedInstanceState.get("mykey")
```
Only safe (?.) or non-null asserted (!!.) calls are allowed on a nullable receiver of type Bundle?

Changing to the safe method call:

```
var value= savedInstanceState?.get("mykey")
```

makes the error message go away, but now value is inferred to be a nullable. In this case `value` is Any?. Notice that if either `get` is null or "mykey" doesn't exist value is set to null.

At this point any null values are not causing a problem. However if we cast the value to a non-nullable type things can go wrong:

```
var value= savedInstanceState?.get("mykey") as Int
```

Now `value` is a non-nullable `Int` and while this compiles it will cause a run time exception if the result is to try to assign a null to a none nullable. The compiler adds an assertion that the value is non-null to protect you and if it is you will see a runtime exception that includes the message:

```
Caused by: kotlin.TypeCastException: null cannot be cast to non-null
type kotlin.Int
```

Alternatively you could cast to a nullable type:

```
var value= savedInstanceState?.get("mykey") as Int?
```

Now `value` is a nullable Int and it both compiles and runs without an exception even if the result is null. Of course if you now try to use `value` you still have the problem that it might be null but now the compiler prompts you to deal with this:

The compiler will not complain if you check for a null before trying to use value:

```
var value= savedInstanceState?.get("mykey") as Int?
if(value!=null)value=value+1
```

A shorthand way of checking is to use the `let` method:

```
value?.let{value=value+1}
```

which only evaluates the expression if the variable is non-null.

The problem seems to be that once you have a null in the system it is difficult to get it out and you have to test and react to it in all of the code where it matters. The only alternative is to replace it with a non-null result that behaves correctly. You can do this in Kotlin using the amusingly named Elvis operator ?:. For example:

```
value?:0
```

is zero if value is null. In general, if you have a value that will substitute for a null then you should eliminate the null as soon as possible.

309

For example, in this case we can use the Elvis operator to make value a non-nullable type:

```
var value= (savedInstanceState?.get("mykey")?:0) as Int
```

Now value is a non-nullable Int and if Java returns a null for savedInstance or the result of get then it has a value of zero.

In many cases it is best to remove the null at its first appearance. So for example, we can make savedInstanceState safe:

```
val safeSavedInstanceState=savedInstanceState?:Bundle()
```

If savedInstanceState is null safeSavedInstanceState is a newly instantiated Bundle. This also allows you to use array access in place of the get.

Notice however that this doesn't get rid of the null problem as:

```
var value= safeSavedInstanceState["mykey"] as Int
value=value+1
```

will compile, but you will generate a runtime exception if mykey isn't in the Bundle as this then returns a null. So you still have to check that result isn't null:

```
var value= (safeSavedInstanceState["mykey"]?:0) as Int
```

Nulls are a common cause of runtime crashes and it is worth spending time working out what should happen if something you rely on in code is null. Kotlin doesn't solve the null problem, but it does give you the tools to solve it.

## Kotlin Aims to Help

There are many more ways that Kotlin, the compiler and the plugin to Android Studio, try to make life easier. There are too many to cover in detail and you can expect both code completion and code prompting to get better as Kotlin support in Android Studio is improved.

Notice that Android Studio takes us beyond pure Kotlin in the range of facilities it provides. Take, for example, the automatic binding of properties of the Activity to the ids assigned to components in the XML files. This is not part of the Kotlin language, but it is very much part of Android programming with Kotlin.

In most cases you should find that the messages and prompts that are issued by Android Studio give you enough guidance to work out what alternatives are on offer and what the solutions to problems actually are.

Always take time to read the prompts and messages as the answer is often staring you in the face.

If you would like to know more about Kotlin, then I recommend my book: ***Programmer's Guide To Kotlin ISBN:978-1871962536***

# Summary

- Kotlin is fully compatible with Java and provides many simplifications for using the Android Java libraries.

- If you are a Java programmer there are many thing you have to get out of the habit of typing – especially semicolons.

- In Kotlin there are no fields, only properties complete with get and set methods. These map to Java fields with get and set methods.

- The Kotlin plugin converts the ids assigned in the XML layout file to properties of the Activity.

- Event handlers are easy to create using either lambdas or objects.

- Data classes are a very easy way to create "record" like data structures.

- Kotlin introduces tools to help you manage nulls from a pure Kotlin program.

- When Kotlin interacts with Java code then nulls are a fact of life and you have to deal with the possibility that a nullable type is indeed null.

# Index

Made in the USA
Middletown, DE
26 January 2021